Financial Deepening
in Economic Development

ECONOMIC DEVELOPMENT SERIES

General Editor
Gerald M. Meier, Professor of International
Economics, Stanford University

Published
HUMAN RESOURCES AS THE WEALTH OF NATIONS
 Frederick H. Harbison
ECONOMIC THEORY AND THE UNDERDEVELOPED
COUNTRIES
 H. Myint

Financial Deepening in Economic Development

EDWARD S. SHAW
Stanford University

New York
OXFORD UNIVERSITY PRESS
London   1973   Toronto

Introduction to the
Economic Development Series

1768122

Two centuries ago it all began with *The Wealth of Nations;* today it is called the Poverty of Nations. If economics has always been asked to propose means of social betterment, and if economists are, as Lord Keynes suggested, the trustees of the possibility of civilization —then the problems of world poverty will persistently challenge each generation of economists. But what is new for this generation is the concentrated effort by so many countries to undertake conscious programs of economic development. With the heightened awareness of world inequalities, development policies have been deliberately adopted on a national basis and supported by international institutions.

The time has come for a reappraisal of this experience. This Economic Development Series has therefore been designed to take a hard look at the central problems and strategic policy issues that have emerged to the forefront of development efforts. Recognizing that it has become impossible and undesirable for any one author to attempt to cover the entire subject of economic development, this series concentrates on a set of special problems analyzed by authors who are widely recognized authorities in their respective fields and who have had extensive experience in the developing countries. Each author offers an incisive study of a specific problem area that now requires more understanding by students and practitioners of devel-

opment alike. The treatment in each volume emphasizes both experience and theory. Taken together, the volumes in this Series formulate
a number of policies that may be better designed to cope with some
of the most troublesome problems of development.

G. M. MEIER

Preface

This is an old-fashioned book. It is neoclassical in insisting that relative price counts in economic development. It is monetarist in insisting that money and its relative prices affect real aspects of the development process. It draws attention to financial markets for the role that they can play in making growth paths steeper for relatively poor economies and more stable. The emphasis that it puts on financial deepening, or accumulation of financial assets at a pace faster than accumulation of nonfinancial wealth, implies a bias toward decentralization of economic choice in a context of either capitalism or socialism. Its focus is on markets and on the seamless web that binds them together in an economic system.

The target of the book is the "lagging economy." The lagging economy confines itself to poverty partly by imposing upon its markets patterns of financial, fiscal, and international economic policy that, in effect, instruct market participants to keep aggregate levels of income and wealth where they are. It depends on the plan, mandate, ration, license, and privilege to optimize resource allocation and use. It resists liberalization of markets, where decentralized decisions could advance economic welfare, even though its government sector is inept. The lagging economy is stubbornly poor.

The substance and spirit of the book may have been affected too much by the author's sample of experiences. A different sample of lagging economies and leading ones might have inspired a different essay, even a testament to the virtues of centralism and contrived markets, to the vices of finance and of "market forces." The odds go the other way: economic incentives and constraints are so much the same everywhere that a different exposure would confirm views set down in the pages ahead.

So many acknowledgments are due! To the teachers of long ago, Bernard F. Haley and Dennis H. Robertson. To Ronald I. McKinnon, for collaboration in antecedents of this volume. To colleagues at Stanford, especially Moses Abramovitz, Emile Despres, and Tibor Scitovsky. To superb public officials who have been patient with me in ventures abroad. To Gerald Meier for personal encouragement and professional editorship. Especially to Elizabeth and Janet.

E. S. SHAW

Stanford, California
November 29, 1972

Contents

Financial Deepening
in Economic Development

1 | Financial Deepening

The theme of this book is that the financial sector of an economy does matter in economic development. It can assist in the breakaway from plodding repetition of repressed economic performance to accelerated growth. If it is repressed and distorted, it can intercept and destroy impulses to development.

The financial sector is a complex of markets for financial assets and financial services. It has its own industries, the monetary system among them, utilizing inputs of productive factors according to relevant technologies. There is a superstructure of regulatory authority with its pattern of policies and array of control instruments. Linkages with foreign financial sectors are inescapable. The sector is unique in the degree to which its markets, prices, institutions, and policies impinge upon all others. Money is the only good that trades against all other goods. Interest rates are the relative prices that have most pervasive relevance to economic decisions.

Numerous decentralized economies with low levels of per capita income and wealth have been attracted at times to a development strategy that results in "shallow" finance. By distortions of financial prices including interest rates and foreign-exchange rates and by other means, it has reduced the real rate of growth and the real size of the financial system relative to nonfinancial magnitudes. In all cases this strategy has stopped or gravely retarded the development process. A new strategy that has the effect, among others, of "deepening" finance—a strategy of financial liberalization—has invariably renewed development. Liberalization matters in economic development. It is *not* our theme that only financial liberalization matters. On the contrary, financial liberalization is appropriately linked with complementary measures that reach beyond the financial sector.

This theme is excluded from dominant traditions of theory and practice in economic development. Some development theory seems to be designed for a barter world. In other models finance is passively adaptive, and its deepening is a by-product of accelerated growth in "real" things. There is doctrine that ranks financial deepening among obstacles to development and recommends financial repression. That guiding beacon of development practice, the Plan, gives scant heed to finance in the usual case. The guidelines that such international agencies as the International Bank for Reconstruction and Development and the International Monetary Fund suggest for development practice are specific and inclusive for public finance through the fiscal budget and for international finance through the balance of payments, but typically there is little in them about purposes and techniques of financial deepening.

NOMINAL FINANCE AND REAL FINANCE

The first step in clarifying the developmental role of finance is to distinguish real values and real rates of return for financial assets from their nominal counterparts—to cleanse the analysis of money illusion. Where the strategy of financial repression is in effect, nominal aggregates of money, for example, or government securities and social trust funds commonly rise at some buoyant rate. At the same time, these aggregates deflated by any broadly inclusive index of prices for domestic goods and services are rising less rapidly or falling. Nominal finance is taking the high growth path, real finance the low one. Then finance in the real sense is shallow, partly because it is being taxed by inflation.

Table I Patterns of growth in money *plus* time
and savings deposits

Indexes of Nominal Values

	Ghana	Thailand	Iran	Uruguay
1963	1.00	1.00	1.00	1.00
1968	1.63	1.96	2.16	8.10

Indexes of Real Values

	Ghana	Thailand	Iran	Uruguay
1963	1.00	1.00	1.00	1.00
1968	1.01	1.74	2.00	0.45

SOURCE: International Monetary Fund, *International Financial Statistics.*

The experience of four countries during 1963–68 illustrates divergence between nominal and real financial growth.

Uruguay realized nominal growth of 710 per cent in money, time, and savings deposits whereas real values declined by 55 per cent. In the race between growth in nominal pesos and inflation, the latter was an easy winner. Ghanaian policy expanded the nominal stock of cedi liquid claims whereas the real stock remained constant. Iran and Thailand achieved financial deepening, real financial growth absorbing the increment in nominal claims. The Uruguayan economy collapsed during 1963–68, and the Ghanaian economy retrogressed whereas both Iran and Thailand realized growth in real income and consumption. Analysis of the bearing of finance on these differences in growth experience starts with the observation that nominal values and real values in terms of the new cedi, rial, baht, and peso took dissimilar relative paths.

Where finance is shallow, in relation to national income or nonfinancial wealth, one finds that it bears low, often negative real rates of return. Holders of financial assets including money are not rewarded for real growth in their portfolios: they are penalized. During 1965–69 the proportion of money balances to gross national product in Ghana declined from 14.4 per cent to 10.7 per cent. The nominal explicit rate of interest on money balances was zero, but the average real rate of return was negative 8 per cent, the realized average rate of inflation.

Table II   Two prices and a rate of interest for money:
the case of new cedis

	Nominal Price	Relative Price	Real Yield (%)
1965	1.00	1.00	—
1966	1.00	.79	−21.0
1967	1.00	.80	1.3
1968	1.00	.83	3.7
1969	1.00	.74	−10.8

SOURCE: Central Bureau of Statistics, *Economic Survey, 1969*, Accra, Ghana, 1970.

Trade unions and employers appreciate the difference between nominal and real wage rates and wage incomes. Financial authorities are rarely as sophisticated about nominal and real financial rates of return, flows, and stocks. They seem to miss the point, for example, that money has four prices. One price is simply unity (column 1, Table II), a decreed price for the money unit—one new cedi, one baht, one rial, one peso. Another price is $1/P$ (column 2, Table II), an index for the purchasing power of money over some assortment of goods and services. The money stock valued at the first unit of account or accounting price is the nominal stock M, whereas the money stock valued at its relative worth in goods and services is the real stock M/P.

If the second price of money and the real money stock are to be positive, the marginal unit of money must yield valuable services. These services may be in kind, including benefits to consumer welfare or to productivity, but they may also take the form of a third explicit price. It is a real deposit rate of interest d, the sum of any nominal rate of interest $\underline{d}$ on money balances and the rate of change $\dot{P}$ in money's second price: $d = \underline{d} - \dot{P}$. For the new cedi in 1969, nominal deposit rate was nil, $\dot{P}$ was negative 10.8 per cent, and so d or the real yield of Ghanaian money balances was also negative 10.8 per cent. The fourth price of money is a foreign-exchange rate, the ratio of exchange between one money, perhaps a new cedi, and another money, perhaps a dollar. Financial analysis would be simpler if there were just one exchange rate between two moneys rather than a real or purchasing-power-parity rate as well as a nominal rate and forward or future rates as well as present or spot rates.

Multiple pricing characterizes all financial assets, non-monetary assets as well as money. The same distinctions arise between nominal and real amounts of finance, between nominal and real rates of return. A distinction exists too, between instruments of financial policy, with some bearing on nominal amounts of finance and some bearing on real amounts. The position to be taken in later chapters is that financial deepening results from appropriate real-finance policy. The principal instruments of this policy bear on real rates of return to real stocks of finance. Shallow finance is partly the consequence of distortions in prices of finance.

MEASURES AND INDICATORS OF FINANCIAL DEEPENING

Numerous indicators or measures register financial deepening. Here it is sufficient to mention only a few. One class pertains to financial stocks. When financial policy has been liberalized and distortions in financial prices have been removed or reduced, reserves of liquidity increase. For example, the central bank typically builds up its international liquidity and takes less recourse to detailed intervention, through rations or licenses, on the foreign-exchange markets. Farmers substitute balances of financial assets for working capital in the form of rice or wheat or other commodity inventories that are costly to maintain. Buyers and sellers in all markets accumulate average balances of liquid assets that make it unnecessary to waste resources on inconveniences of barter. Stocks of financial assets aggregatively grow relative to income or in proportion to tangible wealth, and their range of qualities widens. There is a lengthening of maturities, and a wider variety of debtors gains access to the financial markets. The menu of financial assets is diversified so that borrowers may adjust their debt structures and lenders their portfolios by relatively small degrees at the margin.

Financial flows can be read easily for evidence that finance is deepening. Where it is shallow, for example, an economy depends relatively heavily on its government fiscal budget and on its international capital accounts for the flows of savings that finance capital growth. Deepening eases the strain on taxation and moderates demand for foreign savings. Flight of savings abroad by one device of smuggling or another and demand for construction of dubious social productivity are common evidence of an aversion to finance. Deepening stops and reverses capital flight and diverts savings from those skeletons of partially complete office and apartment buildings. The velocity of money diminishes.

In the context of shallow finance, organized finance is dominated by the banking system and other finance flows through the foreign exchanges or through the curb market of moneylenders and cooperative societies. The banking system behaves as a high-cost, high-profit oligopoly. Finance through the foreign exchanges is dominated by external grants of aid, high-cost suppliers' credits, and direct investment from abroad. The curb is limited to short-term transactions at some high risk from borrower default and governmental repression. The deepening of finance increases the real size of the monetary system, and it generates opportunities for the profitable operation of other institutions as well, from bill dealers to industrial banks and insurance companies. Deepening involves specialization in financial functions and institutions, and organized domestic institutions and markets gain in relation to foreign markets and the curb.

Financial prices are perhaps the least ambiguous evidence. Where finance is shallow, demand for financial assets is repressed by low real rates of interest and supply of primary securities on these terms is repressed by credit rationing. Even the curb market is subject to usury laws and regulations. The financial markets are required to trade at interest rates that overvalue the future in terms of the present. Deepening implies that interest rates must report more accurately the opportunities that exist for substitution of investment for current consumption and the disinclination of consumers to wait. Real rates of interest arc high where finance is deepening. Differentials between rates tend to diminish—for example, between loan and

deposit rates and between rates on the organized markets and rates
on the curb.

Shallow finance is commonly associated with overvaluation of domestic money on the official markets for spot foreign exchange.
Regulatory policy demands a premium on domestic balances in
terms of foreign balances as well as a premium in present balances
on future balances. It discourages exporting and saving but encourages importing and consumption. Deepening ensues when these
biases in relative prices are removed. The evidence one looks for is
a decline of the discount on domestic money in the black markets
and the forward markets for foreign exchange.

OBJECTIVES OF FINANCIAL DEEPENING

Financial liberalization tends to raise ratios of private domestic
savings to income. Some of the gain may be illusory: savings may
be drawn to uses that are counted in national income accounts and
away from capital flight in various forms that defy measurement.
Some of the gain must result from higher rewards to saving—higher
real rates of interest and opportunities for diversifying savers' portfolios of domestic assets. Again, real growth of financial institutions
provides more investors with access to borrowing and gives them
incentive to save and to accumulate the equity that makes borrowing cheaper. Finally, there seems to be a shift of savers' planning
horizons to the more distant future and improvement in income expectations that reduces relatively the attraction of consumption now.

Savings tend to rise in the government sector. When finance is
shallow, in decentralized economies, government savings are characteristically low. Government depends on the inflation tax for command over resources, and the typical inelasticity of tax revenues and
profits of government enterprise to inflation reduces government
savings in the conventional sense. Savings from the foreign sector
also respond to liberalization. Capital flight of domestic funds is reversed, and there is easier access to foreign capital markets when
distortions of such relative prices as interest rates and foreign-

exchange rates are corrected. In some circumstances the inflow of foreign funds reaches proportions that are not easy to absorb at a stable domestic price level.

Liberalization permits the financial process of mobilizing and allocating savings to displace in some degree the fiscal process, inflation, and foreign aid. Fiscal technique is backward in lagging economies. Its capacity to draw revenues is strained by demands for government consumption and, in the usual case, for some minimal social security. Additional demands upon it for the purpose of financing investment tend to have effects upon economic efficiency and social equity that offset benefits of capital accumulation. Foreign aid has been, in some important degree, a substitute for domestic savings: the aid gap is partly an expression of excess demand for savings in economies that employ relative price to repress savings of their own. Technocratic planning models may define ranges of per capita income in which developing economies generate shortages of savings and foreign exchange, but correction of distorted relative prices has a remarkable way of making the models irrelevant.

Liberalization opens the way to superior allocations of savings by widening and diversifying the financial markets on which investment opportunities compete for the savings flow. In the repressed economy savings flow mainly to the saver's own investments: self-finance prevails. In the liberalized economy savers are offered a wider menu of portfolio choice. The market for their savings is extended; a broader range of selection in terms of scale, maturity, and risk becomes available; and information for comparison of alternatives can be obtained more cheaply. Local capital markets can be integrated into a common market, and new opportunities for pooling savings and specializing in investment are created.

The extended capital markets, where prices in the form of interest rates can be used to discriminate between investment alternatives, seem to be a congenial context for appearance of new investing firms and innovative investment projects. They generate competing proposals for the disposition of savings. In this respect, the contrast with financially repressed regimes can be striking. There savings flow through narrow channels which are not subject to the discipline of relative price, into the repetitive projects of established firms, especially government enterprise and traditional trading firms. Too often the search for investment uses of savings is casual and opportunistic, with little reference to comparative rates of return. Financial depth seems to be an important prerequisite for competitive and innovative disposition of savings flows. It is no accident that marginal ratios of investment to output are high where finance is shallow.

Unemployment in lagging economies is partly the result of financial repression. Scarce savings supply labor inadequately with the tools of its trades. To make matters worse, the low interest rates that inhibit savings combine with relatively high minimum-wage rates to guarantee that labor is supplied with the wrong tools. Investment flows to capital-intensive production even though capital is scarce and labor plentiful. The status of labor is not improved by the over-valued exchange rates that conceal the comparative advantage of labor-intensive agriculture and indigenous manufacturing.

Financial liberalization and allied policies tend to equalize the distribution of income. It appears that elasticities of substitution of labor against capital may be high in some lagging economies and that a rise in interest rates and foreign-exchange rates relative to wage rates may both raise employment and increase the wage share of income. Again, liberalization reduces the monopoly rents that flow from import and other licenses to the few importers, bank borrowers, or, for example, consumers of electric power. Furthermore, the twists in terms of trade against farmers, for example, or against workers that are applied in a regime of repression to extract profits and savings for investors can be replaced by measures of finance and taxation that achieve as much growth of capital with less abuse of equity and less hazard for political and social stability.

Liberalization and deepening of finance contribute to the stability of growth in output and employment. There can be less stop-go. One reason for this is that some of the more ample savings flow may be used to finance larger international reserves. More flexible foreign-exchange rates can also absorb some of the shocks of international trading. If both the current balance on international account and the domestic savings flow respond to treatment, the economy becomes less vulnerable to the ebb and flow of supplier credits and foreign aid. From the standpoint of stability, it is perhaps most important that liberalization can reduce dependence on bursts of inflation and the inflation tax to balance fiscal budgets and can bring monetary variables under discipline.

The name of the policy game in repressed economies is interventionism. Because monetary variables are out of hand, there seems to be need for price control in detail. Because the exchange rate is overvalued, complex tariff schedules, import licenses, and differentiated export bonuses are put into force. Because savings are scarce, credit is rationed loan by loan. An economy that immobilizes critical relative prices must fall back upon contrivances of interventionism to clear markets. A burden is put upon the civil service that it cannot carry, and the costs in both inefficiency and corruption are high. It is a principal purpose of liberalization to substitute markets for bureaus.

THE ORIGINS AND CONTEXT OF FINANCIAL REPRESSION

Financial repression has its typical complements in development strategy. It is part of a package. As we have suggested, overvaluation of the domestic currency in terms of foreign monies is another part. Whereas financial policy including inflation reduces real rates of interest and makes savings appear cheap, so cheap that they must be rigorously rationed, exchange-rate policy holds down the domestic price of foreign exchange. There is excess demand for both savings and foreign exchange. In the rationing of foreign exchange, preference commonly goes to capital equipment or, once the equipment has been installed, to its spare parts and replacements and to materials that it processes.

Another part of the strategy reduces relative prices for domestically produced primary products. Industrial raw materials are made cheap for the urban industrial establishment that benefits, too, from low rates of interest and from cheap imports. Foods are made cheap for the urban working class in order to temper its wage demands. Primary products are diverted from export markets, and imports of substitutes have a claim of high priority for scarce foreign exchange when domestic supplies run short.

The strategy produces a dual labor market. A relatively small fraction of the labor force is recruited for capital-intensive industry that benefits from low rates of interest, low rates of foreign exchange, and cheap prices for domestic inputs. Industrial labor unionizes and is granted minimum-wage rates that, despite erosion in real terms during inflation, draw rural labor into urban unemployment. Basic amenities for the urban population impose a growing burden on the government budget and reduce government's contribution to the flow of savings.

Fiscal policy in this context is easy to predict. By one device or another, including marketing boards, substantial revenues are collected from traditional exports. Excises on some items of luxury consumption and duties on imports of goods that compete with products of capital-intensive industry are other ranking revenue sources. Real property is taxed lightly, if at all; various tax concessions are arranged for the industrial enclave; and public enterprise supplies cheaply, or at a loss, various utilities that, like savings and foreign exchange, are rationed in some degree of compliance with a plan of industrialization. Total revenues tend to be inelastic to both inflation and growth in real national output.

Excess demand for savings spills into the capital account of the balance of international payments. In the worst of circumstances, it draws on high-cost, short-term credits until some solution is found for funding. It may be satisfied by direct private investment from abroad and by grants of official aid, some of them with local-currency counterparts that provide a measure of relief for the fiscal budget.

This is a strategy of transformation and structural change. It manipulates a congeries of relative prices—for savings, foreign exchange, basic materials, labor, government services—and it resolves by rationing the excess demands that emerge at these prices. The general purpose, of course, is to break away from relatively low levels of income and consumption by changing the national matrix of products and their inputs. It is an inferior strategy under the best of circumstances and a self-defeating strategy in the usual case: the excess demands or "gaps" that it generates on some markets and the excess supplies that occur especially in markets for labor and for products of capital-intensive industry prove impossible to close at desired or acceptable growth rates of income and consumption. They repress development.

Why countries adopt this strategy of excess demands is not clear. Some of them seem to slip into it by inadvertence. An initial disturbance, such as a turn in the terms of external trade against traditional exports, may generate shortages of savings and foreign exchange. If one response is an increase in the rate of inflation, to cover a government deficit or to finance the bill of imports, and if appropriate changes are not tolerated in relative prices for savings and foreign exchange or for new exports and government services, the process of repression can be off to a fast start.

In some instances the strategy of interventionism with fixed nominal prices and rationing on some critical markets seems to be a deliberate choice. "Market forces" are mistrusted on the grounds that elasticities of response to relative prices are thought to be too high or too low for desired outcomes, that markets are vulnerable to exploitation or that "this country is different." Although markets are mistrusted, there is faith in the capacity of the civil service—especially if it includes a planning commission—to identify and establish the economy's appropriate growth path.

Again, the choice of strategy may be a reflex to experience with colonialism in one form or another. The old regime may have left a relatively strong governmental apparatus, a relatively weak stratum of endogenous entrepreneurship, and comparatively primitive domestic markets, especially for finance. Costs of learning the development process by doing it in a context of effective markets and flexible prices can appear to be unacceptably high, and the quick way to postcolonial economic independence may seem to be the interventionist way.

Class interests are involved in the choice of development strategy. An entrenched civil service, which can make way for recruits from a rapidly growing labor force, may be reluctant to step aside for "market forces." Groups that benefit from the monopoly rents of import licenses, credit and investment permits, tax concessions and cheap supplies of goods and services from government enterprise, urban concentration around subsidized industrial enclaves, and shifts in terms of trade against domestic agriculture have a stake in the excess-demands regime.

Economic myopia may be partly to blame. Possibly it is overlooked that negative real rates of interest that make savings cheap for investors also make savings scarce or that overvalued foreign-exchange rates that make foreign currency cheap for importers also make production and trade unattractive to exporters. Sometimes the point is missed that a government pledge to reduce conventional taxes may commit the government to the inflation tax or, possibly, to expensive borrowing abroad. Micro-economic decisions to benefit one segment of the economy may be taken without due concern for their impact elsewhere.

A PREVIEW

Analysis of financial repression and liberalization—of shallow finance and of financial deepening—is necessarily grounded in monetary theory. Chapter 2 moves quickly through conventional bodies of doctrine, including the Keynesian, regarding money and non-monetary finance in the context of steady growth. Chapter 3 presents a modification of these conventional views that appears to be more appropriate for analyzing finance in the context of economic development. Chapter 4 is a description of the policies that repress finance in lagging economies, and Chapter 5 is a survey of reforms that can deepen finance. Chapter 6 is concerned with interaction between financial and fiscal sectors, suggesting that shallow finance and fiscal inadequacy go together and require simultaneous therapy of financial and fiscal reform. Chapter 7 discusses the regime of "disequilibrium money" in the international sector of lagging economies. The last chapter presents a generalized model of short-period instability in economies that are addicted to shallow finance, fiscal inadequacy, and disequilibrium in the foreign exchanges. Policies that repress growth induce turbulence. Financial deepening along with compatible reform in the fiscal and international sectors may make growth paths both steeper and smoother.

2 | Money, Finance, and Capital Accumulation I. The Wealth View

Monetary reform comes first in financial deepening. Until policy affecting real money has been shifted from restraint and even repression to liberalization, the financial system cannot participate effectively in the development process. Without financial deepening the prospect for escape from the strategy of excess demands and interventionism is dim. Distortion of the relative prices of money is a barrier to development that bad policy imposes but that sound policy can and should remove quickly.

This chapter presents a conventional view of money and finance, the Wealth View (WV) and its Keynesian variant (WVK). WV has not been refined for the subtle context of development, but the conclusions that it reaches regarding money in the simpler context of steady growth have useful implications for lagging economies. Misinterpretation of WV seems to be responsible for some policies that keep finance shallow. Chapter 3 presents another view, the Debt-Intermediation View (DIV), which accepts some parts of WV but rejects others. We find it more adaptable to the context of development.

Balances of real money are obviously wealth for the individual money holder. WV considers them to be wealth for society as well. They are (essentially) costless sources of services, according to

WV, and rightly appear in any catalog of wealth along with nature's endowment of such resources as copper and oil deposits; with human capital; and with produced physical capital of factories and looms and ships. Starting with the definition of real money as wealth, one may move to some striking conclusions. Ministers of finance, hard-pressed for revenues, can tax real-money wealth by excessive issue of nominal money: the inflation tax is a fiscal convenience. Ministers of labor and employment, concerned with chronic unemployment in the labor force, may resent savers' desired substitution of money wealth for reproducible physical capital: as they see it, hoarding magnifies unemployment. On the other hand, the clan of monetarists may insist that increases in the proportion of real money to labor and material capital make everyone better off, at least up to some remote limit. WV evidently has important implications for welfare in both advanced and lagging economies.

The first section below presents the social wealth accounts according to WV. The second section describes the economic regime of WV—its markets, conditions of production, and flows on income-and-product account. The market for money is considered next, and then the market for capital in the sense of savings. Finally, there is a discussion of monetary institutions, techniques, and policies.

SOCIAL WEALTH

The social balance sheet, drawn according to WV, reports four varieties of wealth in three sectors of the economy. The first asset is physical capital K, valued at the real rate of interest that is both the marginal return to investment and the private rate of time discount. It may be held by the private sector as K^p or in the government portfolio as K^g. The second is non-monetary government debt, a perfect portfolio substitute for K, that can be held by the banking sector or the private nonbanking sector. It is reported in the balance sheet below as B/iP, where B represents the number of outstanding annuities of one national currency unit, i the nominal rate of interest, and P the money price of output. The third asset is real money balances,

M/P, an imperfect substitute in private portfolios for K^p and B/iP, and the fourth is the value to the government or private banks of profits from creating money. For a constant real stock of money, this "charter" is worth $\dfrac{(i - \underline{d})M/P}{i}$, where $\underline{d}$ represents the nominal deposit rate of interest paid to money holders. In models that segregate savers and investors, one finds a fifth asset in the form of private debt, equities, or bonds, which is also a perfect substitute for K.

The WV model has one debt item on the balance sheet—government bonds. Net worth may be shared by government if it participates in money issue or if it has acquired physical capital in its fiscal operations, private savers in general, and private savers who are also bankers. These components appear in Table I.

Table I   Social balance sheet in the WV regime

Wealth		Debt	
Physical capital	K	Government debt	B/iP
Real money	M/P	*Net Worth*	
Government debt	B/iP		
Bank charter	$\dfrac{(i - \underline{d})M/P}{i}$	Government	$K^g - B/iP$
		Private	K^p
			M/P
			B/iP
			$\dfrac{(i - \underline{d})M/P}{i}$

According to WV, real money is private and social wealth, yielding a stream of valuable services, measurable by $i(M/P)$, for which money holders are willing to forego services from other items of wealth, human and physical. It is a costless social wealth if it is fiat money rather than bodied money and its services are costless to produce: accumulation of real money—"investment" in money—requires no factor inputs, and the use of money involves neither its depreciation nor application of factor services. Money is not debt of the governmental monetary authority or of the private bankers. If "bank charter" is valuable, there is some degree of monopoly in the production of money, and the differential $(i - \underline{d})$ permits some distortion in the production and distribution of income and wealth away from competitive norms.

All wealth is riskless in the WV model. According to WVK, only money is riskless, whereas physical wealth, government bonds, and bank charters bear yields that private wealth holders regard as subject to perfectly correlated variances. The private estimates of variance increase as yields on these items of wealth fall relative to some critical level. There is no objective risk. Risk is subjective and myopic but nonetheless important in shaping private demands for money in relation to other forms of wealth.

THE ECONOMIC REGIME OF WV

Markets

The economic regime of WV contains six markets. Four of them are explored below: the capital market where savings finance new investment, the market for money, the market for bank charters, and, when issues of fiscal policy arise, the market for government bonds. Two markets remain in the background. The first is the market for homogeneous labor, which is assumed to be in full-employment equilibrium for WV and in underemployment equilibrium for WVK. The second is the market for homogeneous consumption, which also is continuously cleared of excess demand. No market for private securities is present in the WV model because private securities and private physical capital are perfect substitutes: in effect, savers and investors are the same people. This market is retained in adaptations of WV that segregate savers, who hold financial capital, from investors, who hold physical capital, in order to dramatize the difference between decisions to save and to invest.

Each market is a common market for the economy. Trading is costless and results in a uniform price except on the market for money where deposits and currency may bear different yields and on the market for charters when it is imperfectly competitive. Equilibrium everywhere is continuous. In WV there is perfect foresight on all markets. Future prices of consumables, labor, and money in terms of each other are never in doubt. Rates of change in the value of money, the reciprocal of the price level P for output, are perfectly foreseen and need not be deduced from experienced rates of change. Even in the capital market there is perfect foresight with regard to the price of capital in terms of output, the real rate of interest r, and the price of capital in terms of money, the money or nominal rate of interest i. The essential distinction of WVK is that it admits private uncertainty as to the real rate of interest which, given the assumption of a rigid P, is identical with the money rate.

The economy is at the efficient technological frontier in all markets. Technique is most appropriate in production of current output, given the single real wage rate and the only real rate of interest. It is fully refined on the market for money in the sense that production of money is costless and that no techniques exist that would increase money balances demanded at each real deposit rate on money. Monetary policy is costless and gifted with perfect foresight, although not always with good sense. Best techniques are used for implementing fiscal policy: there is costless collection and spending of government revenues. For given objectives the first-best choice between monetary and fiscal policy is always feasible.

WV imposes these market specifications rigorously in growth models. When it comes to analysis of monetary and fiscal policy in developed economies, the specifications are assumed to hold over the long run. Expositors of WV suggest that the regime is not wholly appropriate to the lagging economies.

Conditions of Production

Output is putty in the WV regime, an homogeneous product that can be consumed or used as a productive input. It is produced for a competitive market. The inputs are only labor and putty capital in some versions of WV, but more refined versions count real money as a productive factor. According to the latter, the aggregate production function may be written:

(1) $Y = G\ (K, L, M/P)$

Here Y is output, K the stock of capital, L homogeneous labor-time inputs, and M/P is the stock of real money balances issued either by the monetary authority or by private banks, held either by consumer households or by firms. The marginal products of the three mutually substitutable factors are positive, and returns to scale are assumed away. We may suppose that technological progress is "Harrod-neutral," augmenting labor efficiency, so that L represents inputs of efficiency units rather than natural units of manpower

In the presence of constant growth of population and of sophistication in technology, to yield a steady growth rate n in labor efficiency units, it is convenient to reduce (1) to a per capita or, more precisely, per efficiency-unit basis:

$$(2) \qquad\qquad y = g\ (k,\ m)$$

Output per "head" depends positively on ratios of both physical capital and money wealth to labor. For our purposes it is important to stress that, in this version of WV, an increase in m—money-deepening relative to labor—increases production possibilities for each capital-labor ratio k. Through the production function it has a positive income effect on consumer welfare.

The marginal product of labor along the growth path is the real wage rate w, the marginal product of capital is the real interest rate r, and the marginal product of money is its implicit deposit rate u. According to the usual specifications, the golden-rule growth path equates r with the temporal rate of change $\dot{Y}$ in output and with n and yields the maximum attainable level of consumption per capita. As we shall see, WV adds another condition, that u should be zero because money is costless to produce.

There is also money output in the sophisticated version of WV. Since the real stock of money is wealth, additions to it are necessarily social income whether they come about through increases in nominal money M or through deflation of P. This implies a definition of social income:

$$(3) \qquad\qquad Y' = Y + \Delta\ (M/P)$$

Furthermore, real money yields services of $i(M/P)$ minimally, and these should be added in (3) if they are final services, omitted if they are intermediate inputs. They can be construed as intermediate inputs even for consumer households, and we accept this interpretation here. Whereas these services accrue to money holders, income represented by growth in real money accrues either to the monetary system or to money holders, depending on the explicit deposit rate that the former pays to the latter and on the rate of inflation.

Flows on Income-and-Product Account

Income Y' is distributed between factor shares in this fashion:

$$(4) \qquad Y' = wL + rK + \Delta \,(M/P)$$

Its allocation to consumption, savings, and investment is as follows:

$$(5) \qquad Y' = C + I + \Delta \,(M/P)$$

$$(6) \qquad S_p = I$$

$$(7) \qquad S_m = \Delta \,(M/P)$$

Here S_p is "physical" savings embodied in growth I of physical capital, and S_m is "money" savings embodied in increase of the real money stock. Real money and physical investment compete for total savings S. This implies that in WV money deepening in the production function may have a negative substitution effect, as well as its positive income effect, on consumption per capita. An increase in the money-labor ratio may imply a decrease in the capital-labor ratio. This is a central conclusion of WV, and we return to it in our discussion of the market for capital.

Total income Y' is divided between money holders and money issuer, either the monetary authority or private bankers or both. Since money is costless to produce, no factor earnings are generated in the money industry. If an initial amount of nominal money is distributed as a transfer payment to money holders and thereafter price deflation accounts entirely for growth in real money, the income

$\Delta\ (M/P)$ accrues to money holders and is equal to $-\ \dot{P}\ (M/P)$, where $\dot{P}$ is the temporal rate of change in the price level.

Real money is wealth; hence it is taxable. Somewhat wistfully, Lord Keynes considered the Gesellian stamp tax on money as a means less for transferring income to the money issuer than for counteracting the desire of wealth holders to substitute money for physical capital in their portfolios.[1] He thought of it as an expenditure tax, penalizing desired allocation of savings to money wealth. Inflation is a popular alternative, especially in lagging economics: the rate of tax is the realized rate of inflation $\dot{P}$, and the tax revenue accruing from money holder to money issuer is $\dot{P}\ (M/P)$. To maintain a given M/P, money holders restore from their incomes, at the expense of consumption or of savings not allocated to money, the loss in real-money wealth that inflation has imposed, and the command over nonmoney outputs that they forego accrues in revenue to the money issuer.

One may choose as base for measuring the tax rate a constant price level. Other bases are suggested in this definition:

$$(8) \qquad \Delta\ (M/P) = \Delta\ M/P - \dot{P}\ (M/P)$$

As we have seen, growth in real money accrues as income to money holders when $\Delta\ M$ is zero. Any issue of nominal money by the monetary system appropriates some of the income for the monetary authority or banks, and this flow may be considered as seignorage or tax. If we choose to regard all of it as tax, the base for measurement of the tax rate is the rate of deflation that occurs when M is constant. If we choose to divide the real-income share of the monetary system into two parts, seignorage and tax revenue, the basis for measurement of the tax rate can be a $\dot{P}$ of zero. Then seignorage is the share of the increase in real money that is accounted for by the second term in (8).

Income accruing to the monetary system is distributed to money holders when the monetary authority or banks pay a nominal deposit rate $\underline{d}$—a negative Gesellian tax—equal to $\Delta\ M/(M/P)$. In this

[1] John Maynard Keynes, *The General Theory of Employment Interest and Money*, pp. 353–358.

case the monetary system incurs no factor costs and realizes no revenues precisely as when all expansion of real money occurs through price-level deflation. Except in these two cases, the monetary system is able to produce money and appropriate with it some part of physical output.[2] How this part is allocated between consumption, investment, and transfer payments other than deposit interest depends upon the saving propensity of the monetary system. A familiar argument for the inflation tax and against payment of deposit rate is that the monetary system can be counted upon or required, perhaps by the Monetary Board and Planning Commission, to use its revenues for growth in K or other socially worthwhile objectives.

One may be tempted to the conclusion that, when the monetary system retains no revenues (paying them out in deposit interest) and incurs no factor costs, it is producing nothing, and hence M/P cannot be counted as social wealth. This is wrong, according to WV, since real income is generated by growth in real money and accrues, either by price deflation or by receipts of deposit interest, to money holders.

THE MARKET FOR MONEY

There is a market for money in any economic system for which one can define supply and demand functions for money. In equilibrium on this market the real stock of money is equal to the real stock demanded, the rate of growth in the stock to the rate of growth desired by money holders. A barter society has no market for money; no real money is demanded, and none is supplied; no money wealth and no income from producing and using money appear in the social accounts. WV is concerned with economies so fully monetized that no change in techniques for creating, holding, and exchanging money

[2] As samples of an extensive literature on revenue aspects of money-creation, see Martin J. Bailey, "The Welfare Cost of Inflationary Finance," *Journal of Political Economy*, April, 1956, pp. 93–110; Milton Friedman, "Government Revenue from Inflation," *Journal of Political Economy*, July/August, 1971, pp. 846–856; Robert A. Mundell, "Growth, Stability and Inflationary Finance," *Journal of Political Economy*, April, 1965, pp. 97–109.

could increase the real amount of money demanded at each real deposit rate.

Demand for Money

Demand on the market for money is demand for real money. On this market, as on all others, there is absence of money illusion, a matter partly of simple rationality in that behavioral choices are made by households and firms, including bankers, on the basis of real variables. Absence of money illusion also implies that expectations regarding changes in the price level are not static. People who plan in terms of real money balances do not take it for granted that the price level will stay where it is. They are aware that realized changes at some rate $\dot{P}$ have been a tax on their money wealth if the changes were inflationary, or a yield on their money wealth if the changes were deflationary, and they are alert to prospective rates of change P^*. In WV there is perfect foresight regarding $\dot{P}$, so that $\dot{P}$ and P^* are the same.

Demand for real money is a portfolio demand for one form of wealth. It is limited by total wealth, which we may represent in the WV regime of steady growth by Y'. It is limited, as well, by the attractiveness of consumption as an alternative to wealth accumulation. This can be measured by consumers' rate of time preference r_c. Finally, it is limited by the real rates of return that can be anticipated, with certainty in WV but not in WVK, for wealth in physical capital and government bonds. We designate these rates as r. Despite the wealth constraint on demand for money, despite the drawing power of other uses of wealth, real money is demanded on the basis of its own rate of return r_m.[3]

The rate of return on money is a composite. Evidently it must include P^*. There may be an explicit nominal deposit rate $\underline{d}$. Finally, it includes money's yield of services, indicated by a real marginal product u. In the riskless economy of WV, the marginal product of

[3] Edgar L. Feige and Michael Parkin, "The Optimal Quantity of Money, Bonds, Commodity Inventories, and Capital," *The American Economic Review,* June, 1971, pp. 335–349; Milton Friedman (ed.), *Studies in the Quantity Theory of Money,* pp. 3–24.

each stock of real money represents resources of K and L that are economized in the search-and-bargain and payments process and released for production of putty output. It is the growth of output, given stocks of K and L, that results from a marginal change in real money balances. This marginal product diminishes smoothly, other things being equal, to zero but not less because money is costless to store.

The individual wealth holder evidently optimizes by so allocating his wealth that:

$$(9) \qquad\qquad r_m = r = r_c$$

Given the perfect common markets in the economic regime of WV, it can be assumed that all wealth holders optimize at the same relative prices so that (9) is also a condition for collective optimization. Recalling the definition of r_m:

$$(10) \qquad\qquad r_m = u + \underline{d} - P^*$$

and assuming that $\underline{d}$ is zero, we can see that real money wealth is in the privately optimal amount when:

$$(11) \qquad\qquad u = r + P^* = r_c + P^*$$

That is to say, the marginal productivity of money can be deduced from the opportunity cost of holding money, the nominal or money rate of interest $i = r + P^*$.

From the productivity function that describes money's diminishing marginal u, the wealth constraint and the optimizing condition, one can derive this money-demand function:

$$(12) \qquad\qquad D_m = l\ (Y', r_c, r, r_m)$$

The relationship is positive for Y' and r_m, negative for r_c and r. It is convenient if (12) is expressed in terms of the temporal rate of change in real money demanded and income:

$$(13) \qquad\qquad \dot{D}_m = l'\ (\dot{Y}';\, r_c, r, r_m)$$

The common assumption in WV is that the elasticity of D_m with respect to Y' is unity, that each one per cent change in the growth rate of income induces a change of one per cent in the growth rate of real money demanded. Relative prices in the demand function determine, not the growth rate of money demanded, but the steady-state proportion of money demanded to income or wealth. A change in one of the relative prices induces a once-and-for-all adjustment in D_m/Y' with no effect on D_m. These adjustments are important in WV, and they count heavily in the monetary experience of lagging economies.

The full-liquidity or satiation level of demand for money or of demand for money in proportion to income is important in WV. We may define it from this modification of (11):

$$(14) \qquad u + \underline{d} = r + P^* = r_c + P^*$$

There is full-liquidity demand when u is zero and when nominal deposit rate $\underline{d}$ is equal to the money rate of interest. Then equimarginality between rates of return to different uses of wealth is achieved at a real stock of money for which the marginal product is zero. The same stock of money is desired if:

$$(15) \qquad u - (- P^*) = r = r_c$$

That is to say, expected and realized deflation at rate P^* equal to the rates r and r_c induces demand for money to the limit at which the marginal product of money is zero. When this limit is reached and full-liquidity demand for money is satisfied, the monetary system can retain none of its revenues from seignorage and the inflation tax.

The panels of Figure II.1 may be helpful in illustrating concepts of demand for money.

In Panel A, uu' is the path of money's real marginal product for successively larger amounts demanded, given Y'. An increase in income shifts uu' rightward. The amount demanded is Oa and Ob is the algebraic sum of $r + P^* - \underline{d}$. When this sum is reduced to zero by an increase in $\underline{d}$ or by price deflation expected or both, money is demanded in the satiation amount Ou'. The net private and social welfare accruing as a flow from real-money wealth is measured by the area under $ua'a$ for the smaller amount of real money, by the

Figure II.1   Aspects of demand for money

Panel A   Panel B

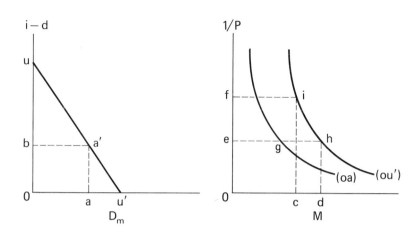

area under uu' for the larger. The larger amount is demanded, and welfare is highest, if the net opportunity cost of holding it, represented by the difference between the money rate of interest and nominal deposit rate, is zero.

The same two alternative amounts of real money demanded are indicated in Panel B by rectangular hyperbolae. Money holders are indifferent as between all possible combinations of nominal money M and its unit value $1/P$ along the curve oa: the point g is not superior to any other. The larger amount ou' similarly may be constituted from the combinations indicated by points i or h or any other. Correspondingly, money holders do not care how any desired rate of growth in real money demanded is achieved: any $\dot{D}_m$ can be satisfied by numerous combinations of $\dot{M}$ and $\dot{P}$ that satisfy the equality $\dot{D}_m = \dot{M} - \dot{P}$.

Supply of Money and Instruments of Monetary Policy

Any stock of real money can be supplied by an indefinitely large number of appropriate combinations of M and P. Any growth rate of the stock of real money $\underline{\dot{M}}$ can be supplied by an indefinitely large number of appropriate combinations of growth rate of nominal money $\dot{M}$ and of growth rate for the price level $\dot{P}$:

$$(16) \qquad \underline{\dot{M}} = \dot{M} - \dot{P}$$

Now, for the long run, there is continuous equilibrium in the market for money, so that:

$$(17) \qquad \underline{\dot{M}} = \dot{D}_m$$

Moreover, the rate of change in prices $\dot{P}$ is determined on the market for money and by the difference:

$$(18) \qquad \dot{P} = \dot{M} - \dot{D}_m$$

The rate of inflation or deflation, a phenomenon of the market for money, preserves equilibrium in that market given the rate of increase in real money demanded by wealth holders and in nominal money supplied by the monetary system. The monetary system can accommodate any growth rate in real money demanded by an indefinitely large number of appropriate combinations of $\dot{M}$ and $\dot{P}$. It exercises its choice by the simple expedient of setting $\dot{M}$. Money holders are indifferent, for any $\dot{D}_m$, between combinations of $\dot{M}$ and $\dot{P}$, so that the monetary system can choose the combination.

Manipulation of $\dot{M}$ by the supplier of money is an instrument of monetary policy because it is the means of regulating $\dot{P}$. Because $\dot{P}$ is perfectly foreseen by money holders, its adjustment by the supplier of money is an instrument for regulation of the expected rate of inflation P^*. In turn, the expected rate of change in the price level is one instrument for regulation of real deposit rate $\underline{d} - P^*$ or d, and nominal deposit rate is the other. Real deposit rate is the ultimate instrument of monetary policy, with M, P, and $\underline{d}$ qualifying only as proximate instruments. Increases in real deposit rate result in money deepening; they raise the ratio of the stock of money demanded to income and, hence, of the equilibrium stock of money relative to income, and decreases reduce the desired and realized ratio. If P is perfectly flexible, as WV commonly assumes, all participants in the market for money must be indifferent among the innumerable combinations of $\underline{d}$ and $\dot{P}$ or P^* that sum to any d.

WV and Optimality of Monetary Policy

The choice of WV and WVK among alternative deposit rates—the nomination for optimal monetary policy—is very simple. For money that is costless to produce, real deposit rate should be set at equality with the real rate of return on physical capital and with consumers' rate of time discount. Then the marginal productivity of money falls to zero, with the real stock of money demanded and supplied at the full-liquidity or satiation level. The marginal productivity at zero is equal to the marginal cost of money, and the income effect of money deepening is maximized.

This ultimate of monetary policy can be achieved, when the price level is flexible, with a constant stock of nominal money. In steady-state growth, with income-elasticity of demand for money at unity, the rates of price deflation and income growth would be equal, and nominal deposit rate would be dictated by the difference between income growth and the rate of return to physical capital. Along the golden-rule path of growth, with equality between $\dot{Y}$, $\dot{P}$ and r, nominal deposit rate could be zero. The monetary authority might issue no increments of nominal money, announce no deposit rate and permit price deflation to assume entire responsibility for maintaining the best ratio of real money to real income and to physical capital. In such a state the monetary authority would have nothing to do. With welfare at its maximum, the monetary authority would be unemployed, technologically displaced by a flexible price level.

We may discard the assumption of downward price-level flexibility. Then price deflation involves a social welfare loss in short-period instability of income and employment and is not acceptable. There is no reason for deviating from the target of full liquidity. Given unit elasticity of demand for money, in terms of income, the monetary authority may set $\dot{M}$ equal to $\dot{Y}$ to preserve price-level stability and fix nominal deposit rate equal to r. With the rate of growth in nominal money and deposit rate at the disposition of the monetary authority, downward price-level rigidity implies no sacrifice of social welfare. To be sure, the monetary authority is busy distributing its seignorage, but it does so costlessly.

Perhaps money-holders stubbornly anticipate some rate of inflation no less than P^*_e. The reason might be that the monetary authority has experimented too long in the past with this rate of inflation, and nothing can persuade money holders that prices will be any more stable. Again there is no reason for deviating from the target of full liquidity. The monetary authority needs only to expand nominal money at the rate of growth in real income *plus* P^*_e and pay a nominal deposit rate on money balances of $r + P^*_e$. The economy can extract the maximum in income effect from real money at any rate of inflation if nominal deposit rate is held at parity with the free-market money rate of interest.

This same story of realized and expected inflation can be rephrased. Perhaps, as a condition for avoiding short-period instability, money-wage rates must rise at the rate $\dot{W}$ though the rate of growth in labor's marginal product is a smaller $\dot{w}$. The difference implies a perfectly foreseen rate of inflation in the price level of output. The rate of increase in nominal money must be $\dot{Y} + \dot{W} - \dot{w}$, and nominal deposit rate must be $r + \dot{W} - \dot{w}$ to achieve full liquidity in money holders' portfolios. Sometimes this phenomenon is interpreted as wage-push inflation. However, the inflation is achieved by the appropriate rate of growth of nominal money, not by the rise in the money-wage rate. The value of $\dot{W}$ sets a target for the rate of inflation, if short-period instability is to be avoided. Moreover, $\dot{W}$ is high because of labor's experience in the past with $\dot{P}$ and so with $\dot{M}$. Wage-push turns out to be a special case of price-level rigidity.

It has been possible to realize full liquidity on the market for money in each of the cases we have considered. Now we turn to a case in which optimality is out of reach. It is assumed that $\dot{P}$ is positive and inflexible downward and that, for some institutional reason, no deposit rate can be paid. The monetary authority must impose and collect an inflation tax, but it cannot return the revenues to money holders as a reward for money holding. Inevitably the desired ratio of money to income must fall below the satiation level, and there is a welfare loss to the economy that exceeds inflation-tax revenues. The excess is indicated by the area $aa'u'$ in Panel A of Figure II.1. As a proportion of the economy's income, this loss rises with the minimal rate of inflation for which deposit rate cannot compensate. To be sure, the tax revenues are available to the monetary authority for some fiscal purposes. Because the same purposes can be achieved without social cost, WV assumes, by other measures than inflation, the economy is inevitably harmed.

Professor Friedman's recent prescription for monetary policy in the United States can be derived from our last two cases. Because of this country's experience with inflation, perhaps also because of the vanities of labor leaders, the least obtainable rate for $\dot{W}$ is zero, not less, and the best rate of price deflation is equal to $\dot{w}$, about 3 per cent. Granted that the steady-state growth in income is 4 per cent and that there is unit elasticity of demand for real money, the appropriate $\dot{M}$ is 1 per cent. If income elasticity of demand for money is higher, perhaps 2, the appropriate $\dot{M}$ is 5 per cent.[4]

The average nominal deposit rate in the United States on the various assets that count in Professor Friedman's definition of money is not high enough to cover the difference between price deflation of 3 per cent and the rate of return on physical capital. The rate $\underline{d}$ is low because money consists partly of currency, on which payment of interest is judged not to be feasible, and because of regulatory ceilings on $\underline{d}$ for deposit forms of money. Hence it appears that full liquidity cannot be obtained, and that the issuers of money, both government and banks, are collecting an uncompensated tax from money holders. Given the restriction on $\underline{d}$, the loss of social welfare must increase if current policy with respect to nominal money and price inflation is so liberal as to raise the minimum $\dot{W}$ and so reduce the achievable rate of deflation below 3 per cent. Expansion of nominal money must be held steadily in the range of 2 per cent.

Professor Friedman has faith in the competitiveness of private

[4] Milton Friedman, *The Optimum Quantity of Money and Other Essays,* pp. 46–47.

banking and its ability to circumvent regulatory ceilings on nominal deposit rates.[5] He is receptive to the suggestion that banks do pay rates above the ceilings by granting services to money holders. If the suggestion is correct and if banks can be counted upon to pay premia that vary with the rate of inflation and expected inflation, stability of money-wage rates is not so important after all for social welfare in the long run, and the 2 per cent rule can be relaxed.[6]

THE MARKET FOR CAPITAL

In the context of all markets the market for money finds the equilibrium stock of real money and real deposit rate. The market for capital finds the equilibrium stock of physical capital and the real rate of interest. Because, according to WV and WK, real money and physical capital are substitutes in wealth holders' portfolios, the markets for money and capital jointly find the equilibrium ratio of real money to capital and the ratio of real deposit rate to the real rate of interest. In this section we are concerned with the market for capital and with its interdependence with the market for money. WV is presented first, then WVK.

WV and the Market for Capital

Output is putty in the WV model, and it may be consumed or invested. Because savers are investors, there is not literally a market for capital with buyer-seller confrontation. Homogeneous saver-investors pit the retention and accumulation of putty capital against the attractions of putty consumption with a third option in mind, the accumulation of money. They arrive at one real rate of interest. Although existing capital is consumable, the analysis below is in terms of net accretions of investment.

Saving-Investment in the Barter Economy. In setting the stage for WV, it may be helpful to consider equilibrium in the capital market of a barter economy:

[5] Milton Friedman, *op. cit.,* pp. 38–39, 47.
[6] Prakash Lohani and Earl A. Thompson, "The Optimal Rate of Secular Inflation," *Journal of Political Economy,* September/October, 1971, p. 981.

(19) $I = sF(K, L)$

Reducing both sides of (19) to a per capita basis, dividing both numerator and denominator of I/L by the capital stock K and assuming balanced growth, we obtain:

(20) $nk = sf(k)$ **1768122**

where n is the growth rate of output, capital, and labor and k is the capital-labor ratio. The propensity to save s is a constant. The expression nk is growth in demand for capital, and $sf(k)$ is savings available to finance it, both on a per capita basis.[7]

Saving-Investment and Deadweight Money. A simple version of WV introduces money as wealth but not as income and not as a factor of production. Its accumulation competes with physical investment I:

(21) $I = sF(K, L) - \Delta (M/P)$

If real money demanded is a constant proportion o of income and if the market for money is in equilibrium, (21) may be written:

(22) $I = sF(K, L) - o \Delta F(K, L)$

Dividing this expression by income, one obtains a vital distinction between the constant propensity s to accumulate wealth in both physical and money form and the "physical propensity" s_p to accumulate physical wealth only:

(23) $s_p = s - on$

The physical propensity to save varies inversely with the money-demand coefficient o.

Now the expression (20), relevant for a barter world, must be adjusted to exclude monetized savings:

(24) $nk = (s - on)f(k)$

---

[7] A particularly helpful reference for the present analysis is David Levhari and Don Patinkin, "The Role of Money in a Simple Growth Model," *The American Economic Review,* September, 1968, pp. 713–753.

This represents in extreme degree a basic proposition of WV and WVK—the substitution effect of growth in real money against growth in real capital. Any increase in the desired proportion o of money to income must result in a smaller capital-labor ratio. Money enrichment is capital impoverishment, and hoarding implies a reduction in consumption along a path of steady growth, assuming that the capital-labor ratio is not above its golden-rule optimum. Because any reduction in k raises the marginal product of capital and the real rate of interest, money accumulation tightens credit. If the money-income ratio o is a positive function of real deposit rate, it follows that the real rate of interest and real deposit rate are directly related as well as that the real rate of interest can be reduced by expected inflation. From observation of the capital market only, one may conclude that consumer welfare is improved by a low, even negative real deposit rate, and the analysis suggests that welfare is highest when there is no money at all.

Saving-Investment with Money as Income and as a Factor of Production. The conclusion that an economy is better off with barter and without money is unacceptable in WV and WVK. One knows from analysis of the market for money that welfare benefits when demand for money is sated. The dilemma that optimality on the market for capital implies no money at all whereas optimality on the market for money calls for money satiation is easily resolved. The first step is simply to count growth in real money as income. Then (22) may be replaced by:

$$(25) \qquad\qquad Y' = F(K, L) + o\Delta F(K, L)$$

$$(26) \qquad I = s\,[F(K, L) + o\Delta F(K, L)] - o\Delta F(K, L)$$

Proceeding in the same manner as with (22), we obtain these replacements for equations (23) and (24):

$$(27) \qquad\qquad s_p = s - (1 - s)on$$

$$(28) \qquad\qquad nk = [s - (1 - s)\,on]\,f(k)\text{[8]}$$

---

[8] Special acknowledgement is due at this point to Professor James Tobin for his pioneering work in monetary growth theory: "Money and Economic Growth," *Econometrica,* October, 1965, pp. 671–684.

The result of counting growth of real money as income is to increase the physical-savings ratio. Money displaces consumption, not physical savings alone, in a fashion that we term the WV savings effect, a partial offset for the substitution effect.

The second step in escape from the optimality dilemma is to introduce the income effect of growth in real money. In the manner of equation (1), real money is included as a factor in the production function, which becomes $G(K, L, M/P)$ rather than $F(K, L)$. The monetized society achieves a higher level of putty output than the barter society for each combination of physical capital and labor. The real interest rate, real wage rate, and putty output per capita are determined on a superior frontier of production possibilities.

The definition of the physical-saving propensity remains unchanged from (27), but the condition of equilibrium on the capital market (28) is revised:

$$(29) \qquad nk = [s - (1 - s)\ on]\ g\ (k, m)$$

We know that $g'(m)$ is positive so that each increase in real money per capita increases the flow of physical savings per capita to the capital market, expressed on the right side of (29), and hence for each steady growth rate n in output and labor force permits a higher capital-labor ratio k. An increase in the money-demand coefficient o does tend to raise the real rate of interest on the capital market: real deposit rate and real rate of interest are positively related through the income effect. However, the real rate of interest tends to rise because capital is more productive, not because it is more scarce, and the associated gain in income per capita assures more physical savings and a higher k at each real rate of interest. Money lifts capital-labor and consumption-labor ratios along the golden-rule path.

Public Policy and the Dilemma of Optimality. Because of the substitution effect, growth in real money deprives the capital market of savings. Because of the savings effect, a part of this diversion of savings is restored. Because of the income effect, labor and putty capital become more productive, and the higher level of income per capita for each capital-labor ratio recovers still more of the savings diversion. The net result for savings flows to the capital market is ambiguous, but the best or golden-rule capital-labor ratio is raised.

According to WV, public policy has the perfect, costless solution for the dilemma that money satiation occurs at the expense of optimality on the capital market. An economy can have optimal money and optimal capital too—the best m and the best k. The key to optimal money is a real deposit rate that reduces the marginal product u of money to zero. The key to the best k and r is the physical-savings propensity s_p. If k lies below the golden-rule target, the fiscal authority may save more of its income from state-owned enterprise, and it may tax private incomes, both saving and investing a larger proportion than the taxpayers would prefer. If k is too high, the fiscal authority may spend on public consumption or reduce tax rates. Monetary technique affecting d and fiscal technique affecting s_p are socially costless and combinable for the purpose of removing the last shreds of the optimality dilemma.

Evidently money is not neutral in the WV regime. Any change in real deposit rate affects the production function, the savings and consumption functions. It implies some appropriate adjustment in tax rate and government consumption and investment. Variations in nominal money that do not affect real deposit rate are neutral, to be sure, and the rate of inflation does not matter if nominal deposit rate is adapted to it. The stock of real money, its rate of change, and its yield are not neutral, and public intervention is required if the optimal deepening of both money wealth and physical wealth is to be achieved.

WVK and the Market for Capital

In his *General Theory of Employment Interest and Money,* Lord Keynes was subjecting capitalism to static-equilibrium analysis, probing for the structural defects that could result in chronic under-employment of human and physical wealth. His diagnosis identified deadweight money and other liquid wealth, costless to produce, as one weak spot. In his fix-price model, with $\dot{P}$ zero, money's own yield is certain and unable to fall below zero for any stock of real money, however large. The real rate of interest on the alternative disposition of savings, physical capital, is regarded by private investors as uncertain, subject to variance. This subjective risk attached to physical capital and its rate of return has no social basis: private myopia regarding the rate of interest is the second weak spot.

With real money available as an abode for private savings, any decline in the real rate of interest on physical wealth relative to its mean expected level can reduce the private physical propensity to save. There is desired substitution of money wealth for physical wealth, on grounds of risk avoidance. This liquidity-preference demand for money implies both a substitution effect upon real capital accumulation and an employment effect. Demand for money induces no employment, because money is costless, and is suppressed by a fall in employment of existing capital and labor unless public policy intervenes. Money, in the presence of uncertainty about the real rate of interest, has an employment effect. There are solutions for these defects of capitalism that can achieve optimality, from the social point of view, on the markets for money and capital.

Lord Keynes emphasized that there are two savings decisions in the private sector. Wealth holders decide s, the share of income not to be consumed, and s_p, the share of savings to be applied to growth in physical wealth, relative to s_m, the share of savings destined for growth in real money balances. The importance of duality in the savings decision was dramatized by a distinction between savers and investors who are linked by a market in private securities, but this distinction is not important to the Keynesian diagnosis of capitalistic frailty. On the Keynesian market for money, a related distinction is drawn between money demanded for transactions purposes and money demanded as a shelter from risky investment of physical savings.

Equilbrium in the market for money is written:

$$(30) \qquad \frac{M}{P} = o_1 \, F(K, L) + o_2 \, (i)$$

where transactions demand is positively related to real income and liquidity-preference demand is negatively related to the money rate of interest, becoming infinitely elastic at some low level of i. The money rate is identical with the real rate of interest only in the fix-price regime.

The prescription for equilibrium on the capital market is:

$$(31) \qquad I - sF(K, L) - o_1\Delta\, F(K, L) - \Delta\, o_2\,(\iota)$$

Incremental transactions demand for money, as between one static-equilibrium level of income and another, and incremental speculative demand, associated either with a shift of the function o_2 or with a fall in i, reduce the desired ratio of physical savings to income:

$$(32) \qquad s_p = s - \frac{o_1\Delta\, F(K, L) + \Delta\, o_2\,(i)}{F(K, L)} = s - s_m$$

Now (31) becomes:

$$(33) \qquad I = (s - s_m)\, F(K, L)$$

The substitution effect of growth in real money, common to all variants of WV, is apparent in (33). At alternatively higher levels of income and lower levels of i, with s given, the desired physical-savings ratio diminishes toward zero, depressed by desired money savings s_m. In particular, savings tend to fall into the liquidity trap $[o_2\,(i)/F(K, L)]$.

There is equilibrium on the market for output when:

$$(34) \qquad F(K, L) = C + I + G$$

Here C is private demand for consumption, and G is government demand for physical output. The components of effective demand may be rewritten:

$$(35) \quad F(K,L) = (1 - s)F(K, L) + s_p F(K,L) + (s - s_p)F(K, L)$$

This suggests that output can be at full-employment level if seignorage from the creation of money is spent by government, in deficit finance, but the seignorage can be applied to demand for output in the private sector; for example, through loans from the monetary system, if the privately expected r is not so low that incremental private demand for wealth is demand for money-wealth only. If the differential $s - s_p$ at full employment is not accommodated, equilibrium on the goods market must be found at a lower level of output. Because s is an average ratio that falls with income, output may decline until s is zero and incremental demand for money, financed by savings, has been destroyed. If $s - s_p$ is not accommodated by government spending, autonomous shifts in private demand for output, or decrease in liquidity preference, the differential must be wiped out by underemployment of existing physical and human wealth.

With static equilibrium in the markets for money, savings, and output, there may be chronic excess supply in the market for labor. A fall in money-wage rates and output prices P is of no use in restoring full employment. Its effect, given r, is to reduce the money rate of interest i, intensify demand for money, raise s_m and increase the differential $s - s_p$. That is to say, expansion of real money through price deflation simply makes money wealth more attractive relative to physical wealth. Expected price deflation is a real deposit rate on money.

Keynes disclosed in the *General Theory* his standards of market optimality and techniques of policy for achieving them. For the labor market optimality means full employment. For the capital market optimality means euthanasia of the rentier, with the capital-labor ratio above its golden-rule level. On the market for money optimality is satiation of demand for money in the sense that real deposit rate and the marginal utility of money are zero.

WVK, expressed in the *General Theory*, was a sophisticated variant of WV, introducing the concept of risk on markets for wealth and tracing the impact of the substitution effect of demand for money upon employment in static equilibrium. Subsequent developments of WV have added the savings and income effects. A superb monetary theorist, Lord Keynes was fully aware that real money contributes to welfare and undoubtedly took the income effect for granted.

WV AND THE MONETARY-FINANCIAL STRUCTURE

Money wealth in the preceding discussion has been governmental fiat money, homogeneous in quality and costless to produce. We consider briefly in this section alternative forms of money and non-monetary financial assets in the WV regime. For each new asset there is a new market with its own specifications of optimality.

Deposit Money and Currency

For reasons that are not evident in the frictionless economy of WV, money might be differentiated between deposits subject to transfer by check and pocket currency. The only new issue to arise is that payment of a nominal deposit rate on pocket currency might not be feasible, although a real deposit rate common to both forms of money could be arranged by price-level deflation. If deflation is ruled out so that a full-liquidity deposit rate can be paid only on deposits, the result is that the public demands too little currency and satiation of money demand is impossible. Presumably differentiation increases the income effect of growth in real money, but this advantage cannot be fully exploited.

Bodied Money

Fiat money is costless to produce and maintain. It is net wealth on the social balance sheet. Commodity or bodied money is not costless. It is not an addition to social wealth but a diversion of wealth from other uses. After resources employed in producing and servicing money have been reported as wealth, it would be duplication to report the real money stock, too.

The optimal stock of bodied money is not the full-liquidity stock. The reason is simply that at full liquidity the marginal social utility of money at zero would lie below the marginal real cost of producing money. Bodied money is inefficient in the WV regime because it is expensive and because there is no reason why giving body to money should increase demand for money. Fiat money is clearly preferable to, say, gold. Rational preference against fiat money must be based on rigidities, immobilities, and imperfections of rationality and foresight that are excluded from the WV regime.

Inside-Outside Money

There is no place in WV for any distinction between outside and inside money. Real money is wealth whether produced by the state or by private bankers or by the American Express Company in the form of traveler's checks. It is wealth no matter how its producer puts it into circulation. The full-liquidity rule of optimality applies for all varieties of costless money. The income and substitution effects of growth in real money are the same in all cases, and the savings effect is the same if different money issuers spend seignorage in the same way.

Private Banking

The monetary system need not consist of the monetary authority alone. There may be private banking, and the money supply may consist of both high-powered issue by the monetary authority and bank money or of bank money alone. We consider here only two among numerous possible arrangements: one is money issue by private monopoly, and the other is competitive private banking in conjunction with the monetary authority. In both cases there is a new market for bank charters with its own conditions of supply and demand and its own socially optimal price.

A private money monopolist would be free of money illusion, with no concern for the stock of nominal money M and the price level P. The monetary authority would necessarily designate a base-period aggregate of M. Then the monopolist could be relied upon to find the rates of change $\dot{M}$ and $\dot{P}$ and the nominal deposit rate that would maximize his flow of real revenues and, given the real rate of interest, the capital value of his charter. He would fix real deposit rate so that the stock of real money, on a per capita basis, would be the stock demanded at the point of unit elasticity on money holders' demand schedule for his product. Evidently the full-liquidity deposit rate would not be to his taste. The monetary authority can impose the full-liquidity rate upon him by a new instrument of monetary control, a tax liability equal to the product of the money rate of interest and the satiation stock of real balances. This is a liability that exceeds his revenues from each stock of real balances less than the satiation stock. The tax would reduce the value of the monopoly charter to zero, and a sensible monopolist would throw his charter away.

Alternatively, the monetary authority may experiment with delegation of responsibility for money issue to a banking industry consisting of numerous firms. The monetary authority would issue charters on request at zero price but would specify for each banker the initial issue of nominal money. The authority would not specify deposit rate or impose it by tax. Because banking is costless in the WV regime, perfect competition among bankers would establish a full-liquidity rate. Competition would compel each banker, operating his business with no factor inputs, to return to money holders his entire revenues from money issue. Optimality is achieved, for the case in which the monetary authority is money monopolist, if the authority fixes real deposit rate equal to r. It is achieved, for all cases of private banking, if bank charters are a free good. This implies that there is no place for rational private bankers in the WV regime.

Proposals for a reserve requirement of one hundred per cent upon private bankers fit into the context of the WV of money. Such a requirement permits bankers to issue nominal money, but it appropriates for the monetary authority the real revenues from issue that, in a state of full liquidity, the authority should pass on to money holders. It is a substitute for monopoly of money issue by the authority, for a full-liquidity tax on a private money monopolist, and for free competition in banking. It makes bank charters worthless.

Non-monetary Financial Assets

In the regime of WV there is no place for part moneys, for instruments that combine in varying proportions the qualities of money and of equities in physical capital. Any wealth holder may achieve the portfolio he wants, with some wealth in money form and some in physical form, and there are no costs to be economized by adding a crossbreed form of wealth. Moreover, the monetary authority is not so blind to optimality in the market for money that it imposes deposit rate below the full-liquidity level, in effect inviting bankers to differentiate money and invent new forms on which higher deposit rates pass the authority's inspection. Money is unambiguously and homogeneously money.

No rational basis exists for non-monetary financial intermediation. No economies of scale are to be realized in acquiring and holding equities in physical wealth, no special advantages in access to information about returns to physical capital on the basis of which intermediaries could sell their indirect debt at a rate of interest lower than r. In the WV regime one cannot find assets that are partly money and partly intermediary debt. There are gilt-edge equities, and there is money. We shall wish to inquire, in the next chapter, whether WV needs money.

If the regime were to distinguish savers from investors, so that private securities would appear, maturity dates would be unimportant. Any maturity would do, and the real rate of interest would be uniform for all issues because the marginal product of capital is constant and perfectly foreseen. If the monetary authority adopted a constant rate of inflation, the money rate of interest would be uniform for all maturities of security. A variable rate of inflation would create maturity differentials between money rates of interest, but rates of inflation would be perfectly anticipated in forward rates. The market for securities would be an homogeneous market. It would also be an unnecessary market.

CONCLUSION

The regime of WV is remote from lagging economies, the regime of WVK a little less remote because of its allowance for risk and risk aversion. Some elements of WV and WVK are vulnerable to criticism even in the context of steady growth. For example, it is not clear how money can enhance production possibilities along a frictionless growth path. Again, as we suggest in the next chapter, the substitution effect is fictional. On the other hand, various things that WV and WVK have to say about markets for money and capital are pertinent to lagging economies. A case in point is the emphasis on the relative price of money, its real deposit rate, and its significance for money deepening. Failure to heed some of the lessons that emerge from WV and WVK have cost lagging economies dearly. The purpose of the Debt-Intermediation View, to which we turn now, is to adapt WV and WVK so that they can be used to find and correct mistakes of monetary and financial policy.

BIBLIOGRAPHICAL NOTE

The theory of growth in a monetized economy is not burgeoning: it has burgeoned. The list of references below is a modest but fairly representative sample. Each reference pushes the level of analysis beyond the point that we have considered necessary for our purpose of bringing some basic notions of monetary theory into discussion of policy for developing or lagging economies.

Phillip Cagan, "The Non-Neutrality of Money in the Long Run: A Discussion of the Critical Assumptions and Some Evidence," *Journal of Money, Credit and Banking,* May, 1969, pp. 207–227.

Harry G. Johnson, "Inside Money, Outside Money, Income, Wealth, and Welfare in Monetary Theory," *Journal of Money, Credit and Banking,* February, 1969, pp. 30–45.

Allan H. Meltzer, "Money, Intermediation and Growth," *The Journal of Economic Literature,* March, 1969, pp. 27–56.

Jerome L. Stein, "Monetary Growth Theory in Perspective," *The American Economic Review,* March, 1970, pp. 85–106.

3 | Money, Finance, and Capital Accumulation II. The Debt-Intermediation View

The strategy of repression—of excess demands and interventionism—is imposed in regimes that are radically unlike the regimes of WV and WVK. Its effects are to intensify the contrast, twisting the path of development in lagging economies away from steady and optimal growth. The strategy of liberalization including financial deepening can perform no miracles in cleaning up the debris of distortions in markets for money and capital, for example, or labor and foreign exchange. What it can do is difficult even to measure and describe precisely, given the context of disarray in which it is applied. Nonetheless, the signals that it gives do invoke changes in market structure and market behavior that make steady, optimal growth a more relevant dream for the lagging economies.

The Debt-Intermediation View (DIV), discussed in this chapter, is adapted, partly at least, to the regime of frustrated growth. Output is not putty, for example, nor is foresight perfect. DIV differs in a second way from WV and WVK, regarding money, not as wealth, but as debt of the monetary system. Still, in a number of circumstances, it calls upon the classic conclusions of WV and WVK to explain the advantages of the shift in development strategy from repression to liberalization and especially of deepening of finance.

The first section below is a study in contrasts, between the DIV regime of lagging economies and the regime of steady, optimal growth. The second section discusses social accounts and conditions of production in the DIV mode. The third section brings us once more to the market for money, an area of disagreement between DIV and WV or WVK. Markets for non-monetary financial assets are the topic of the fourth section, and the capital market appears again in the fifth section. There follows a brief discussion of financial organization.

CONTRASTS IN ENVIRONMENT:
STEADY GROWTH VS. LAGGING DEVELOPMENT

The economic regime of WV is blandly homogeneous, difficult to enjoy but easy to aggregate. The labor market trades in homogeneous units of effective labor. Output and physical capital are putty. Production applies a single, best technology that evolves at a steady rate. Excess demands for physical wealth, money, and a government perpetuity are continuously cleared at a single real rate of interest. In contrast, the regime of lagging economies is notable for segmentation of markets. It is not a collection of common markets, not even for money.

The markets of lagging economies do not report uniform prices. Not just one real wage rate exists, but many—for urban labor and rural labor, native and foreign labor, unionized and unorganized labor. The relative price of money in goods and services cannot be specified unambiguously because one item bears different prices and because buyers' baskets of purchases are dissimilar. The capital market is perhaps the most fragmented of all because frustrations from capital scarcity have generated especially pervasive and discriminatory intervention. Differentiated prices in the various markets are commonly not competitive prices: market power is applied by government and by private market participants as well.

Temporal horizons are short in the lagging economy. Capital scarcity is one reason: there are high returns to short-lived investment of scarce savings. Experience with instability in real rates of return to physical and financial assets is a second reason. Unforeseen instability in the past has generated aversion to far forward commitments, a sense of high and unpredictable variance in returns to forward contracts beyond some short horizon. This aversion is especially apparent in markets for financial assets. There short-term instruments predominate, and long-term instruments are small in real volume, bearing high relative yields when low yields are not imposed by authority. Because financial markets do not establish a wide span of forward rates of interest, investors in physical wealth are conscious of risk in successive refinancings of durable investments.

A continuous, imperfect adjustment is present in the DIV regime of expected prices and rates of return to unforeseen experience with changes in prices and yields. On the market for money, rates of price inflation $\dot{P}$ do diverge from expected rates P^*. The result is that assets bearing unescalated nominal yields, and money in particular, are subject to imperfectly foreseen changes in real value. The risks associated with these assets divert portfolio demand from patterns that real social rates of return would justify and depress demand for wealth relative to consumption and demand for domestic wealth relative to wealth abroad.

Information is expensive and incomplete regarding yields for both physical and financial assets. Investors, savers, even tax collectors, work under a handicap of ignorance about yields and costs of wealth holding. Benefit-cost analysis for new projects, firms, and industries depends in no small degree on sheer divination. Allocative waste could be reduced appreciably by even modest new investment in data banks at the expense, for example, of new construction for commercial banks.

Mobility is costless in the WV regime: there is no friction in substituting superior for inferior uses of resources, and there are no distributive consequences in correcting for misallocation. DIV is necessarily concerned with long-run effects of error in accumulating and allocating resources. The assembly of wealth is a progressive phenomenon, and the qualities of an existing labor force or capital stock affect new allocations in the market for savings. Some governmental interventions in markets for, say, money or savings or labor represent attempts to escape social costs of past mistakes.

In a WV regime savings need not pass through financial markets other than markets for money and government securities. Savers are investors, and the savings function describes both the diversion of resources away from consumption and the diversion into investment. There are no scale economies in producing putty input, no lumpiness in capital accumulation that justifies specialization between savers and investors. Entrepreneurship is part of the homogeneous labor force, and all entrepreneurs have the same costless access to relevant information and best technology. DIV is preoccupied with a quite different world in which investment opportunities are not homogeneous and in which there are risks differently measured and differently regarded by savers and investors. DIV necessarily makes a place in its analysis for diverse financial markets and for financial innovation that both responds to and creates a changing distribution of yields on capital accumulation.

Best practice is the rule in WV. Optimal technology is known to all producers, and there are no lags in adjustments of the capital stock, the labor force, and relative factor prices to technological progress. Instruments and techniques of monetary and fiscal policy work without friction or cost. Goals of policy can be specified precisely, and an equal number of instruments is at hand for costless implementation. Where DIV applies, diffusion of technology is slow and expensive, and one counts partly upon reform of financial and other markets to assist in accelerating it selectively. One allows, too, for constraints on public policy that include real costs in monetary and fiscal systems, ambiguities in policy objectives and delays in policy impact. First-best is typically out of reach in production, finance, and government intervention.

The WV regime is sectored very simply. There is a private inside sector and a public outside sector. Private entities, in indefinitely large number, keep busily concerned with maximizing micro-welfare. The state attends to macro-goals of optimality. This clear sectoral demarcation is blurred in a DIV context. There is mixed public-private enterprise. Powers of the state are appropriated for discrimination between classes, clans, and regions. The state's capacity to tax and borrow is closely bounded. In many respects the state resembles a private sector in its behavior. One implication for us is that debts of the two sectors may be treated alike in analysis of the lagging economy's markets: the distinction between outside debt and inside debt is dropped.[1]

The list of differences between the putty world and the lagging economies is much longer, but the ones mentioned here are especially important for the analysis to come. It is to be emphasized that the differences do not invalidate lessons about money that can be drawn from the simple world of steady growth for the contorted world of underdevelopment. There are markets for money in both contexts, interrelated with other markets, and all of the special features of underdevelopment cannot justify the substitution of "structuralist" irrationalities about monetary phenomena for principles that emerge in analysis of steady growth.

WEALTH, PRODUCTION, AND INCOME

Distinguishing characteristics of DIV appear in the social accounts and in the aggregative production function of the lagging economy. Real money is not counted as social wealth nor growth in real money balances as social income, and money is not a productive factor. A distinction is drawn between saving and investing sectors, and these sectors are linked by a collection of financial markets. Finance is not costless in terms of factor inputs. To explain these and other differences between DIV and WV, there is first a schematic social balance sheet, then a production function, and finally some social flow accounts.

---

[1] For examples of the role that this distinction has played in economic analysis, see Lloyd A. Metzler, "Wealth, Saving and the Rate of Interest," *Journal of Political Economy,* April 1951, pp. 93–116 and Robert A. Mundell, *Monetary Theory: Inflation, Interest and Growth in the World Economy,* pp. 14–22.

Private and Social Wealth

Social accounting in the DIV manner, approximately relevant to lagging economies, is a tangle of ambiguities. Segmented markets produce different prices for labor, wealth, and consumables, and market imperfections result in discrepancies between private and social valuations. Alternative methods of valuing and aggregating stocks and flows can yield substantially different estimates of real growth rates or of ratios between labor, physical wealth, output, and financial assets. Sectoring the economy generates financial assets bearing different rates of return. The nice simplicity of the WV balance sheet is gone.

A sectored social balance sheet appears in Table I. One part of it is for an investing or deficit sector that holds part of physical wealth K and of the money stock on the basis of retained earnings and of primary debt. A second statement is for a surplus sector that holds money, non-monetary indirect financial assets NM, a portion of outstanding primary debt and real equity in financial institutions. A third statement is for the monetary sector that holds physical wealth and primary debt, owes the money stock as its debt, and reports the difference between assets and debt as equity. The final statement is for the non-monetary intermediaries. They own physical wealth, money, and primary debt, with their assets financed by non-monetary indirect debt and retained earnings. For present purposes, no distinction is drawn between state and private sectors: the state can be fitted into any or all sectors. If these statements are consolidated, the surviving entries are the capital stock K and the sum of equities for the nonfinancial sectors. Money does not survive, because it is counted as intersectorial debt but not as wealth.

Money is identified on the social balance sheet as the means of payment, an instrument for economizing on services of human and physical wealth in the search-and-bargain process. Depending on the expected level and variance of its real deposit rate, it may substitute for physical wealth, primary debt or "bonds," corporate equity, and claims an non-monetary intermediaries as a store of value in

Table I   Sectored social balance sheet

Deficit Sector (a)		Surplus Sector (s)	
Assets	Debt	Assets	Net Worth
K^a	B	$\dfrac{M^s}{P}$	E^s
$\dfrac{M^a}{P}$	$\overline{iP}$	$\dfrac{NM}{P}$	
	Net Worth	$\dfrac{B^s}{iP}$	
	E^a	E^b	
		E^c	

Monetary Sector (b)		Non-monetary Intermediary Sector (c)	
Assets	Debt	Assets	Debt
K^b	$\dfrac{M}{P}$	K^c	$\dfrac{NM}{P}$
$\dfrac{B^b}{iP}$		$\dfrac{B^c}{iP}$	
	Net Worth	$\dfrac{M^c}{P}$	Net Worth
	E^b		E^c

private portfolios. Elasticity of substitution for other assets against money varies along a continuum, in the financially developed economy, from nearly unity toward zero. If money is defined more broadly, as an abode of purchasing power yielding such nonpecuniary services as pride of possession, it can be related only by some strong stretch of imagination to policies and instruments of monetary authority in the usual sense. "Money" yields private and social services because it is the one good for which all others exchange, and its use permits escape from search-and-bargain processes that are more costly in factor services. As the means of payment, in reserve for expenditure, it may dominate other abodes of purchasing power.

Money in any form—coins, notes, or deposits—is debt of the issuer, whether monetary authority or private bank. The issuer is committed to providing facilities for the payment process, and there is an appropriate deposit rate of interest for each stock of real money. Moreover, the issuer is committed to redeem real balances that money holders do not desire, at a stable or falling price level, by withdrawing nominal money, or to repudiate them through inflation.

Real money is not costless. Supplying it is expensive in resources. The expense includes the minor items of minting coins, printing notes, and establishing bank accounts. It includes, too, the costs of allocating the real savings that flow into the accumulation of money balances; the "fiscal" aspect of monetary expansion is costly, particularly in the lagging economy with its segmented capital markets and its paucity of information regarding investment opportunities. Creation of real money requires real resources, and so does the provision of the services of money as a means of payment. The money industry draws physical and human wealth from other uses and sustains a technology of producing the national income that is more productive than technologies associated with barter.

The monetary system is a financial intermediary attracting savings from spending units that forego consumption to acquire increments of real money. It allocates these savings to other spending units, some for private or government consumption and some for private or government investment. In addition, it exchanges its own money debt for the primary debt of spending units wishing to augment real money balances. Finally, it intermediates between savers repaying their primary debt to the monetary system and new borrowers. It reduces social wealth and income by diverting factors into its own employment. It increases social wealth not including money and social net income not including increments in real money or the services of money if factors remaining with other industries, including households, are deployed more efficiently than barter permits.

The monetary system is one part of the financial system for which place must be made in the social accounts. No new principles are involved in accounting for other intermediaries: there are factor costs and risks in their operation, and a part of the community's income from its capital stock is distributed to them and through them to savers. Their debts are claims for distinctive services to the creditors, and these services count as intermediate inputs to producers of final outputs, in some cases, and to ultimate consumers in others. Markets for primary securities, the third component of the financial system, yield their own services at a cost, and direct finance through them occurs at a "bond" rate of interest lower than the marginal return to capital by a margin sufficient at least to cover their cost.

Money may be state as well as private issue. It may involve a simple exchange of the state's money debt for the primary debt of the private sector. Alternatively, it may involve an exchange of increments in real money balances for private savings that the state can redirect to the private investing sector or utilize for its own purposes including capital accumulation, consumption, or transfer payments. The provision of state money involves costs in supplying services of the payments mechanism and in allocating the real proceeds of money issue. The state may exercise monopoly power and may hold for itself a valuable charter or may dissipate the value of the charter in dividends to recipients of its choice.

Conditions of Production

The lagging economy produces within the consumer household, for both subsistence and trade, as well as within the private firm and in government enterprise. Inputs and technologies are heterogeneous, markets for outputs and inputs are segmented, and uniform prices do not prevail. Conceptually and statistically, national net product or income is difficult to specify. Sidestepping difficulties of definition and aggregation, we write conditions of aggregate production as follows:

$$(1) \qquad Y = H\ (K_1\ .\ .\ .\ K_n, L_1\ .\ .\ .\ L_n;\ T)$$

Here Y is real income; the K's are production goods; the L's are heterogeneous labor services. Subscripts indicate the employing industries, and T is a collection of production processes. Some production goods (K_m, L_m) are employed in the money industry, some in nonmonetary finance (K_n, L_n), and T defines technology in the financial production function. For the time being, it may be supposed that (1) is not affected by economies of scale, and usual marginal relationships apply. The marginal products are competitive standards, within industries, for real wage rates w and real interest rates r. Since common, competitive markets do not enforce one price for each factor, a golden rule of capital accumulation cannot be defined.

The real stock of money does not appear in (1) as a factor of production. Output Y of non-monetary goods and services is related instead to factors employed in the money industry and to monetary technology. Services of the money industry are intermediate inputs for other industries including household industry: balances of real money both extend boundaries of markets and release labor and physical capital from the search-and-bargain process and from "abodes of purchasing power." On the basis of (1), DIV defines a dual income effect of growth in real money. A negative component exists because growth in real money draws labor and capital away from other industries to the money industry. The positive component is the same as suggested by WV, a contribution of growth in real money to the average and marginal products of factors producing Y.[2] Growth in the stock of real money extends production possibilities within any constellation of related markets, and it makes feasible the extension of market boundaries.

It appears in (1) that full liquidity in the WV sense cannot be the target of optimality for growth in real money. First, there is no single nominal rate of interest to set the standard for money's deposit rate $\underline{d}$. Second, real monetary expansion incurs marginal factor costs so that at full liquidity the marginal yield of money would lie below marginal cost, and there would be a social sacrifice of some attain-

[2] Productivity gains from the existence and use of money are analyzed in an extensive and increasing body of literature including: W. J. Baumol, "The Transactions Demand for Cash: An Inventory Theoretic Approach," *Quarterly Journal of Economics*, November, 1952, pp. 546–556; Karl Brunner and Allan H. Meltzer, "The Uses of Money: Money in the Theory of an Exchange Economy," *The American Economic Review*, December, 1971, pp. 784–805; Edgar L. Feige and Michael Parkin, "The Optimal Quantity of Money, Bonds, Commodity Inventories, and Capital," *The American Economic Review*, June, 1971, pp. 335–349; Sir John Hicks, *Critical Essays in Monetary Theory*, pp. 1–60.

able output. The goal of full liquidity does not allow for the negative income effect of money.

Flows on Income and Product Account

We are defining net national income by factor shares as:

$$(2) \qquad\qquad Y = rK + wL$$

The rate of return r is a vector of disparate rates on the heterogeneous pile of physical wealth. The rate of return w to human wealth is no less complex where markets for wealth are imperfectly linked. Because it cannot be supposed that factor markets are competitive, interpersonal income distribution is affected not only by productivities of owned factors but also by market power, and it is affected too, of course, by fiscal redistributions and transfers. It will be noted that growth in real money is not included in (2) whereas earnings of factors employed in financial industry are included.

The aggregative allocation of income to consumption, savings, and investment is:

$$(3) \qquad\qquad Y = C + I = C + S$$

Income is consumed or invested, and investment is financed by savings. Growth in the money stock does not count as an addition to wealth, and the savings aggregate is physical savings, with no component of savings applied socially to growth in real money. There are no final services of money or of other financial assets as a part of consumption.

Money and non-monetary financial assets do appear in sectoral measurements of the allocation and disposition of income.[3] An intermediary sector, consisting of the monetary system and nonmonetary financial institutions, attracts savings of a surplus sector, where savings exceed investment in physical capital, by issue of its

[3] Raymond W. Goldsmith, *Financial Structure and Development,* Chapters 1 and 2; John G. Gurley and Edward S. Shaw, *Money in a Theory of Finance,* Chapters I–III; John G. Gurley and Edward S. Shaw, "Financial Structure and Economic Development," *Economic Development and Cultural Change,* April, 1967, pp. 257–268.

own debt including money. It applies these savings to its own accumulation of physical capital and, in exchange for primary securities or "bonds," to accumulation of capital in a deficit sector, where investment exceeds savings for self-finance. The intermediary sector absorbs savings, too, from repayment of bonds by some of its borrowing customers. It stands ready, finally, to exchange money and other claims upon it against primary securities when no savings flows but only portfolio readjustments are involved.

Desired savings are demand, in part, for additions to real money balances and other financial assets. Desired investment is supply, in part, of additions to the real stock of primary securities. The monetary system and other financial institutions intermediate by incurring real-money and non-monetary indirect debt that savers wish to hold and by buying real primary debt that investors wish to owe. Intermediation increasing the stock of real money may occur by way of an increase in nominal money or by a decrease in the price level with corresponding changes in the number of bonds B or in the real value of each bond in the monetary system's portfolio.

The monetary system receives as its gross income a share of rK^a (Table I) equal to B^b/P. It incurs costs in depreciation of its own K^b, in wage costs of labor that it employs, in costs of other inputs and in interest payments to money holders at real deposit rate d. The gap between r and d is a measure of unit costs in maintaining the payments mechanism and intermediating, of reward for risk taking to bank shareholders and of monopoly power. Reducing the gap to a competitive minimum is an objective of monetary policy, but reducing it to the full-liquidity of WV by raising d to equality with r is inefficient.[4] Monetization and intermediation are not costless and risk-free. Similarly non-monetary financial instituitons realize a rate spread between r and their own deposit rate $d,$ and it is one objective of financial policy to maintain this spread at a competitive level.

In the preceding chapter the rate of increase in nominal money was defined as a tax on money holders, refundable by payment of

[4] John Hicks, *Capital and Growth,* Chapter XXIII.

deposit interest. In the absence of refund the tax appropriated income for the monetary system from production of money wealth. According to DIV, money is not wealth, and increments in its real stock are not income. Yet, if money holders are not compensated by deposit interest, intermediation that involves expansion of nominal money rather than price deflation diverts gross revenues of the monetary system away from money holders to the deficit sector or to owners of bank equities. The inflation tax redistributes a portion of rK, reducing the reward to savings that flow through the intermediation of the monetary system to capital accumulation.

The social accounts trace the distribution of rK to compensation of factors employed in the financial process and to savers. The returns to savers flow at the rate r in self-finance, at the rate $i - \dot{P}$ in direct finance, at the rate d to money holders and at the rate d_n to holders of claims on non-monetary intermediaries. Holders of bank equities receive incomes that banks can command for entrepreneurship and risk assumption or appropriate from either borrowers or money holders by imperfectly competitive activity on markets for primary securities and money.

THE MARKET FOR MONEY

Substantial differences exist between WV and DIV regarding the market for money. These differences arise partly because the regimes are so dissimilar, partly because real money is regarded as wealth in one case, and as debt in the other. However, from both points of view, money is not neutral. On the contrary, optimal monetary policy is important for social welfare.

Demand for Money

There can be no money wealth in WV models unless services of money generate a demand for it. We can detect no services for money to perform in the WV regime. Putty output and wealth are riskless to hold and costless to move. Full liquidity is in the WV regime without money: the marginal product of real money in the social production function is zero for all amounts of money. WVK assumes a chronic myopia of wealth holders regarding the rate of return to physical wealth, as a basis of demand for money, but myopia is unlikely to survive long-run steady growth. WV and WVK are not a fruitful context for analysis of banking because it would require no factor services and pay no factor rewards for producing a product that no one wants.

In the WV regime the homogeneous output would be generally acceptable as a medium of exchange. In the regime of DIV money alone is generally acceptable, at a uniform price in the unit of account, in exchange against all other goods. The boundaries of the market for money are a currency area, and in this area spending units use money to clear surpluses of net selling and deficits of net buying in other markets. The basis of demand for money is the service it performs in clearing the area's payments matrix.

The lagging and underdeveloped economy may comprise more than one currency area, and imperfect "foreign-exchange" markets between the areas may reduce the scale of common markets in output, wealth, labor, and securities. In some regions common markets are reduced to the small size that barter can accommodate, where monetization is primitive. Improvement in conditions of supply of money and in the payments and intermediation functions of the monetary system is prerequisite to consolidation of these segmented markets. As this improvement merges currency areas in the economy, the amount of real money demanded rises. Conversely, mismanagement of money supply and inefficiency in provision of services in the payments and intermediation processes have been known to cause reversion to segmented markets and barter.

The amount of real money demanded depends positively upon the services of money as a means of payment. These services are one element of u, included in money's real own-rate of return r_m. Their marginal value is high for small stocks of real money, measured in relation to wealth. The chance of default by a spending unit on markets where it incurs deficits increases as real money balances are held in lower average volume. This risk can be diminished if the spending unit has access to borrowing facilities, but borrowing is expensive. Risk of default and expenses of borrowing can be diminished if the spending unit holds other disposable assets than money, but trading in these assets involves costs that do not affect the medium of exchange, and holding the assets in inventory involves storage costs and changes in value that are larger than those associated with money. These risks and costs can be reduced if spending units adjust payments intervals or contract the payments matrix, but these solutions are also expensive. The service of money in economizing costs and risk of settlement diminishes marginally as the real stock of money increases relative to wealth.

Accumulation of money is one form of saving. It is a substitute for saving through self-finance of physical investment, purchase of primary securities or acquisition of non-monetary indirect financial assets. It delegates responsibility for allocation of savings to the loan officers and investment committees of the monetary system. Capital and labor employed in the monetary system provide not only the services that facilitate the use of money as a means of payment but also the services of intermediation. Their advantages in skill and scale can reduce both costs and risks that savers incur in disposing of their savings. These costs and risks avoided are another element of money's return u.

No asset is riskless in the lagging economy. The rate of return on money *ex-post* includes the realized rate of inflation $\dot{P}$, and $\dot{P}$ is neither stable nor perfectly foreseeable in the DIV regime. Monetary systems in lagging economies do not compensate money holders for changes in the price level with changes in nominal deposit rate. Money is a risky asset, but there may still be risk aversion or liquidity-preference demand for it because the variance of its real rate of return is small and predictable relative to variance in returns to other assets. Monetary policy that adds to the risk of money holding drives risk aversion demand to physical wealth, consumption, or foreign assets.

Money yields services as means of payment and as a store of value for working capital and risk-aversion purposes. These services represent both private and social economies in resources of capital and labor. Demand for money is induced by them and by real deposit rate. The rate of price-level change is not subject to perfect foresight in the DIV regime: $\dot{P}$ and P^* are not the same. Expected rates of change and their probability of occurrence are deduced from experienced rates and from other observations of money holders regarding, for example, the behavior of the nominal money supply or of governmental budgetary deficits or of money-wage adjustments and foreign-exchange rates.

Money yields returns u, P^*, and $\underline{d}$. Holding money for the sake of these rewards, that add to r_m, involves opportunity costs, indicated in the WV model by the single rate of return r to homogeneous physical wealth and government debt and by the consumer rate of time preference r_c. The DIV regime has a variety of opportunity costs. Segmented capital markets require us to reinterpret r as a vector of opportunity costs. Non-monetary indirect financial assets are a counter-attraction to money, and their rate of return d_n is an opportunity yield in the money-demand function.

Demand for money depends upon own-yield and opportunity yields. It depends, too, on wealth or permanent income, the expected stream of returns to wealth. This stream is not perfectly foreseen, and it is subject to revaluations by income recipients. It may be revalued downward in recurring periods of crisis and economic constraint, and demand for money falls correspondingly. It may be revalued upward when public policies take a turn that implies renewal or acceleration of economic growth, and demand for money rises correspondingly. Casual evidence indicates that revaluations can be large, with significant discontinuities in the stock real money demanded relative to current income.

Determinants of instantaneous demand for real money may be summarized in this equation:

$$(4) \qquad D_m = l\ (Y_p, r_c, r, d_n, r_m, t)$$

where positive effects on money demanded are associated with Y_p, r_m, and t. The argument t is included to suggest the stimulating effect on demand for money of technological improvement in the money industry, of increases in the currency area, and of resulting gains in monetization of the economy. It may be interpreted as a trend term, but there are occasions when, for example, major improvements in the monetary mechanism or rapid shifts of population into the cities should be indicated by some large change in t. The remaining arguments are all subject to uncertainty, and the rates of return are not uniform among money holders nor even homogeneous for each spending unit.

Absence of money illusion is assumed in DIV as in WV and WVK. Demand for money is demand for real money and can be satisfied by various combinations of M and $1/P$. Price-level expectations are not static. The money-demand function of WV is modified in four ways. A discounted sum of income expected to the money holder's horizon is substituted for current income because of the latter's variability. There is a new substitute for money yielding d_n. All of the determinants of money demand are subject to uncertainty, and allowance is made for technological change.

Supply of Money and Instruments of Monetary Policy

The function of the monetary system is to supply the appropriate stock and rate of growth of real money balances, providing services of the payments mechanism in which these balances are used. Insofar as growth in real money balances attracts savings of money holders, the function of the monetary system is also to intermediate, allocating the savings between alternative investments in physical wealth or to dissaving. Savings are intermediated, too, between investors repaying debt to the monetary system and investors incurring new debt. There is a "monetary" function and a "fiscal" or intermediative function. The former brings the monetary system to the market for money, the latter to the market for capital.

For the long-run analysis of this chapter, we assume continuous equilibrium on the market for money, with the rate of growth in the stock of real money equal to the rate of growth in the stock demanded:

(5) $\dot{\underline{M}} = \dot{D}_m$

Because growth in real money and maintenance of the money stock
is not costless, we may visualize a real-money supply function:

(6) $\underline{M} = \dfrac{M}{P} = q\ (i,\ \underline{d},\ P^*,\ w,\ e,\ g,\ t)$

Primary rates of interest i less the expected rate of inflation P^* are
the reward that the monetary system can extract by provision of its
services according to the technology t. Deposit rate $\underline{d}$ less P^*, or d,
is a real cost to the monetary system. The spread between primary
rate and deposit rate is absorbed by real wage costs w, real user
costs e of physical capital and by an additional cost g that suggests
the supply price of risk assumption in banking by private enterprise
or by the state.

DIV accepts the quantity-theory interpretation of the price level:

(7) $\dot{P} = \dot{M} - \dot{D}_m$

Because there is no evidence of money illusion in the money-demand
function (6) or in the money-supply function (8), it is the responsibility of the monetary authority to specify nominal money M and its
rate of growth in order to determine P and, without the precision that
is assumed for the WV regime, the expected rate of inflation P^*.

According to WV, the ultimate instrument of real money policy is
real deposit rate, and it can be manipulated through P and either
nominal deposit rate or charter policy. Responsibilities of the monetary authority are more complex in the lagging economy. There one
normally cannot count upon charter policy to enforce competition
in the banking industry. As a result, the authority may need to induce economies in factor inputs, enforce competitive levels of loan
and deposit rates, and press for acceleration of technical change in
monetary and banking service. It is up to the authority to determine
whether a private money industry supplies net worth sufficient for
preventing default on money debt and whether special measures for
insurance of money balances are in order. Economies of scale can

occur along some portions of the money-supply function that would justify state subsidy of banking enterprise on a temporary basis, and the argument may be made that some externalities of growth in real money also justify subsidy. In economies where DIV applies, one can find imperfections and abnormalities in markets for money, primary securities, and bank charters that seem to require instruments of monetary control in addition to $\dot{P}$ and $\underline{d}$.

Optimality of Monetary Policy

DIV commits the monetary system to participation on both the market for money and the market for capital. Optimality of monetary policy is an issue on both markets. We consider new criteria for optimality on the market for money and return later to "fiscal" criteria for the monetary system on the market for savings.

In a WV regime, in which the price level of output is flexible and perfectly foreseeable, $\dot{P}$ can be a matter of indifference. In a DIV regime there are narrow limits within which the monetary authority can elect a $\dot{P}$ that is both feasible and desirable. Output is heterogeneous, and the various prices that enter into any index P are not equally flexible: for some period any change in the growth rate of P involves relative changes in output prices that would not otherwise occur. Labor is heterogeneous, and the various money-wage rates that enter into an index W of the general wage level are not equally flexible so that variations in W result in relative changes of real-wage rates. Deviations of $\dot{P}$ and $\dot{W}$ from familiar paths have consequences in the price structure that affect stability of income, distribution of income, and its rate of growth.

Foresight regarding $\dot{P}$ is blurred in the DIV regime. If it is permitted by the monetary authority to fluctuate in some random way, real yields implied in any present money rate of interest are uncertain. Erratic changes in $\dot{P}$ result in uncertainties regarding P^* that, for those averse to risk, divert demand from money and from wealth, particularly from wealth yielding long-term streams of income. One concludes that $\dot{P}$ should be stable. An escalation clause in all forward contracts could protect markets for money and capital against price-level variability, but escalation is costly to administer and, judging from the fact that escalation has not been widely adopted nor always retained after trial, it is an imperfect substitute for a stable rate of change in the price level.

Conditioned by long experience with inflation, lagging economies are even less amenable than developed economies to pressure from the monetary authority for price level deflation secularly. Real deposit rate cannot include a negative P^*. The choice of $\dot{P}$, then, is for a stable rate not less than zero and not higher than can be accommodated by flexibility in spot prices and escalation in forward contracts. The likelihood is that for most economies the appropriate $\dot{P}$ comes close to price-level stability. The argument for stability is strengthened by the fact that deposit interest cannot be paid easily on pocket money. In comparison with deposits the optimal amount of coin and currency may be relatively high in lagging economies so that penalizing demand for coin and currency can retard monetization significantly.

According to WV the optimal nominal deposit rate is equal to the money rate of interest. This relationship is not appropriate in lagging economies because there is not just one money rate of interest and because the monetary system incurs real costs. Instead, interest allowances to depositors should exhaust earnings of the monetary system after provision of all costs. The costs include factor payments and a competitive return on net worth. They should include as well premia for insurance of money holders against default by private money issuers. Because a private market for insurance is unlikely to develop in the lagging economy, the monetary authority must assume responsibility for fixing the premium, administering the insurance fund and defending the markets for money and capital against the shock of banking failure. Premia varying among banks according to their loss experience may be an efficient substitute for expensive and not always perceptive governmental supervision of banking practice.

These specifications for nominal and real deposit rate do not imply full liquidity in the sense that the marginal utility of money would be driven to zero. However, they are as close an approximation to the standard set by WV as is possible when money is expensive to produce and maintain, when capital markets are segmented and when risk is attached to bank portfolios. Their intent is to exploit fully the positive income effect of growth in real money subject to the negative income effect that growth in money entails real social costs.

MARKETS FOR NON-MONETARY FINANCIAL ASSETS

In the WV regime no economic opportunity exists for financial assets other than money and government debt. Physical capital is homogeneous and costless to hold, its rate of return perfectly foreseeable and subject to no scale economies. Money and government debt provide yields equal to the return on physical wealth. Neither factor productivity nor consumer utility has anything to gain from further portfolio diversification.

In lagging economies real money and real government debt are in small volume relative to income and physical wealth. Direct long-term finance of investment is slight, and non-monetary indirect financial assets exist in marginal amounts. Private and governmental self-finance of physical wealth are found, and apparently substantial but unknown amounts of financial assets are generated in short-term curb markets. Our point in this section is that economic opportunities may exist for deepening not only in money but in other financial assets, too.

Economic opportunity for a financial asset other than money occurs if it yields services and a pecuniary return at a real rate d_n that diverts savings from money, self-financed investment, direct finance, and consumption and if the differential between this rate and the yield to physical wealth r allows competitive remuneration, for the real volume in which the financial asset is demanded, to factors employed in supplying the asset and its services and in allocating the savings flow. Demand and supply functions may be defined, comparably with functions (4) and (6) for money. The critical issue is whether there is an equilibrium stock and rate of growth at an interest rate "gap" $r - d_n$ that compensates for factor costs.

Some differentiation in financial assets has occurred, in more and less developed economies alike, as the result of imperfect competition and nonoptimal regulatory policy in the monetary system.[5] Banks and their regulators have put low ceilings on money's yield r_m that create a market opportunity for a different asset and its issuing institutions. Other cases occur in which d_n has been supported by subsidy at levels attractive to savers. Again, some institutions have been developed for captive groups of savers, especially government employees, who could be forced to accept low deposit rates. Financial differentiation induced by one variety or another of market imperfection is sometimes wasteful of factor inputs to financial industry; it is not effective in raising rates of saving; it does not commonly improve savings allocation. It is not financial deepening.

Some differentiation, then, has been superfluous. Some kinds of differentiation are irrelevant in lagging economies because, perhaps, of social and legal phenomena. Others are involved in a vicious circle of capital shortage: they require an investment of capital in human skills, in facilities for finding and using information, in market-place facilities; but, because capital is not available for their own purposes, they cannot perform their function of attracting savings to ease capital shortage for investors. Constraints in the demand and supply functions for financial assets in lagging economies limit efficient differentiation and justify primary emphasis on real growth in the monetary system.

Even the issues of monetary systems have been differentiated in a degree that only exercise of the banks' monopoly powers can fully explain. To be sure, there are costs and risks to banks in issue of demand money debt that can be economized by issues of longer maturity, and deposit rates rising some small number of steps from the basic rate on money can be justified. The case seems to be a strong one, for simplifying the financial-asset menu for savers by permitting the monetary system to exercise its competitive capacities in selling a lean selection of demand and term obligations.

[5] "The President's Commission on Financial Structure and Regulation: A Symposium," *Journal of Money, Credit and Banking,* February, 1971, pp. 1–34.

Economic opportunities for finance are bound to occur that the monetary system cannot exploit as efficiently as other financial institutions can.[6] At one extreme a cooperative credit union may win its share of the market because of special services that it can provide to both savers and investors and because it economizes explicit factor inputs. At the other extreme, in a sufficiently large economy, a stock market with its retinue of brokers, dealers, information specialists, and others may give savers access to rates of return on primary securities that, even with due allowance for risk, can divert demand from indirect financial assets including money. Economies of scale may occur in supplying some indirect assets, yielding distinctive nonpecuniary services, that justify specialized financial enterprise. Areas of investment may be found, closed to the monetary system at any modest premium for deposit insurance, to which savings can be drawn by intermediaries that are especially adapted to measurement and assumption of high risk.

There remains good reason for a lean selection of financial assets. On the side of demand, the wealth constraint in lagging economies as well as savers' inexperience in estimating yields and savers' traditional commitments to some forms of self-financed investment imply that a fat selection of assets would simply subdivide the total market into inefficiently small pieces. On the side of supply, the scarcity of resources for financial industry implies that there should be specialization in a few markets. On the side of regulation, government is strained enough in fulfilling basic functions without distraction for supervising a complex financial system. If savers are to receive the highest average of deposit rates, on various assets including money, for each set of social opportunities to invest in growth of the capital stock, the case against a complex financial system is persuasive.

Import substitution and autarky can be as objectionable on markets for financial assets as on markets for goods and labor. Some domestic financial industry can yield fully competitive returns to factor inputs once it has acquired skill and scale—infant industry

[6] James Tobin, "Notes on Optimal Monetary Growth," *Journal of Political Economy,* July/August, 1968, Part II, pp. 839–859.

that can be given a running start by insurance of its debt. Other domestic financial industry is bound to be a burden indefinitely on the capital market. In order to avoid its high factor costs, its demand for subsidies, and its misallocations of savings, the lagging economy may import financial services. Experience even in the more developed economies suggests that comparative advantage or disadvantage among economies, in provision of financial services, may have long-term staying power.[7] Free trade in finance is a sounder basis than subsidy, in some circumstances, for wealth accumulation.

THE MARKET FOR CAPITAL

According to WV equilibrium growth in real money generates the savings that wealth holders wish to invest in real money. Given wealth holders' target proportion of total wealth—money, government securities, and physical capital—to income, this accumulation of money can displace some accumulation of physical wealth, diverting to consumption some savings that would otherwise flow through the capital market to productive instruments. If the money-income ratio is raised to the satiety level by an appropriate increase in real deposit rate, the result is a rise also in the rate of interest r: money deepening is at the expense of capital deepening. However, according to WV, this effect may be reduced, even reversed, if money wealth adds enough to the social productivity of human and physical wealth and to consumers' utility both to raise income and, given the target ratio of all wealth to income, to increase physical capital demanded at each rate of interest. That is to say, the income effect of money and an allied savings effect may offset or overpower the substitution effect on wealth portfolios. Whatever the balance of effects, the optimal ratio of physical wealth to income can be achieved by costless fiscal policy.

DIV does not grant the *substitution effect* because it does not count real money as social wealth or growth in real money as social income

[7] Organization for Economic Cooperation and Development, Committee for Invisible Transactions, *Capital Markets Study: General Report.*

and savings. DIV puts more emphasis than WV upon the *positive income effect* of growth in real money because it is concerned with a regime that has not exploited monetization to the full and has not achieved a common currency area by full employment of the technology of money. It finds a *negative income effect* of growth in real money because the services of the monetary system require inputs of physical capital and labor.

DIV does not assume for its regime a given target ratio, for private savers, of total wealth to income and of total savings to income. It suggests a *savings effect*, different from the WV savings effect, of growth in real money and financial deepening upon the private propensity to save. DIV introduces, too, an *investment effect*. Growth in real monetary and other finance is associated with intermediation that unifies segmented capital markets and raises accessible rates of return to wealth. Finally, DIV does not grant the frictionless perfection of fiscal instruments but finds that government's fiscal devices in lagging economies intensify capital shortage, that fiscal devices effectively available are imperfect substitutes for monetary and other intermediation in eliciting and allocating savings and that fiscal performance benefits from financial growth.

Financial Growth and the Rate of Saving

Changes in private and social rates of capital accumulation are among the striking features of the development process. When an episode of quickened development comes to a close in a lagging economy, both private and public budgets shift away from capital accumulation to consumption. When the pace of development picks up once more, accumulation accelerates. These discontinuities can be associated in part with financial constraint and liberalization.

Some of the gain in savings that comes with financial deepening may be illusory. Savings may be drawn to uses that are counted in national income statistics and away from capital flight in various forms that defy measurement. For example, because measurement of inventories is notoriously imperfect, savings applied to inventories may escape count while the same savings drawn to finance by increased rates of return would be reported. Income and savings from smuggling are in a statistical no-man's land, but exports drawn to normal channels by exchange-rate and interest-rate adjustments are easily identified.

The gain in savings is not wholly illusion. To some limiting stock of real money per capita the positive income effect of growth in real money outweighs the negative income effect so that incomes rise. Given private propensities for saving and rates of taxation, the higher level of income implies a higher flow of private and public savings and investment relative to the existing capital stock. The extension of market matrices and the economies achieved by money in the search-and-bargain process cannot fail to raise factor productivities, incomes and savings flows.

Some of the gain in savings associated with liberalization seems to be transitory. The increase represents a temporary acceleration in demand for wealth, at the expense of consumption, perhaps to restore inventories that have been drawn down during a period of inflation with, say, an overvalued foreign-exchange rate and import licensing—perhaps to replace capital equipment for which maintenance has been neglected. It is a once-and-for-all adjustment of the wealth portfolio to desired levels that lifts the savings-income ratio temporarily and, once done, has no lasting effects on capital intensity.

However, good reasons explain a permanent effect on the private and public savings-income ratio. New investment opportunities appear, possibly because restraints are lifted on agriculture and exports, because imports can be liberalized or because there are changes in relative prices of factor inputs including capital and labor, and these opportunities encourage saving for self-finance of investment. An increase in the real stock of money permits bank credit to flow more freely, even though at higher rates of interest, and borrowers to build up their equities to qualify for loans.

Measures to raise real rates of return on financial assets, to reduce the variance of returns, and to improve financial technology, along with allied measures in nonfinancial areas, extend savers' horizons over both space and time. Wealth portfolios that seemed appropriate at each level of income are too small when savers can diversify more efficiently in an integrated capital market and when the flow of returns to wealth can be anticipated with greater precision for relatively long periods. If the savers' future is less obscure, they can be expected to lower their rates of time discount.

Observation of savings behavior in developed economies particularly suggests a relatively small or even perverse influence for rates of return to savers' portfolios on desired savings-income ratios.[8] However, the range of experienced rates is small in comparison with the range of rates in lagging economies as they shift between significantly different growth rates in real income, different rates of inflation, and different financial policies. One suspects that savers do respond through self-finance, direct finance, and indirect finance as yields to wealth fluctuate between the negative and positive levels that are reported. Savers may ignore a possibly transitory increase from, say, 4 to 6 per cent in rates of return, but they are less likely to maintain consumption-saving patterns when rates of return change, in a context of economic reform, from negative levels to positive 10 or 15 per cent and more. Given the relative scarcity of wealth in the lagging economies, the income effect of higher rates of return should not be expected to overwhelm the effects on substitution of more wealth for less consumption now.

For various reasons, financial deepening and associated measures tend to change the distribution of income within the private sector as

[8] Irwin Friend, "Determinants of the Volume and Composition of Savings with Special Reference to the Influence of Monetary Policy," in Commission on Money and Credit, *Impacts of Monetary Policy,* pp. 649–688; K. L. Gupta, "Personal Saving in Developing Nations: Further Evidence," *The Economic Record,* March, 1970, pp. 243–249; John Maynard Keynes, *The General Theory of Employment Interest and Money,* p. 93; Ryutaro Komiya, "Japan," in National Bureau of Economic Research and The Brookings Institution, *Foreign Tax Policies and Economic Growth,* pp. 60–61; Warren E. Weber, "The Effect of Interest Rates on Aggregate Consumption," *The American Economic Review,* September, 1970, pp. 591–600; Colin Wright, "Some Evidence on the Interest Elasticity of Consumption," *The American Economic Review,* September, 1967, pp. 850–855.

well as between private and public sectors. There tends to be a shift in favor of labor against property, as we note in the section below. There is a decline in monopoly rents to importers, for example, or banks and bank borrowers. The public sector gains from higher profits to public enterprise as well as from increases in tax revenues and even from economies in welfare and other consumption expenditures. It is not clear that the redistribution of income within and against the private sector must shift the social savings-income ratio, but the bias seems to be toward an increase, if we may judge from the experience of each country in which liberalization has been tried.

Financial deepening eliminates the uncompensated inflation tax on monetary and other financial assets. Some evidence from experiences of hyperinflation indicates that the tax raises rates of return to physical wealth and so stimulates saving.[9] But contrary evidence indicates that savings are reduced by the tax because it drives savers from real money and other financial assets and shrinks the flow of intermediation, because total real tax revenues are adversely affected and also because of its adverse income effects from demonetization. Perhaps inflation can raise temporarily the relative prices of capital goods that permit economies in money balances and stimulate savings to finance them, but the long-run effect of substituting a less efficient for a more efficient payments matrix can be only impoverishing, reducing both consumption and saving.

Undoubtedly, appropriate real-finance policy, reducing the spread in interest rates $r - d$, has an immediate effect in stepping up the real stocks of money and non-monetary indirect financial assets demanded. Whatever the effect on desired savings in all forms and on any steady-state rate of saving, the effect on demand for real money and relatively close substitutes in the short run is substantial. If the monetary authority is ready for the increase in demand and if it supplies appropriate increments in nominal money, there is an immediate bonus flow of savings to borrowers in the intermediation process. If the monetary authority is asleep, the discontinuity of real stocks

[9] Reuben A. Kessel and Armen A. Alchian, "Effects of Inflation," *The Journal of Political Economy,* December, 1962, pp. 521–537.

of financial assets demanded can be deflationary. Financial deepening that lifts growth paths of accumulation may involve some stormy experiences for monetary, fiscal, and international economic policy.

Investment Effects of Financial Growth

In the WV regime capital is homogeneous, and the best technique is applied to its use. Information is costless; foresight is perfect. There can be unambiguous measurement of the aggregative wealth-output ratio, and the optimal ratio is unmistakable. None of these conditions applies in lagging economies. As a result, there are opportunities for financial growth to improve the investment mix, to reduce savings and investment required at each growth rate of output, and to raise the rate of return to wealth.

Financial growth permits unification of the capital market. It reduces interregional and interindustry differences in investment yields and increases mean yield. In the wider market inferior investment opportunities have a smaller chance in the competition for savings at each bond rate of interest. Moreover, policies that induce financial growth diminish uncertainty regarding forward rates of return on both physical and financial assets so that more rational choice can be made between short-lived and durable instruments. The temporal widening of the capital market and the liberation of interest rates from low ceilings can moderate the investment dualism that is sometimes apparent in lagging economies, with deep investment where real rates of interest are held administratively at low or negative levels and shallow investment where rates of interest are free to reflect savings scarcity. Unlike policies that involve unexpected changes in the rate of inflation, with imperfect adjustment in nominal rates of interest and foreign exchange, liberalization policies minimize the part played in investment decisions by windfall gains and losses.

Financial growth is conducive in other ways to more discriminating choice between investment alternatives. Larger lumps of investment are feasible in the private sector when savings are pooled in financial markets. Diffusion of superior technologies can be faster on the basis of information and experience that is accumulated in financial institutions, and complementarities between investments may be exploited more quickly than is possible on segmented capital markets. Integration of capital markets is the basis for integration for labor, land, and product markets with benefits from more effective utilization of resources and from economies of scale and comparative advantage in outputs, and the result again is to improve the mix and mean yield of capital formation.

Capital markets in lagging economies have difficulty in detecting and discriminating among investment opportunities. They do not reward continuous and critical search for projects especially in the private sector. All too often, when a new flow of finance from the fiscal budget or from foreign sources becomes available, there is a hasty, *ad hoc* assembly of projects with only rough approximations of possible yields. So much of profit from investment depends upon success in bargaining with control agencies for an import license, upon a ration of credit, upon a tax concession, or upon other advantages that investors do not bother to generate the flow of bids for savings that comes to a deep and competitive capital market.

Except for some inventories, buildings, and land, physical wealth is not easily marketable in lagging economies. It is a frozen asset. Financial deepening opens new facilities for disposing of partial equities in wealth or for shifting ownership completely. Whether through intermediaries or through the market for primary securities, wealth holders can achieve liquidity for some forms of wealth that raises their rates of return. When existing wealth has an effective market, values put upon it under competitive conditions are a useful clue to new investment opportunities. Imaginative entrepreneurs can shift their equities from established firms into new investment that might otherwise go unheeded. Firms that are family enterprise can tap new sources of equity funds and expand to a larger, perhaps more efficient scale of operation.

The savings effects of financial deepening tend to increase wealth-income ratios and hence, for a given mix of wealth, to reduce its rate of return. The income and investment effects raise rates of return. In lagging economies all of these effects are unambiguously desirable objectives of financial reform.

Capital and Employment

The essence of financial liberalization and deepening is release of real rates of interest to disclose the scarcity of savings and to stimulate saving, to raise accessible rates of return on investment, and to discriminate more effectively between investments. The outcome is a rise in interest rates and, given the production cost or import price of capital goods, a rise also in the cost of using them. Where substitution between capital and labor can occur, or between capital and land, this increase in the rental rate of capital induces replacement in some degree of labor intensive or land intensive for capital intensive processes and outputs. An increase in interest rates gives the signal that capital is scarce, and the rational response of an economic system is to use capital more sparingly but labor and land more liberally.

It is even possible that higher ratios of labor to capital can shift the distribution of income, raising labor's share. This depends, of course, on the elasticity of substitution between factors in the production function. Elasticity is defined:

$$(8) \qquad e = \frac{-\ \Delta\ (L/K)}{L/K}\ /\ \frac{\Delta\ (w/r)}{w/r}$$

where r is the rental rate of capital rather than the rate of interest. Where e is higher than unity, any decline in w relative to r increases labor employed for every unit of capital utilized. It results also in a rise of wL relative to capital's share of income and output. Then income is reapportioned in favor of labor.

Some conventional analysis of economic development takes it for granted that elasticities of factor substitution approach zero. Then there is no place in the analysis for financial deepening as a device for putting more labor into employment at reduced real wage rates for a higher income share. The same analysis is likely to suppose that the elasticity of savings to the rate of interest is negligible. There is no place in the analysis for financial deepening as a device for putting more labor into employment by eliciting savings for more factories and machines and inventories—the K that the production function specifies. If there is a third assumption, that employers' demand for savings is interest-elastic, the conclusion must follow that financial deepening does not raise the wage rate of labor but does reduce employment. it impoverishes the working class to no one's benefit and discourages accumulation of physical wealth.

In view of growth rates for population and labor force in most lagging economies, the prospect for rapid and socially placid development is dark indeed if interest-rate elasticities are low for the substitution of labor against capital and of savings against consumption, with aggregate investment sensitive to the price of savings. Then there is no escape in the long run, except possibly by foreign assistance, from grossly high rates of unemployment, with the unemployed clustering around urban enclaves of capital-intensive production. And labor must depend largely on extra-market processes to protect its share of income.

Except in unusual limiting cases, then, financial deepening has an *employment effect*, perhaps even a *distributive effect*, in addition to its income, savings, and investment effects. Technologies and tastes are not the rigid constraints that they are sometimes assumed to be. Comparable goods are produced by different combinations of factors. Composition of output does respond to inducements of relative price. Saving behavior is not insensitive to the reward for saving.

THE STRUCTURE OF MONEY AND FINANCE

In the WV regime with perfect mobility, price flexibility, foresight, and competition, a financial system serves no purpose. The regime needs markets only for putty and labor. The regime of lagging economies is a different matter. It generates both real advantages and real costs of financial accumulation, and rates of return on financial portfolios of wealth holders are relative prices that affect consumption, the flow and disposition of savings, the employment and reward of labor. Finance matters. In this context the organization of finance can be important for desired growth of finance.

One can design an indefinitely large number of institutional arrangements for finance in the lagging economy. The choice among them is to be based on the principle of maximizing income, savings, investment, and employment effects. On the markets for money and other financial assets, this implies the highest real rates of return to savers consistent with a competitive return to equity investment in financial enterprise. The return to equity may be computed inclusive of any subsidy that can be justified by externalities of growth in finance that financial enterprise does not foresee or expect to share. Maximizing real rates of return to savers implies economy in inputs of real resources by financial industry, efficiency in selection of financial technologies, and an approximation of perfect competition. On the capital market the central consideration is selectivity by financial enterprise among the numerous alternative dispositions of savings. Because there is no one rate of return for all investment opportunities and because no rate of return can be foreseen with certainty, the portfolio performance of financial enterprise depends upon its absorption and unbiased use of information about capital productivity.

The two critical issues of organization are the degree to which the state shares in financial enterprise and the manner in which the state regulates private financial enterprise. At one extreme financial industry may be private, at the other governmental. The spectrum includes any share, for government, from zero to unity in issue of money and other financial assets and any share in the financial system's portfolio. Whatever the shares, financial regulation is not simply regulation of nominal money and its components of high-powered and private or low-powered issue. Its boundaries are defined in the demand and supply functions for real stocks of financial assets. The concern of financial regulation is market rates of interest, real factor costs and technologies of finance, market values of financial charters, selectivity by financial institutions among investment outlets for savings. Modes of regulation are discussed in the next two chapters.

4 | Financial Repression

The lagging economies have repressed real financial growth. Social losses have resulted. Income might have been higher with more thorough monetization. Savings-income ratios might have risen if savers had been offered feasible rates of return. Savings allocation might have been more effective if interest rates had been used to discriminate ruthlessly among investment options. Employment could have been higher if capital had been substituted less often for labor. Possibly the distribution of income would have been less unequal if less reliance had been placed on the strategy of repression and interventionism.

This chapter is concerned, first, with techniques of financial repression. They are simple but numerous, widely known, and widely practiced. The principle that guides them is to establish unattractive yields on domestic financial assets and so to repel demand. The chapter is concerned, second, with some of the doctrine and circumstances that explain why repressive policy is adopted. Ample basis for it is found in doctrine, from the Old Testament and the Koran to the *General Theory*. Circumstances are everywhere the same: capital is scarce; free-market rates of interest seem ominously high; subsidy at the expense of some savers appears necessary for desired investment; and there is confidence that direct controls can succeed in the saving-investment process.

TECHNIQUES OF REPRESSION

In some economies real financial growth cannot occur. Natural and social considerations may stand firmly in the way. The land may be too arid, the location relative to world markets too remote, the people too isolated from financial sophistication by lack of education. The natural and social environment may repress yields on physical and human wealth so that saving, investment, and financial accumulation are pointless. There may be economies where marginal returns to wealth are so depressed, but they are few and do not concern us here.

The typical lagging economy, short of physical and human wealth, is long of investment opportunities at high real rates of return. The evidence can be found in aggregative data, not too precisely perhaps but adequately, if changes in national income are divided by concurrent or lagged investment and the result multiplied by capital's share in income. The results of this calculation for the Republic of Korea (South Korea) indicate returns during 1962–67, excluding income of unincorporated enterprise, on the order of 17 to 29 per cent net of depreciation and indirect taxes. Evidence can be found as well in project data to report marginal rates of return to physical wealth that dwarf average returns in developed economies, and the evidence comes from such disparate regimes as Chile, Ghana, and India. There is no shortage of investment opportunities: there is a shortage of savings for their finance, especially for the best ones among them.

Deposit, Loan, and Inflation Rates

Economic policy in the lagging economies is intricately involved in price manipulation on virtually all markets. The degree of intervention seems to reach its peak in markets for financial assets, partly because they are so ingenious at evasion. A standard package of intervention consists of a positive and variable inflation rate along with stipulations of loan and deposit rates at banks and other institutions of the "organized" financial market. The realized inflation rate reflects public policy in fixing a rate of growth in nominal money that exceeds growth in real money balances demanded. The expected in-

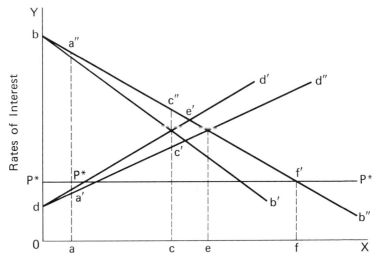

Figure IV.1   Interest rates and rationing

Rates of Interest
Flows of Supply and Demand for Financial Assets

flation rate, which enters into the real loan and deposit rates that concern us here, is a projection by asset holders of experience with inflation modified by their interpretation of other evidence, such as shortages of import goods or new wage contracts, bearing on prospective rates of change in nominal money and real money demanded. The stipulations of nominal loan and deposit rates take sometimes the form of ceilings, sometimes the form of specific percentages.

Figure IV.1 may be helpful in visualizing the impact of inflation and rate control in organized financial institutions including the monetary system.

The curves *bb″* and *bb′* are arrays of average and marginal loan rates at which financial institutions can accumulate primary securities, while *dd″* and *dd′* are arrays of average and marginal deposit rates at which financial institutions may sell their own indirect debt. The curves represent the market opportunities of a representative imperfectly competitive financial institution. Nominal rates are measured from the base axis OX, real rates from the axis $P*P*$, with $OP*$ measuring the expected rate of inflation. Real factor costs of financial enterprise are neglected in this chart, but we do consider them shortly.

We imagine that a nominal ceiling of aa' is imposed on deposit rate, a real ceiling of negative $a'P*$. A high real loan rate would appear to be the corollary of low real deposit rate: the loan rate that would clear the market in Figure IV.1 is aa'' less the inflation rate or $P*a''$. Instead, it is common policy in the lagging economies to put low ceilings over nominal loan rates, for example, at ff' where real loan rate is zero. In effect, asset holders are required to pay a real rate of interest for their indirect financial assets, for lending to banks and, for example, pension funds, postal savings institutions, and insurance companies. Their reward for substituting against other forms of asset or against consumption turns out to be a penalty. On the other hand, borrowers can dispose of their primary debt into the portfolios of financial institutions at low or negative real rates of interest: they are provided with free loanable funds or paid to take them away. The institutions of the organized market are compensated by the spread $a'P*$ between loan and deposit rates. In Figure IV.1 the tax on depositors is the revenue of the intermediary. It appears that the intermediary's preferred position would be at loan and deposit rates of cc'' and cc', with marginal revenue equal to marginal cost.

The figure is too simple for realism on a number of counts. For example, there is typically a scale of deposit rates with arbitrary differentials in favor, for example, of longer maturities or of rural as against urban owners. There is typically a scale as well for loan rates, with the lowest rates accorded to government, exporters, and other borrowers ranking high in planning priorities. Reserve requirements are imposed on intermediaries, and their effect in the figure is to steepen the revenue curves of the intermediary, moving the point b' leftward, unless interest is paid on reserves. The requirements, in effect, appropriate a share of the funds flowing from depositors for lending by the monetary authority. Again, the schedules of yields and deposit rates are subject to uncertainty by reason both of possibilities of loan default and of unforeseen changes in the rate of inflation. Tax effects can shift the curves about.

Simple though it is, the figure indicates the chronic excess supply (*af*) of primary securities in lagging economies that results from the combination of investment opportunity and controls over interest rates in intermediation. Various ways are found of dispelling excess supply. One of them is credit rationing among borrowers, sometimes according to the dictate of monetary or other authority, sometimes according to the preferences of the intermediaries. The intermediary, alternatively, may raise loan rate toward *cc″* by concealed charges and, at least for some depositors, illicitly raise deposit rate toward *cc′*. Borrowers denied accommodation and savers subject to negative deposit rate in the organized market may come together in direct finance either through formal security exchanges or in the curb markets. Some borrowers find funds in the government's fiscal budget, either directly or indirectly through development "banks." Both savers and investors seek better accommodations on foreign financial markets. Despite foreign-exchange controls, savers can and do accumulate assets abroad through capital flight. Investors find substitutes for domestic funds in foreign credits, perhaps short term and very expensive, perhaps long term from various forms of international aid.

Demand for real money balances and some other assets of the organized financial markets appears sometimes to be inelastic to real deposit rate and specifically to inflation. One explanation is that some changes in the rate of inflation do not affect the mean expected rate or its variance significantly: they are a familiar experience and have been absorbed into asset holders' expectations. Another explanation is that money holders have been driven to such economies of money balances that the marginal utility of money rises very sharply with each additional unit foregone. They have reached the stage of money starvation, where further economizing involves unacceptable losses of welfare at least until more ways of using money substitutes can be

arranged or the payments matrix contracted. We consider the inflation inelasticity of demand for money as evidence of financial
repression.

Demand for some financial assets may be less sensitive to real
rates of yield than one would expect, in view of opportunities for
substitution, because it is compulsory demand. In lagging economies
the practice is common of forcing financial assets upon savers, at
negative real yields. Earnings of foreign enterprise are blocked in the
form of deposits or government securities. Government employees
are subject to income withholding, compulsory saving, for retirement
and pension funds, funds for health insurance and education and
finance of national monuments. Importers must accumulate advance
deposits, exporters their proceeds of sales abroad, farmers their revenues from sale to the agricultural marketing corporation. Mandates
to hold financial assets at low or negative real yields are substituted
for rates of return that report to savers the productivity of investment.

Low or negative and uncertain real deposit rates repress voluntary
and total demand for real stocks of claims, including money, against
financial intermediaries. Devices to make indirect finance shallow,
they reduce the capacity of this financial process to provide savings
for investment. The harm that they do is not undone by illicit bonuses to some depositors, and nonpecuniary compensation in the
form of lavish financial buildings or numerous branches or colorful
advertising is an imperfect substitute, as depositors see it, for interest
income and an expensive substitute from the social point of view.
The street markets and regulated exchanges for direct finance can
supply only imperfect substitutes for indirect financial assets even of
non-monetary varieties. The presumption must be that repression of
indirect finance reduces total desired stocks of financial assets and,
given constraints on self-finance of investment, the private domestic
ratio of savings to income.

Low or negative real loan rates leave it to rationing to eliminate
excess bids for loans at intermediaries. Because loan rate is not used
for discriminating among bids for loans of Of in the chart, to sort out

Oa from the total, either public authority or the intermediary must do it. Rationing is expensive to administer. It is vulnerable to corruption and conspiracy in dividing between borrowers and officers of the intermediary the monopoly rent that arises from the difference between low, regulated loan rate and the market-clearing rate. It can be frustrated by borrowers who simply do not repay loans and keep their places in the ration queue by extending maturities. The rationing process discriminates poorly among investment opportunities along the curve *bb''*, and the social cost of this misallocation is suggested by the high incremental ratios of investment to output that lagging economies report.

Effective low ceilings on real loan rates intensify risk aversion and liquidity preference on the part of intermediaries. Banks and others keep a privileged place in their portfolios for established borrowers, especially trading firms with a long record of stability. They have little incentive to explore new and less certain lending opportunities. They are content to pass on some large share of their funds to the monetary authority, through excess reserves, or to the finance ministry, through holdings of government securities. Then, on occasion, the authorities pass the funds along one more step, to development banks. Some of the expensive layering of financial institutions in lagging economies is the direct consequence of controls on loan and deposit rates. There have been instances in which the authorities, while wanting to maintain the share of the central bank, the ministry of finance, and the development banks in total lending by intermediaries, criticize commercial banks in particular for their risk aversion and liquidity preference, and urge upon them more liberal lending in new directions—to fishing cooperatives, for example, or indigenous exporters and low-cost housing projects. Because depositors do not desire an increase in the real value of indirect financial assets, this portfolio expansion could result only in expansion of nominal money and non-monetary indirect debt and, as a result, in the pace of inflation. The effect would be still more repression of financial growth in real terms.

The general level of loan rates is low at intermediaries, with some set to yield real subsidies to borrowers in especially privileged classifications. These subsidies are an assessment upon depositors: they are biased against savers. They are a bonus for products and processes that utilize capital intensively: they are biased against labor. They sometimes go to investors with projects that score badly in terms of anticipated rates of return: they are biased against factor productivity. They have frequently turned out to be wasteful of foreign exchange, encouraging imports of capital equipment or stimulating exports that depend on imported inputs and realize small, even negative value added in terms of international prices. The subsidized loan rate represents repression at its worst.

Patterns of nominal loan and deposit rates in organized finance are often intricate, with differentials of, for example, one-half of 1 per cent common. Yet the other element of real realized rates, the rate of inflation, is permitted to behave erratically, and the expected rate of inflation is more stable in only limited degree. So, in the Republic of Korea during 1969–70, interest rates on government advances by the Bank of Korea were 2 per cent, rates on loans for exports 3.5 per cent, rates on rice-lien loans 4 per cent. Meanwhile, rates were reduced for commercial bills from 22 to 21 per cent, for loans against imports from 5 to 3.5 per cent. In the same period, the rate of inflation increased from less than 10 per cent to more than 13 per cent. There is money illusion in administration of nominal interest rates that results in erratic behavior of real rates. Unstable inflation renders any mean real deposit rate less palatable to savers, any mean loan rate more costly to investors, and any mean real spread less rewarding to intermediaries. It tends to shift leftward the loan-supply and deposit-demand curves of Figure IV.1.

Costs and Profits of Financial Institutions

If financial authority in lagging economies were to let deposit and loan rates alone, for the market to determine, other sources of financial repression would still exist in organized finance. For very small economies diseconomies of scale are inevitable in some varieties of finance, and the relatively high unit costs of financial operation widen the spread between deposit and loan rates. These diseconomies mean, too, that domestic finance can supply, at any given rate spread, only an abnormally lean selection of assets for savers and cannot efficiently accommodate the differences in savers' wealth, taste for risk, and other circumstances that emerge as per capita income rises.

Charter policy does not make the most of competition among banks and other financial institutions, with all of the usual consequences. Unit costs tend to be relatively high among institutions, when finance is repressed, even with allowance for diseconomies of scale. Wide rate spreads reduce pressures for cost economizing. They still leave room for wide profit margins between loan rate and deposit rate. It is a fair surmise that oligopoly is exploited, with the central bank participating, to return attractive profits in the typical repressed financial system. Financial palaces are a common feature on the represssed financial system's landscape, and bankers' associations do not encourage competitive pricing.

Captive finance has been experienced in many financial systems, but it is another standard feature in the lagging economies. Under common ownership with private nonfinancial enterprise, banks and other institutions serve as collectors of savings for the group. Allocation of savings fits the group's requirements, and this allocation is not tested against competitive alternatives. It may be more frequent that banks and some other institutions such as pension funds are captives of government, which draws the flow of savings through them into required reserves, forced loans to enterprise with high plan priority, and compulsory holdings of government securities. They may simply be the deposit windows of development banks. "Organized" finance is organized so that few remnants of competition can persist to affect levels of loan and deposit rates and unit costs. No force is driving to reduce spreads and costs.

Direct Finance

Traditional street or curb markets antedate the paraphernalia of intermediation. They are an escape from repression in the organized financial sector. Savers with no taste for negative real deposit rates and borrowers excluded from credit rationing in the organized sector can meet on the curb with or without assistance of brokers. Their contracts are at short term. The rates of interest are shockingly high, from the point of view of organized finance. Rates reflect the shortage of savings, the high rates of return to investment, risk of default and the costs of search and bargain for loan renewals.

The high rates of interest reflect, too, risks associated with evasion of usury laws and regulations. Repression extends to these markets, but it is evaded at a cost. Although information about curb markets is limited, one does not gain the impression that monopoly power of lenders has much to do with the level of interest rates. Because entry to the market is not limited by scarce charters, monopoly profits tend to be small and temporary. Because savings are mobile, rate differentials between segments of the curb markets must be relatively small, at least after allowance for factors of loan size, maturity, and risk.

The effect of repression in organized finance is to increase amounts of funds demanded on the curb at each rate of interest. The effect of repressive measures on the curb is to reduce funds supplied there at each rate of interest. The only consequence can be that repression raises rates of interest in traditional markets. For strong borrowers who satisfy part of their demands for savings in repressed intermediation and the remainder on the curb market where savers and brokers must dodge prohibitions against usury, the effect of intervention is to make capital more expensive, precisely contrary to the government's intent. Weak borrowers find that the government's expressed concern for them makes matters worse.

Long-term direct finance without compulsion upon savers is rare in the lagging economy. A stock exchange may exist, but it trades in few issues including the issues of the stock exchange itself, of one or another government corporation, possibly of predominantly foreign-owned trading corporations. The domestic stock of physical wealth is too small in the usual case and its growth rate too low for diversified trading in equities. The counter-attractions for savers of investment in simple forms of wealth or assets abroad are too strong in view of costs and risks in a domestic security exchange. The cost of funds to potential borrowers is too high, in terms of interest charges or potential loss of control over enterprises, given the alternatives of self-finance or loans from intermediaries and foreign sources and perhaps from government assistance. The long horizons of saver and investor anticipation that are necessary for security exchanges are too obscure, given uncertainties regarding, for example, the inflation rate or public policies regarding taxes and international trading. The complex fabric of law, accounting, and other elements of sophisticated trading in long securities are too expensive for operations on the small scale that a repressed financial system achieves.

Indirect Measures of Repression

Both savers and investors are given incentives in tax law and administration to use the financial process sparingly. As if the inflation tax were not enough, other taxes discriminate against income from financial assets. Such income is conspicuous, unless it flows through the street market, and easily reached by the tax collector. Schedular taxation applied to income from easily assessed claims on financial intermediaries together with the ubiquitous stamp taxes on transactions in these claims is an effective reduction in real deposit rate. The claims on intermediaries are easy to tax, and so are the intermediaries relative to other forms of business enterprise. The spread between loan and deposit rates is difficult to reduce, for the benefit of investors and savers, when allowance is made not only for high unit costs in finance and a significant degree of oligopoly profit but also for taxation of the intermediaries revenues.

Taxation in lagging economies tends to be gentler with forms of wealth that are competitive with financial assets. Taxation of real property is a case in point. Typically real property is not effectively subject to tax. It may be exempted or, if not, assessments lag behind increases in property values as result of both inflation and crowding or urbanization. On various counts, real property is an attractive vehicle for savers as they reach toward their desired wealth-income ratios. It is exempt from tax; real mortgage rates of interest are negative, partly because interest may be tax-exempt; and real property gains in relative value from an assortment of public policies. Real property is an attractive way for savers to reach their desired wealth positions with a modest effort to save.

In a number of ways taxation is gentler with self-finance than with intermediation or direct finance. Retained business earnings are often exempt from tax. Export taxes draw savings away from an agricultural sector for investment in public industry or infrastructure. Import licenses yield monopoly rents for industry that are an implicit tax on other sectors. Savings of public enterprise are, in effect, taxed away through allowance of subsidy prices on electric power, transportation, or docking facilities to some favored buyers. Economic surplus is moved away from saving to investing sectors by nonfinancial means while public policy discriminates against financial technique.

International economic policy is biased against the domestic financial process. Overvaluation of the domestic currency on the foreign exchanges is undervaluation of foreign financial assets. They are cheap to import, and they bear relatively high deposit or yield rates. Moreover, with the domestic currency likely to be depreciated and undervalued in due time, there is a capital gain in prospect. The saver incurs costs in obtaining foreign assets, by evasion of domestic regulations, but the typical volume of capital flight from lagging economies suggests that the cost is not a relatively high one.

Although public policy creates incentives for domestic savings to slip abroad, it facilitates access of domestic investors to foreign savings: savings are exported in capital flight and imported because capital is scarce. The monetary authority seems to find no incongruity in setting negative real deposit rates and overvalued exchange rate, while guaranteeing expensive short-term importer credits. It has one view about the rewards that are appropriate for domestic savers, another about compensation for foreign savers.

The analysis returns in later chapters to the unholy alliance of financial and nonfinancial policy in repressing finance. Once repression is decided upon, an indefinitely large number of ways can be found to make it effective. Capital is so fungible, so slippery for regulation to cope with, that there is a strong tendency to multiply restrictions.

THE LOGIC AND ILLOGIC OF FINANCIAL REPRESSION

Financial liberalization is rare because so many reasons have been found for financial repression. We arrange these reasons in four groups below, but we do not pretend that our count is exhaustive. Perhaps somewhere financial repression exists because it gives civil servants something to do or because it can provide monopoly rents to an in-group of bankers or borrowers at banks. Perhaps lagging economies do it simply in emulation of more mature economies or even of international agencies. The first reason we discuss below is the historic antipathy to usury. Second, effective control has not been established over rates of growth in nominal money and rates of change in the price level. Third, various models of aggregate economic behavior, which are applied in development policy, minimize or misinterpret the role of finance. Finally, the empirical judgment is made that the potentially beneficial results of real financial growth are not worth the costs involved and that alternative solutions of capital scarcity are superior.

The Prohibition of Usury

Lord Keynes took his stand beside "natural man" and against the "classical school of economic theory" in the matter of anti-usury laws:

. . . the rate of interest is not self-adjusting at a level best suited to the social advantage but constantly tends to rise too high, so that a wise government is concerned to curb it by statute and custom and even by invoking the sanctions of moral law.[1]

[1] John Maynard Keynes, *General Theory of Employment Interest and Money,* p. 351. For a critique of anti-usury laws, see Rudolph C. Blitz and Millard F. Long, "The Economics of Usury Regulation," *The Journal of Political Economy,* December, 1965, pp. 608–619.

Statute, custom, and moral law against interest rates that rise "too high" are widespread in the lagging economies—and elsewhere, too. Perhaps there is a Keynesian motive to restrain the liquidity premium on assets other than productive physical capital. Another motive is to protect the poor against outrageous terms on consumer or farmer or small-business loans and to frustrate monopoly powers on the part of lenders. High rates of interest are considered to be exploitative, and the obvious solution for them, as for some other social evils, has appeared to be prohibition. Again, high rates of interest sometimes are considered to be inflationary. If owners of physical capital pay high rates of interest, it is argued, they must pass on the charges, with a cost-push effect upon prices of final outputs. The burden that these arguments put upon anti-usury laws is a heavy one—to prevent stagnation and underemployment, to protect the defenseless against exploitation, and to contain inflation.

Lord Keynes' advocacy of interest-rate ceilings was of a piece with his support for the Gesellian stamp tax on money. If capitalism is to achieve optimality on the market for savings, with capital's marginal product at zero, something must be done to curb the substitution effect of growth in the real stock of financial wealth demanded or to counterbalance it with government investment of its profits from money creation. Ceilings and stamp taxes were instruments of real policy to inhibit growth in financial wealth at the expense of physical wealth. They were appropriate complements of governmental deficit spending. We have preferred the view that money is not wealth and that there is no substitution effect. Money is debt, and growth in the real stock involves intermediation by the monetary system between savers and investors. DIV requires a positive deposit rate on money rather than a Gesellian tax, and it is firmly set against ceilings over either deposits or loan rates of interest.

Explicit ceilings are put over nominal rates of interest. Explicit ceilings less the expected rate of inflation are the real ceilings. In keeping with the fix-price context of the *General Theory,* Lord Keynes did not distinguish between nominal and real rates of interest or between explicit and real ceilings. The distinction is clear in the lagging economies, where inflation is commonplace. There real ceilings can be low or negative, sounding out to savers and investors false signals about the scarcity of savings and physical capital. They deal so harshly with liquidity preference that monetization is inhibited and savings are discouraged and misallocated.

Rate ceilings and capital rationing are Siamese twins where there is capital scarcity, because ceilings are low in real terms relative to both consumer-time preference and investment productivity. Rationing is the perfect vehicle for borrower exploitation. The right way to protect borrowers is not to put ceilings over loan rates but rather to raise real deposit rates and adopt policies, including enforcement of competition on financial markets, that reduce the margin between loan rates and deposit rates.

Because savings are mobile, evasion of interest-rate ceilings is routine in lagging economies. Capital flight away from domestic asset markets, where yields are depressed by ceilings, and around an overvalued exchange rate to foreign asset markets is an expensive result of the statute and custom and moral law that tell excess demand for savings to behave itself and vanish. Needless to say, the borrowers hurt most by capital flight are the poor and weak. One suspects that, on balance, evasion of ceilings is socially productive but also costly in resources applied, and it is objectionable on grounds of equity.

The argument that high interest rates induce inflation and must be repressed to keep commodity prices stable typically disregards the distinction between nominal and real rates of interest. It misses the point that, when high interest rates and inflation coexist, inflation is cause and not result: inflation realized is the basis for inflation expected and for the high P^* in nominal rates of interest i. A second objection is that high interest costs on capital in use are fixed costs and irrelevant for price formation in the short run. A third objection is that, given the flow of savings, high interest rates can prevent substitution of expensive capital for cheap labor and, as a result, can bring output prices down. Fourth, high interest rates are an efficient protection against wastage of savings on plant and capacity that are

doomed to underutilization by the small size of domestic markets
and by various obstacles to growth in exports. Finally, high loan and
deposit rates of interest are relative prices that attract additional
savings, permit increases in efficient proportions of capital equipment to labor and land, raise real output and income, increase real
money demanded, and, for each stock of nominal money, lower the
price level. Effective ceilings over rates of interest are inflationary.

Deficiencies in Control of Nominal Money

Real financial growth and deepening do not occur unless nominal
money is under effective constraint or unless inflationary effects of
monetary indiscipline are compensated by changes in relative prices
including especially interest rates and foreign exchange rates. Uncompensated expansion of nominal money, we know, is a tax on real
balances, and rational holders of financial assets evade the tax by
shifting to forms of wealth that are less vulnerable. Lagging economies have their characteristic episodes of monetary indiscipline. Let
us consider three of the various reasons for this. In some instances
the reason is simply that no technique of monetary control is established. In other cases techniques have been defective, unable to cope
with forces working against stability. Finally, some lagging economies have stumbled into combinations of policy that make financial
repression appear unavoidable and irremediable.

Although everyone else is concerned with real variables including
real money and its rate of return, a monetary authority in the guise
of central bank, monetary board, or robot working by rule must take
nominal money seriously and regulate it. Someone must be affected
with money illusion. Instances have occurred in which a country has
broken away from a gold or foreign-exchange standard or from the
dictates of a colonial monetary board and left control of nominal
money to a commercial bank or to the minister of finance. A commercial bank is indifferent as between alternative stocks of nominal
money although it does have a stake in rates of change in the nominal money supply and the price level, because $\dot{M}$ affects $\dot{P}$ and P^*
and hence the amount of real money demanded, the real size of the

banking portfolio, and the flow of real revenues to bank stockholders. Ministers of finance have been known to regard fresh printings of nominal money as perfect substitutes for real tax revenues. Until 1965 the Banco do Brasil attempted three roles at once—commercial bank, central bank, and lender to the government. The only possible outcome was monetary chaos. Uruguay next door played out the same drama in 1967. No one was in charge of M.

Sometimes the monetary authority has been technically ill equipped to manage nominal money. For lack of instruments appropriate to the regime of markets around it, the authority has failed to anticipate, prevent, or offset undesired changes in nominal money that originate with, for example, the commercial banks, the government budget, or the balance of international payments. In 1970 there was excessive monetary expansion in Ghana partly because the central bank, the Bank of Ghana, was obliged to pay off debts of state corporations to commercial banks. The commercial banks disregarded a mandate to increase their reserve ratios. Fortunately, suitable instruments of monetary control can always be contrived. If a monetary authority is permitted to regulate nominal money in the cause of financial liberalization, technical obstacles need not stand in its way.

The issue of effective monetary control would not arise if the lagging economies, which are always small in terms of wealth and income, were also open. Then, given their real stocks of money demanded, their stocks of nominal money would be essentially at the mercy of the world outside. However, lagging economies enclose themselves within various barriers to trade that preserve substantial exogeneity of domestic nominal money to external pressures. Their revealed preference is to keep the inflation tax under their own jurisdictions.

Even when the stock of nominal money is essentially free of external influences, control over it may be compromised by various mixtures of domestic economic policy. The objective of financial deepening may be subordinated to other objectives. As our first illustration, we suppose that the nominal rate of interest i has been fixed by decree at i'. One recalls the definition:

(1) $i' = r + P^*$

Here r is the real rate of interest charged to investors. Public policy is that r must be appropriate to a target rate of investment I. With inflation perfectly foreseen and, given the real stock of money demanded, perfectly in pace with growth in nominal money:

(2) $i' = r\,(I) + \dot{M}$

Evidently any tendency for the marginal productivity of investment to fall must be accompanied by a decline in r and an increase in the rate of nominal-money issue, inflation, and expected inflation. Nominal money has become endogenous, determined by the fixed level of the money rate of interest, the specified level of real investment and the behavior of demand for real money. Fortunately, escape from the predicament is easy: control over i can be removed or, as a second-best solution, the ceiling over i can be lowered. The Bank of Korea has become adept in sensing the moment when either a reduction in i' or an increase in $\dot{M}$ and $\dot{P}$ is essential, but data suggest that the bank does not always prefer to lower the interest-rate peg.[2]

Management of nominal money can be and often is the victim of fiscal policy.[3] We return to this point in Chapter 6 and, for the moment, may be content with a simple illustration. We imagine that the government considers itself committed to real expenditures G_t in the current fiscal period, to nominal expenditures $G_t P_t$. Its nominal revenues depend upon a tax rate q, on the community's real income Y, which is assumed constant, and on the price level P_{t-l} prevailing one period earlier: there is a lag between tax assessment and collection. Fiscal policy calls for a balanced budget, with $G_t = qY_t$, but expenditures are to be maintained even though there turns out to be

[2] The Bank of Korea, *Monthly Economic Statistics,* Number 1, 1972, pp. 44–46.

[3] Mario Henrique Simonsen, "Brazilian Inflation: Postwar Experience and Outcome of the 1964 Reforms," in Committee for Economic Development, *Economic Development Issues: Latin America.* Dr. Simonsen remarks (p. 327), ". . . anti-inflationary policy must start with the progressive restraint of government deficits."

a deficit that can be financed only by expansion of nominal money. Initially we assume that, with real income given, real money demanded and the real money stock are constant at $\underline{M}$. Finally, we interject a current private expenditure of nominal X that is financed by monetary expansion.

Growth in nominal money is:

$$(3) \qquad \Delta M_t = G_t P_t - q(Y_t P_{t-1}) + X_t$$

Since G_t and qY_t are equal:

$$(4) \qquad \Delta M_t = G_t (P_t - P_{t-1}) + X_t$$

Dividing by the current price level:

$$(5) \qquad \frac{(\Delta M)_t}{P} = (G\dot{P})_t + \underline{X}_t$$

$$(6) \qquad (\dot{M} \cdot \underline{M})_t = (G\dot{P})_t + \underline{X}_t$$

Substituting for $\underline{M}$ an expression of real money demanded as a positive function of real income and a negative function of expected inflation, and removing the subscript $_t$:

$$\dot{M} = \frac{G\dot{P} + \underline{X}}{l(P^*)Y}$$

Some initial impulse, perhaps from an increase in X, of excess money supply can result in a governmental deficit that must be financed by the inflation tax $\dot{M} \cdot \underline{M}$. The tax imposed in any period requires reimposition in succeeding periods. The danger inherent in the process is that it can gather cumulative force.[4] For one reason, expected inflation adjusts to inflation experienced; the real amount of money demanded declines; and the inflation tax must be increased, with the result that the inflation rate rises. For a second reason, the tax collection rate q typically tends to fall in accelerating inflation, increasing deficits for the inflation tax to cover. Again, the techniques of financial repression that are born in the inflation sequence tend to

---

[4] For a sophisticated model of inflation propelled by government deficits, see Dean S. Dutton, "A Model of Self-Generating Inflation: The Argentine Case," *Journal of Money, Credit and Banking*, May, 1971, pp. 245–262.

reduce Y, and the government may feel impelled, by increasing economic dislocation, to raise G.

The rate of increase in nominal money is endogenous in this illustration, dictated to the monetary authority by real fiscal policy, by inflation, by the public's response to inflation, and by factors tending to reduce real income. If the monetary authority were to defy demands upon it by government for monetary expansion, there would be danger of a stabilization crisis and a short-period recession of income and employment, and important objectives of fiscal policy, perhaps fulfillment of a cherished economic plan, would be sacrificed for the indefinite period before $\dot{P}$ and P^* could fall to zero.[5] The temptation is strong to supply the nominal money that the minister of finance and planning demands, to impose administrative controls over prices including rates of interest and to resolve excess demands for goods and savings by rationing. The beneficial effects of real financial growth are foregone, presumably in the hope that efficient applications of G to growth in capital equipment, improvements in fiscal administration that raise q, and injections of foreign savings that reduce dependence on the domestic inflation tax will make monetary restraint unnecessary.

Deficiencies in Guides to Financial Policy

Paths to financial repression are well marked, and easy for monetary authorities to follow, in numerous models of aggregate economic behavior. We draw on only a few samples to illustrate how doctrine can tempt policy away from the objective of financial deepening.

An incautious interpretation of Lord Keynes' *General Theory* is the first sample. It can be represented by equation (8), describing equilibrium on the market for money, and equation (9), describing equilibrium on the market for savings.

$$(8) \qquad\qquad M = l\ (Y,\ \mathrm{r}).\ \bar{P}$$

$$(9) \qquad\qquad x(r) = sY$$

[5] Robert A. Mundell, *Monetary Theory: Inflation, Interest, and Growth in the World Economy,* Chapter 7.

This is a fix-price regime, in which the price level P is given and constant and the supply of output wholly elastic to demand for it. Functional relationships have the textbook signs.

Expansion of nominal money is the right instrument, it appears, to eliminate capital scarcity. The monetary authority has only to expand M in order to reduce the marginal liquidity yield of real money and the bond rate of interest r. Then a higher level of output must increase the flow of savings and the stock of capital, with a falling marginal product of capital, a rising real wage rate and per capita consumption level. Of course, at some minimum of the liquidity yield of real money, no further savings can be generated for physical investment, and monetary policy has run its course.

If this model were valid for lagging economies, there would be no lagging economies. Monetary expansion would have put idle resources to work, generating savings for the capital expansion that would lift income from poverty levels. Unfortunately, the monetary system issues nominal money, not real money, and acceleration of issue has resulted in inflation realized, inflation expected, higher rather than lower nominal and real rates of interest. In the context of the long run, the fix-price model is a disastrous guide to policy, assuming an elasticity of output and savings to issue of nominal money that can exist only during short periods of underutilized capacity in place.

It is only a small step from the model of equations (8) and (9) to a model of "structural" inflation that rationalizes repressive financial policy in a number of lagging economies.

$$(10) \qquad\qquad M = l\,(Y, r).\,P^e$$

$$(11) \qquad\qquad P^e > 0$$

$$(12) \qquad\qquad x(r) = sY$$

Here the price level P^e is inflexible downward but capable of increases that are determined elsewhere than in the market for money. Because of the "structure" of markets for, say, labor or agricultural produce or foreign exchange, it tends chronically to rise independently of excess money supply. Each increase generates excess demand for money that must result in a higher real rate of interest, reduced investment, savings, and income—unless the nominal supply of money is increased equiproportionally. Structural inflation raises real rates of interest, but its effect can be offset by growth of nominal money. If rates of interest do not respond to monetary treatment, the right solution is placing ceilings over them. The guide to policy is clear: protect r against P^e and usury.

In equations (10) and (12), there is money illusion on the part of money holders and investors. The equations suggest that inflation is not foreseen, that expected inflation does not affect real demands for money and physical wealth, that nominal rates of interest are also real rates. They can be improved, as follows:

$$(13) \qquad\qquad M = l\ (Y, i).\ P^e$$

$$(14) \qquad\qquad x\ (i - P^*) = sY$$

If households and firms are free of money illusion, the price level rising at some rate $\dot{P}^e = P^*$, because of structural factors, must induce an excess of i over the real rate of interest r. The theory of structural inflation suggests as the guide to policy, in such a model as this, that M should increase at the same rate as P^e and, in order to reduce r, even higher. Interest-rate ceilings may be appropriate if expected inflation exceeds realized inflation and raises i unduly or if there is reason to believe that lenders are exploiting borrowers in an unstable capital market.

Equations (8) through (14) are in the WV tradition. Their emphasis is upon the substitution effect of growth in money, and their solution for the retardation that the substitution effects puts upon growth in physical capitals is simply expansion of nominal money. The theme is that growth in real income, a fall in r, or inflation imposed exogenously on the market for money creates an excess demand for money in private portfolios—a high marginal s_m, and the excess demand must be satisfied either in the right way, by growth in nominal money, or in the wrong way, by reduced demand for investment, reduced employment and output and reduced savings to finance investment.

As we know, growth in nominal money is essential for economic progress. However, it is not the only condition of progress, and excessive growth inhibits progress by reducing real money and sacraficing the income, savings, investment, employment, and distribution effects of real money. Equations (8) through (12) do not distinguish between growth in nominal money and growth in real money and overlook entirely the significance of real deposit rate. Equations (13) and (14) are clean of money illusion, but they miss the importance of compensating for the effect of realized and expected inflation upon real money demanded. They ignore the effect of low money-income ratios in the production function, the savings and investment functions. This family of models is the perfect rationalization for uncompensated inflation and for other devices, such as interest-rate ceilings, that intensify capital scarcity. They can persuade the monetary authority to ignore inflation, to accept it as inevitable, even to want it as a way of softening the substitution effect of real money.

We do not accept the view that the relative price of money $1/P$ is, for the long run that concerns us here, determined on markets other than the market for money. Some expositions of structuralism ignore the market for money and hence must contrive a non-monetary account of P and changes in it. Others, failing to allow for the role of demand for money in the inflation process and finding unstable relationships between nominal money and the price level, conclude that P must be a non-monetary phenomenon. Still other versions of structuralism are based upon selected sequences of change during the inflationary process in short periods. For example, inflations in which money-wage rates are leaders, for the interval selected, are wage-push inflation or, when agricultural prices are in front, the structure of agriculture is at fault. Identifying all things that happen first as causes of all things that happen later is analytical anarchy that misses a common source of disturbance, which is excess money supply in the case of inflation. Structuralism also finds support in the observation that excess money supply, positive or negative, has initial effects on output and employment. It misses the point that these are not lasting effects and that inflation foreseen and compensated in neutral.[6]

A popular form of structuralism alleges that the rate of change P is a function of the percentage rate of unemployment in the labor force relative to an arbitrary measure of full employment. A stable trade-off, on terms likely to be unique for each economy, is said to exist between inflation rate and unemployment rate so that there can be price stability at some "high" unemployment rate and progressively more rapid inflation at successively lower unemployment rates. The implication for the monetary authority's nominal-money policy is clear: if its own characteristic trade-off does not permit both price stability and full employment, an economy must accept inflation as a datum and its monetary authority must provide the growth in nominal money that, through its effects upon the real rate of interest charged to investors, can assure investment compatible with full-employment output.

One agrees that, in the presence of underutilized productive capacity, increase in the growth rate of nominal money may induce increases in output and employment, depending on whether it is excess demand for money but not for something else that is restricting output. It is true also that output and real demand for money respond progressively less to the stimulus. This means that successive increases in the growth rate of nominal money result in still more rapid increases in the growth rate of excess nominal money and in the impulse to inflation. This outcome can be expected when price-level expectations are static and P^* is zero. However, expectations do not remain static and, as they adjust to experience with inflation, the economy's terms of trade-off between inflation rate and unemployment rate shift so that a higher inflation rate is associated with every unemployment rate. "Full" employment then depends, not on a stable rate of increase in the price level, but on a rising rate of in-

[6] Martin Bronfenbrenner and Franklyn D. Holzman, "Survey of Inflation Theory," *The American Economic Review,* September, 1963, pp. 593–661.

crease in P and hence M: for the sake of real employment effects, $\dot{P}$ must stay ahead of $P*$.[7]

A monetary authority beguiled by trade-off structuralism is committed to a rising rate of inflation, the rate depending on the target level of full employment. If this monetary authority seeks to stabilize both the employment rate and the money rate of interest while $P*$ is rising, the accelerating rise in nominal money has potentialities for explosive inflation. Matters are still worse if monetary expansion to stabilize i is reenforced by interest-rate ceilings for financial assets and by the inevitable specific capital-market controls that result. Trade-off structuralism is a prescription for repressed finance. Successive increases in M are not the long-run cure for chronic underemployment. The durable solution is found in growth of physical wealth, improvement in skills and mobility of labor, and other real determinants of output, including money deepening.

The neo-Keynesian models discussed above call for uncompensated inflation and other measures of financial repression as a means of putting idle resources to work so that rising income, with a given propensity to save, can supply growth in the capital stock. It seems to us that they distort the Keynesian model, emphasizing a part of it but missing the essence. In a slight modification of equation (33) in Chapter 2, we interpret the General Theory to say:

$$(15) \qquad I = [s - s_m(i, d, n)] \, F \, (K, L)$$

Here the physical propensity to save is the expression within brackets, and it is reduced by the propensity s_m to save in real-money form, as affected positively by the growth rate n of real income and by deposit rate d, negatively by the money rate of interest i. No money illusion appears in this equation for equilibrium on the capital market. Moreover, it is wholly pertinent to a situation of growth with full employment. Its message is that the substitution effect of growth

---

[7] Milton Friedman, "The Role of Monetary Policy," *The American Economic Review*, March, 1968, pp. 1–17; Robert E. Lucas and Leonard A. Rapping, "Price Expectation and the Phillips Curve," *The American Economic Review*, June, 1969, pp. 342–350; James Tobin, "Inflation and Unemployment," *The American Economic Review*, March, 1972, pp. 1–18.

in real money reduces the equilibrium capital-labor ratio and raises the marginal product of capital r. To be sure, if demand for real money wealth is not satisfied at full employment, chronic underemployment can result. Even if that disaster is avoided, however, satisfied demand for money wealth is impoverishing. Employment can be at the full, and the substitution effect of growth in real money can be avoided by uncompensated inflation that raises i relative to d or by a Gesellian tax that reduces d. However, these measures are inefficient if they induce economies in transactions balances of money and sacrifice the income effect of money. In his writings Lord Keynes indicated his full awareness of the importance of real money to economic efficiency. A social optimum exists when the marginal utility of money is zero and when fiscal policy so increases s relative to s_m that the capital-labor ratio rises to the satiation limit, with r equal to zero. This view of economic development is a far cry from the view suggested in equations (8) through (14).

As we see it, the *General Theory* has been interpreted wrongly as support for complaints, in lagging economies and elsewhere, against hoarding–demand for real money balances. It has been used to rationalize distaste of monetary authorities and others for pillowcase and mattress balances of coin and currency and for low-velocity deposit balances. In ways that surely would have aggrieved Lord Keynes, it has been called upon to justify financial repression. WVK, WV, and DIV do agree that money deepening is essential in lagging economies, that it need not be capital impoverishing, even that pillowcases and mattresses may be the monetary authority's best friends!

The doctrines we have been discussing are not the stuff, to put it mildly, from which financial liberalization evolves. Neither is the doctrine of development that simply ignores finance. One observes cases in which development policy is preoccupied with planning the rate and quality of investment, mobilization of labor, agricultural reform, and other nonfinancial things. Given target rates of growth in output and an estimate of a constant marginal propensity to save, foreign funds have been sought in support of aggregate investment, and the mix of investment has been arranged according to planning-model estimates of rates of return. The assumption has been that requisite domestic savings must appear somehow through some of the usual channels including the inflation tax: investment and savings are, after all, necessarily equal *ex-post*. The assumption has been, too, that the savings can go to the right places if only enough specific controls are applied. It is needless to fret about the markets for money and capital. Our rejoinder is simply that lack of these policies represses finance and that a thin financial system frustrates plans for capital accumulation and increases reliance on foreign aid.

A Case for Financial Repression—and a Rejoinder

One more explanation of financial repression remains. The basis for it is a set of empirical judgments, all pointing to the conclusion that financial deepening is part of an ineffective development strategy while financial repression fits well into a powerful strategy of structural transformation. A case may be made for financial deepening at some late stage of economic maturity, so the argument goes, but it is premature in lagging economies. It is irrelevant if they are aiming at centralized socialism.

Real financial growth is said to be expensive in terms of scarce factors of production: it seems to call for marbled buildings and regiments of more or less skilled personnel to fill them. Moreover, financial growth depends upon a framework of law and of sophistication in portfolio management that lagging economies do not have and cannot achieve quickly. The sufficient answer to this argument is that financial growth can be economical where high interest rates force it to use expensive human and physical capital sparingly, where competitive pressures prevent the oligopoly profits that do go into lavish equipment and where differentiation of finance is not induced by regulatory intervention. Financial growth can be concentrated in relatively simple institutions, including the monetary system and street markets. Threadneedle and Wall Street need not be copied everywhere.

Another basis for deferring real financial growth is that it works only where markets are susceptible to the disciplines of relative price. "Market forces do not work here" is a common justification for strategies that repress finance. Presumably supply and demand curves are flat or perpendicular or inverted, subject to irrational shifts and incapable of generating stable equilibria. Misleading prices are generated in the market process, issuing signals that would divert the economy from its appropriate development path. Critical relative prices must be administered. One relative price, the rate of inflation, is imposed mainly by structural factors and cannot be managed efficiently as an instrument of growth. Markets and relative prices in open markets cannot be used to promote development: they work well as a result of development.

It is true, of course, that financial growth and evolution of market processes go together. For example, the income effect of money is the result of assistance that money gives in extending markets, perfecting them, reducing costs of trade. The polices that induce financial deepening move an economy increasingly far away from stages of production for subsistence, barter, and regionally narrow self-sufficiencies. "Market forces do not work here" in many cases because financial repression prevents and distorts them. If market forces are weak, the case for financial deepening is strong. Furthermore, there is persuasive if casual evidence that economic behavior can be rationally sensitive to relative price at very early stages of development. The Ghanaian farmer was quick to exploit his relative advantage in becoming the dominant producer of cocoa. The Oriental peasant has demonstrated his alertness to relative prices of different crops and to change in employment opportunities away from the farm. The extent of smuggling where markets are repressed suggests that market forces may be too strong for market intervention to deal with. Market forces are ready to work toward development if given the opportunity.[8]

[8] Robert C. Hsu, "The Demand for Fertilizer in a Developing Country," *Economic Development and Cultural Change,* January, 1972, pp. 299–309; John Isbister, "Urban Employment and Wages in a Developing Economy: The Case of Mexico," *Economic Development and Cultural Change;* Harry G. Johnson, *Money, Trade and Economic Growth,* Chapter VII.

Financial deepening, it is alleged, is premature for lagging economies, and financial repression does well, with complementary instruments, in generating economic surplus and using the surplus for
appropriate capital formation. The argument points to a "Pakistan
strategy" that may be illustrated by a simple model. A leading sector
a is assumed to possess special qualifications for leading an industrial transformation. A traditional sector b provides labor, raw materials, and savings to a. A monetary system supplies money to both
sectors, buying primary securities only from a at a money rate of
interest i and paying on all deposits a deposit rate $\underline{d}$. The monetary
system also transmits external aid F, at the same rate of interest i, to
sector a. The policy issue is how best to achieve a desired high ratio
of investment in a Karachi-like sector a to national income Y.

Equilibrium in the capital market is represented as:

$$(16) \; X \, (r_a{}^*, i - P^*) = sY_a \, (\dot{P}, v) + \dot{P} \, (M/P) + \Delta \, (M/P) + F$$

The left side of (16) represents demand of the leading sector for
investment as a positive function of the expected real rate of return
$r_a{}^*$, a negative function of the real loan rate of interest $i - P^*$. The
rate of return is raised, in the calculations of industrialists, by effects
of inflation, including perhaps overvaluation of the domestic currency
on the foreign exchanges. The nominal loan rate of interest i is administered by the monetary authority, and the real rate reflects an
expected rate of inflation in domestic prices of sector a's output.
Investment in sector b is presumed to be traditional, static, and self-
financed, and it is ignored in (16).

The flow of savings to the leading sector is described on the right
side of (16). There is self-finance, depending on the sector's own
marginal propensity to save s and its share Y_a of the national income.
This share depends positively on the realized rate of inflation $\dot{P}$, perhaps because money-wage rates lag behind product prices. The income share depends as well on other instruments v of public policy
for income distribution, such as taxes or twists in the terms of trade
against sector b exports of commodities and labor services to a. The
second term on the right side of (16) is the inflation tax on real

money balances, and the third term is increases desired in real money balances. The proceeds of the inflation tax and of growth in real money along with the flow of external aid F are passed through the monetary system to industry in a. We suppose that equilibrium prevails in the market for money, with nominal deposit rate $\underline{d}$ at zero and real deposit rate at some negative figure $\underline{d} - P^*$.

The model provides four instruments of financial policy: the rate of change $\dot{P}$ in the price level, the expected rate of change P^*, nominal loan rate i, and nominal deposit rate $\underline{d}$. Strategy calls for a variable and imperfectly predictable rate of inflation as well as for low or negative real loan and deposit rates. Loans are to be rationed by the monetary system according to the specifications of an industrial plan and of contracts for foreign aid. Since firms in a may need funds from the curb markets, anti-usury laws are to be enforced. This is a strategy for financial repression.

Advantages claimed for the strategy are familiar. Enterpreneurial zest is aroused in the industrial sector by the effect of inflation and other measures on yields to investment. These yields discounted at some very low $i - P^*$ excite animal spirits to accumulate physical capital even though the prospect of utilizing it to capacity is dim. Investment can be financed substantially with investors' own savings, and recourse to borrowing through the monetary system is cheap. Loan committees of the monetary system can be expected not to intervene in management of expanding industry, and sources of external aid can be only pleased with rapid transformation of a backward agrarian economy to an industrial economy with exciting growth rates of Y. The inflation tax on money balances is bound to yield a relatively stable, even rising flow of finance since money-income ratios are already so low as to be inelastic to P^* and since there is a chance for substantial growth in real money as industrialization increases the volume of transactions. Of course, sector b is victimized as a supplier of savings, goods, and labor, but this is temporary. After the big push prosperity of the leading sector can filter down, distributing benefits by linkages this way and that. Short-run strategy circumvents the constraints of traditionalism on capital accumulation, at some pain for b, but a later strategy for the long run can sweep sector b along in the development process.

Financial repression in this model is a matter of choice. The income effect evidently is considered to be small, at least in relation to the income effect of shifting from traditional to capital-intensive production. The saving effect is ranked as inferior to the effect of inflation in transferring income to a capitalist sector with a high propensity to save. The costly investment effect of repression seems to be minor if investment is policed by plan. Effects toward maintaining or raising unemployment and concentrating the distribution of income and wealth are regarded as necessary and regrettable but transitional.

We may be brief with the rejoinder, expanding it in later chapters. Income effects of the repressive strategy are surely underestimated by its advocates.[9] Holders and users of money balances M/P, taxed at a rate $\dot{P}$ of sufficient severity to do what the strategy wants it to do, are bound to be economical in savings committed to increments in real balances $\Delta M/P$. The Taiwanese were not unique in evading an inflation tax of 24 per cent in 1952 by holding their money-income ratio low, at 5.5 per cent.[10] Money holders elsewhere, when the rate of tax is reduced, behave much as the Taiwanese did in raising real money balances by 91 per cent as inflation declined to 9 per cent and real income rose by 33 per cent during 1952–56, by another 410 per cent as inflation declined to one per cent and real income rose by 180 per cent during 1950–68, attaining a money-income ratio of 14.2 per cent. An end to repression results in a quantum jump of real money demanded. This is a quantum jump in use of the services of money for search and bargain. The result is to increase productivities of labor and physical capital, pushing outward the community's frontier of production possibilities. A minimal esti-

[9] Milton Friedman, "Government Revenue from Inflation," *Journal of Political Economy,* July/August, 1971, pp. 846–856; Anand G. Chandavarkar, "Some Aspects of Interest Rate Policies in Less Developed Economies: The Experience of Selected Asian Countries," in International Monetary Fund, *Staff Papers,* March, 1971, pp. 48–112.

[10] Fu-Chi Liu, *Studies in Monetary Development of Taiwan,* Monograph Series, The Institute of Economics, Academia Sinica, October, 1970, p. 16.

mate of Taiwan's gain in moving from the money-income ratio of 5.5 per cent to the ratio of 14.2, given a marginal opportunity cost of 25 per cent in holding money, would be a permanent gain of 2.5 per cent in national income, and a reasonable figure could be some small multiple of this minimum. At least a comparable gain in productivity must have accrued to the Republic of Korea as it shifted from an inflation rate of 22.3 per cent in 1961–64 to 11 per cent in 1965–68, with money holders reducing real balances at the rate of 8.4 per cent annually in the first period, raising real balances at the rate of 19 per cent in the second period.[11]

Savings effects of the repressive strategy seem to be disappointing. For one thing, the monetary system is made to penalize saving through growth in real money and other claims. Again, the effect of inflation in transferring income from sectors with low propensities to sectors with high propensities to save depends on expectations: the traditional sector's expectations of inflation must lag behind the realized advance of prices, and the leading sector's expectations should sense the bonanza of windfall profits to come. Widespread experience now suggests that traditional sectors do not suffer the income transfer patiently and for long. They work fewer hours, plant less cocoa, slaughter more breeding stock, smuggle more exports, and in various other ways defend their terms of trade against inflation in prices they pay and controls on prices they receive. Moreover, it becomes less obvious, as savings data are perfected, that traditional sectors are characteristically disposed to low savings-income ratios rather than forced into them by experience with low rewards to saving.

Investment effects of the repressive strategy have not been encouraging. Restraint of investment in traditional sectors retards agriculture and increases import demand for foods and raw materials, to be financed partly by foreign aid F. Restraint on indigenous industry in small production units retards exports, with dependence on F again increasing. Some investment in the leading sector involves high capital-labor ratios, unfamiliar technologies, and chronic excess

[11] The Bank of Korea, *Monthly Economic Statistics.*

capacity. Industry is concentrated in urban areas with the result that substantial savings are required for infrastructure. The strategy throws domestic savings away and stacks up a backlog of indebtedness to savers abroad.

Employment effects of the strategy are notorious. Repression in traditional sectors impels labor migration to the city. There capital-intensive growth absorbs just a portion of the migrants into an enclave with relatively high wage rates. The labor force not absorbed builds its slums. Distribution effects result in an urban elite, an urban proletariat of underemployed, and a rural class on a flat or falling trajectory of income and wealth. The filter-down or spillover or linkage effects from urban industrialization have yet to be impressive in any economy that commits itself to techniques of repression. A leading sector nourished on repression continues, it seems, to require nourishment by the measures that prevent financial deepening.

5 | Financial Reform

At a slow but perhaps accelerating pace, financial reform and other reform complementary to it are occurring despite the formidable traditions that favor repression. From Mexico and Taiwan on to Korea, Indonesia, Yugoslavia, Brazil, Iran, Malaysia, and others, these traditions have been challenged, and policies for financial deepening have increased real stocks of financial assets relative to wealth and income. No country has liberalized its financial system to efficient limits, and some measures invoked in the cause of liberalization simply add new distortions to the old, but the grip of repressive policy is being loosened. Lagging economies that climb aboard the reform bandwagon should test the hypothesis of Sir John Hicks:

> The beginning of a process of expansion . . . might occur because of real factors (inventions and the like) raising the real (prospective) rate of profit. But it might also occur because of financial improvements . . . ; thereby permitting access to funds, for improvements which could have been made earlier, if the necessary funds had been forthcoming. It is not savings only that are required, but a channel of communication between potential savings and potential real investment.[1]

This chapter is concerned with broad contours and some illustrative details of financial reform. It begins with the monetary system

[1] John Hicks, *Capital and Growth*, p. 290 n.

113

because measures for non-monetary financial development are pointless, for the long run, until there is money deepening. It turns next to the street and curb markets that, despite laws against usury, have an important function in the saving-investment process of all lagging economies. Non-monetary intermediaries are third in line, both the intermediaries that can assist in the transition to developed finance and the intermediaries that are hothouse products of restraint on the monetary system. Fourth, there is a discussion of "capital markets" in the narrow sense of exchanges for long-term securities. Finally, a brief section is added for some special "banks" that are not banks. Consideration of reform for the sake of short-period stability is deferred along with analysis of linkages between financial reform and reform affecting fiscal and international budgets.

THE MONETARY SYSTEM

Dormant or shrinking monetary systems are not revived by faster expansion of nominal money: the public can reject it, in real terms, by bidding higher the rate of inflation. They are not revived by multiplication of branches, which can raise real unit costs and widen the spread between loan and deposit rates. Grant of charters to foreign banks is not the remedy nor is nationalization of banks: banks of any ownership can languish under repressive monetary policy. Compulsory savings in blocked bank deposits are a clear warning that financial assets can be perilous to hold. It is the goals and instruments of the monetary authority, concerned with stimulating demand for money, that count most in monetary reform.[2] We consider, first, goals and instruments of the authority on the markets for money and capital. Then we consider the organization of the monetary system. The final topic of this section is the costs and profits of the monetary system.

Goals and Instruments on the Market for Money

The monetary system is a participant in various markets. Sometimes it buys on the art market, acquiring decorations for the walls

[2] Andrew F. Brimmer, "Central Banking and Economic Development," *Journal of Money Credit and Banking,* November, 1971, pp. 780–792.

of the governor's office; it participates in the labor market, the market for foreign exchange, and the markets for various kinds of securities. Its characteristic domain, of course, is the market for money, where it confronts the public's demand for real money balances. The monetary system supplies nominal money, and it brings its instruments to bear upon the arguments or variables of the public's demand function for nominal money valued at its relative price $1/P$. The immediate goal in the lagging economy is to induce more rapid growth in real money balances that the public desires to hold and to use as means of payment. The farther goal is the income, saving, investment, employment, and distribution effects of money deepening. What the turnabout from monetary expansion to liberalization looks like is suggested in Table I.

Table I   First stages in money deepening: Korea 1961–68

Rates of Growth (Per cent)

	Nominal Money[1]	Price Level[2]	Real Money
1961	40.0	15.5	24.9
1962	18.6	13.4	5.2
1963	1.5	28.2	−26.7
1964	17.4	31.9	−14.5
1965	33.1	7.6	25.5
1966	30.1	12.9	17.2
1967	42.5	10.5	32.0
1968	24.8	12.0	12.8

[1] Nominal money is defined in the sense of won means of payment.
[2] Gross national product deflator.
SOURCE: The Bank of Korea, *Review of the Korean Economy*.

The eight years, 1961–68, in Korean experience comprise two distinct intervals. During 1961–64, the real size of the money stock was diminishing while the nominal size increased. During 1965–68, money holders ceased their flight from real balances and, at a diminished rate of inflation, accepted a rising rate of nominal-money issue. Economic authority in Korea evidently found a way in which to stimulate demand for money in real terms.

The Growth Trajectory of Demand for Money. The route for a monetary authority to follow during liberalization is charted in the real-money demand function of private spending units. By one means or another, government may induce expectations of rising real income and higher per capita wealth. Because the wealth-elasticity of demand for money is positive, the effect is to establish on the part of the public a larger demand for nominal money at each price level. The monetary authority may induce expectations of a diminishing rate of inflation and hence of a rise in the real deposit rate of money. If the prospect of comparative stability is offered to them, spending units can be counted upon to discount the future less harshly and to change the rate of substitution between assets in general, including money, and consumption. Demand can be shifted to domestic money balances from such alternative assets as foreign balances or rice inventories or hoards of cigarettes if a correction of the foreign-exchange rate makes foreign balances more expensive and if rice and other goods are made to seem less precious now by the prospect of more ample supplies later. The likelihood that investment in greater variety will become more profitable in a rationalized regime of markets can excite the desire to build, partly through money holding, a base of equity for later borrowing. The payments facilities of the monetary system can be offered more cheaply and conveniently, with fewer hours for money holders to waste idling at bank counters and with fewer stamps to buy for each transaction. The simplest device, of course, is to pay a positive rate of interest at least on checking accounts. The device, deposit rate, is rarely used perhaps because imperfectly competitive monetary systems count on this and related pricing practices to appropriate the consumer surplus in money holding.

Korean authorities took their step in money deepening in early 1963 with the decision to minimize finance of the central government's fiscal budget by money issue.[3] This was a decision to count

---

[3] Research Institute for Economics and Business, Sogang University, *A Study of Money Market and Industrial Investment Financing,* pp. 9–10.

less on the inflation tax and more on growth in real balances as a source of funds for the program of government investment. This budget decision and later measures including foreign-exchange reform and sharp increases in interest rates on the organized financial markets carried the conviction that national income would rise and the rate of inflation fall, reducing expected inflation and raising real deposit rate.[4] Keys to increasing real money demanded were found and used.

Monetary growth begins with an awareness by the monetary authority that there is a money-demand function, and the next step is estimation of the function. For some obscure reason, the money industry is the only industry or, at best, one among few industries that typically has not taken explicit account of the demand for its product. During the interval when policy is shifting from repression to liberalization, precise estimates of the demand function are impossible if only because statistical observations do not extend over the relevant ranges of values for the function's arguments. As a result, serious dangers do arise that growth in money demanded may be underestimated and that excess demand for money may precipitate a deflationary crisis or that growth may be over estimated and that excess supply of money through new issues may rekindle inflation. However, there are signals that warn of both hazards and, once the critical transition is past, growth in real money demanded can be expected to take a comparatively stable trajectory.

The Inflation Target. The essential instrument of policy on the market for money is real deposit rate. Given their reluctance to use nominal deposit rate, monetary authorities are left with two ways of reaching the yield of money r_m. One is measures affecting the payments services supplied by the monetary system. The other is $\dot{P}$ and P^*, the experienced and expected rates of inflation. This option is available in any economy that is not so "small," so "open," and so

---

[4] Irma Adelman and Kim Mahn Je, *An Econometric Model of the Korean Economy (1956–66),* pp. 27–30; Anand G. Chandavarkar, *op. cit.,* p. 97; Research Institute for Economics and Business, Sogang University, *op. cit.,* Chapter IV.

inflexible in its menu of imports and exports that it must share in the price-level experience of the world outside.

Monetary authorities differ in their preferences among alternative rates of inflation under conditions that they regard as stable or sustainable or compatible with steady growth. Table II offers a sample of preferences from Korea, Malaysia, and Taiwan for the years 1965–70.

Table II   Choices among rates of inflation, 1965–70
(*Per Cent*)

	Korea[1]	*Taiwan*[2]	*Malaysia*[3]
1965	13.6	1.50	−0.1
1966	12.1	2.44	1.4
1967	10.8	4.02	4.1
1968	11.1	1.14	0.0
1969	10.1	3.28	−0.1
1970	12.7	3.79	1.3

[1] The Bank of Korea, *Review of the Korean Economy 1969,* p. 166. Data represent the Seoul Consumer Price Index.
[2] *Taiwan Financial Economic Monthly Report.* Data represent the price deflator for gross national product.
[3] Bank Negara Malaysia, *Quarterly Economic Bulletin,* December, 1970, p. 48. Data represent the West Malaysian retail price index.

It was suggested in Chapter 3 that optimality in the market for money requires some low variance in the rate of inflation in order that the risk involved in financial deepening for holders of financial assets can be minimized. It was suggested, too, that the optimal rate of inflation must be low in view of the reluctance of monetary authorities to compensate for inflation by appropriate adjustments in such other relative prices as nominal deposit and loans rates, foreign-exchange rates, and prices for outputs of government enterprises. Korea's choice of an inflation rate of 10–12 per cent annually during 1965–70 did not match neatly the decision to appreciate the won price of the dollar by only 17 per cent over the entire period. The outcome had to be accumulating tensions that finally were relieved in 1971 by a leap of 20 per cent in the won-dollar exchange rate.

The optimal choice among inflation rates in liberating finance is not wide when other relative prices are comparatively rigid.[5]

Exogeneity of Nominal Money. Nominal deposit rate and the rate of inflation are instruments for regulation of real deposit rate. Nominal money is the instrument for regulation of the price level: given the long-run growth rate of real money demanded $\underline{\dot{M}}$, one recalls, the rate of inflation is determined by $\dot{M}$. Unless $\dot{M}$ is at the discretion of the monetary authority and is adapted by it to the economy's choice among inflation rates, long-run financial deepening is at best improbable. Deepening requires exogeneity of the money supply to the economy's real sectors: the decisions regarding M and $\dot{M}$ must belong only to the one agency with money illusion, the monetary authority.

Competition for control over nominal money is intense in every economy. Control has been lost by monetary authorities to commercial banks, ministers of finance, the labor market, the foreign sector and others.[6] It was lost by the Bank of Ghana to the cocoa sector in 1963⁻65. Producer prices paid in the 1963–64 crop season by the Cocoa Marketing Board, a government agency, exceeded the board's export prices, and the monetary system was called upon to finance the losses by loan expansion and the inflation tax. During 1964–65, there was monetary expansion to finance withholding of the cocoa crop from a weakening world market. The outcome of these ventures, in 1964 and 1965, was acceleration of both $\dot{M}$ and the rate of inflation.[7] The Bank of Ghana came out second best again in 1969–70, this time to a broader sample of government corporations and to the commercial banks:

[5] Henry C. Wallich, "Money and Growth: A Country Cross-Section Analysis," *Journal of Money, Credit and Banking,* May, 1969, pp. 298–300.

[6] Eduardo Garcia D'Acuna, "Inflation in Chile: A Quantitative Analysis," unpublished Ph.D. dissertation, Massachusetts Institute of Technology, 1964; Thomas J. Courchene, "Recent Canadian Monetary Policy," *Journal of Money, Credit and Banking,* February, 1971, pp. 35–56; Donald R. Hodgman, "British Techniques of Monetary Policy: A Critical Review," *Journal of Money, Credit and Banking,* November, 1971, pp. 760–779.

[7] Naseem Ahmad, *Deficit Financing, Inflation and Capital Formation: The Ghanaian Experience, 1960–65,* pp. 63–64.

In January and June, two payments . . . were made to the (commercial) banks on behalf of the Government to settle outstanding indebtedness of some State Corporations. To avert leakage of these amounts into the credit stream, the liquidity ratios of the banks were raised in February, 1970 to absorb the additional liquidity inherent in the debt settlement. This objective has been defeated by the banks by underfulfilling the cash ratio. Associated with the cash deficiency, there has been a considerable increase in commercial bank credit.[8]

Excess supply emerged in the Ghanaian market for money toward the close of fiscal 1970, and this first result of slippage in monetary control led inexorably toward the usual consequences including balance-of-payments difficulties and a rise in the inflation rate. Ghana had yet to find its way from monetary repression to monetary deepening.

The traditional way of maintaining an exogenous money supply was independent central banking. That tradition was badly bent if not broken during the 1930's and after the Second World War, and no one alternative has come into general use. More commonly than not, perhaps, monetary authorities are now monetary boards dominated by ministers of finance and planning. Whatever the organization may be, the goal of growth in real money demanded is out of reach unless there is someone to regard growth in real money as important, to select a narrow band of relatively low inflation rates, and to protect the exogeneity of money.

Goals and Instruments on the Market for Capital

According to the Wealth View real money is private and social wealth, and growth in real money is social income that can be appropriated by issuers of nominal money as profits or seignorage. The profits may be spent in the capital market where savings finance investment, and perhaps it is optimal that they should be spent there until the social capital-labor ratio approaches some golden-rule limit. We have adopted the alternative view: money is debt of the monetary system that may be issued to buy existing wealth, to finance

---

[8] Bank of Ghana, *Report of the Board for the Financial Year Ended 30th June, 1970,* p. 45.

governmental and private dissaving, or to draw savings from money holders to capital accumulation. The monetary system is a financial intermediary, both borrower and lender of savings. In this section we are concerned with the monetary system as lender on the capital market, disposing of savings that flow to it through growth in real money balances or through proceeds of the inflation tax.

In the tradition of repressive monetary policy, savings are scarce yet must be priced cheaply, at low or negative real loan rates of interest. Low rates of interest, cheap imports of capital goods, tax concessions for investment, tariff protection for capital-intensive production, are among the preferred instruments in lagging economies for reaching the goal of economic growth. The argument for liberalization in finance is that scarcity prices for savings increase rates of saving, improve savings allocation, induce some substitution of labor for capital equipment, and assist in income equalization. Our purpose now is to consider means of putting liberalization into effect at the loan counters where savings accruing to the monetary system flow into investment.

Among both lagging and developing economies monetary systems are assigned dissimilar roles in the capital market. At the extreme of centralism the monetary system is a deposit window. Savings flow into it and out again, at the dictate of reserve requirements, to the planning or finance ministry or to specialized loan windows called development banks, agricultural banks, and the like. At another extreme, with Japan a striking example, the issuers of money dominate the capital market.[9] We put aside this matter of financial organization for the moment, to discuss a few aspects of trading terms in the market for savings.

Rates of Return to Investment. Savings are scarce in lagging economies in the sense that excess demand for them can be found, at loan rates prevailing in more developed economies, in investment projects with acceptable degrees of risk. The capital market can be cleared of excess demand at some structure of loan rates that is

[9] Jiro Yao (ed.), *Monetary Factors in Japanese Economic Growth,* Kobe Economic & Business Research Series Number Three, 1970.

"high." Unfortunately, demand functions for savings can be estimated by only the crudest of techniques in the lagging economies, and approximations of market-clearing loan rates are necessarily primitive. Still the approximations are preferable to low rate schedules that are normally imposed.

Various indicators of rate levels that minimize the need for loan rationing can be found. There are the rates of the curb markets that do distinguish between borrowers and between projects seeking finance. These rates, however, exceed a target level that would be appropriate for the monetary system. For one thing, they must compensate lenders for the hazard of prosecution under anti-usury laws. There can be sample estimates of investment yields in a range of firms and industries. Even aggregative production functions can suggest whether 20 per cent is closer to the mark than 10 per cent is.

A market for treasury bills or certificates of deposit is a cheap device for testing potential yields of investment opportunities if there is no intervention by the central bank or other authority in the market's determination of yields.[10] With even commercial banks excluded from participation, such a market can suggest the opportunity cost of allocating savings to tangible capital. However, this rate is below the target level that would be appropriate for the monetary system because it is unaffected by risks of investment. The target level lies between rates on the curb and rates on the bill market, and experience at the loan counters of a growing monetary system can reduce the margin of error.

Gestation of Loan Demand. In lagging economies where liberalization is being contemplated warily as the alternative to the existing regime of control and repression, doubts are expressed that loan demand would emerge at scarcity prices for savings. Even government corporations, it is said, incur losses at far lower loan rates. The minister of finance cannot afford higher interest charges: they would simply force him deeper into deficit finance. Private firms in industry and agriculture and fishing or mining do not have the managerial

---

[10] Antonin Basch and Milic Kybal, *Capital Markets in Latin America* (special complimentary edition), p. 135.

skills or technologies or labor force or equity for risk bearing to generate investment opportunities at high yield. Only the larger and older trading firms, their roots established in some earlier colonial period, can supply the loan opportunities and pay scarcity rates. Too often these doubts seem to be confirmed in the experience of international agencies whose funds for project loans accumulate unclaimed for acceptable ventures.

If these doubts were justified, the lagging economy is destined always to be a lagging economy. Fortunately, the doubts are exaggerated. The experience of liberalizing economies is that investment opportunities emerge when firms need to put less effort and expense into obtaining loan rations or import licenses, export permits, or foreign-exchange allowances from an overburdened civil service. Projects that are unattractive at arbitrary prices become viable when price distortions are removed and transactions costs of investing are reduced. Repressive policies inhibit both sides of the capital market.[11]

Some responsibility for gestation of loan demand rests upon the monetary system itself. Typical banking in the lagging economy is inert, content to service traditional borrowers and to extract its oligopoly profits from wide margins between low real loan rates and much lower real deposit rates. Some of the inertia is to be explained by risk aversion at low loan rates and would disappear if official ceilings on loan rates were removed. More would disappear if competitive conditions were imposed on banking by appropriate charter policies and if smaller and more predictable shares of banking portfolios were appropriated by public authority for forced and guaranteed loans.[12] A wider range of loan opportunities can be explored where it is recognized that the stock of money is a debt in perpetuity of the monetary system and need not be backed mainly by liquid assets.

No less than markets for new exports, the market for expanding

[11] Juergen B. Donges, Institut für Weltwirtschaft, Kiel, *Brazil's Trotting Peg,* pp. 24–26.
[12] Banco de la Republica, *El Mercado de Capitales en Colombia,* pp. 183–195.

loans to both old and new borrowers requires cultivation. A learning process for lenders and borrowers involves social costs of factor inputs and risk taking. It is part of the process of capital accumulation, and its costs are properly counted in the costs and rates of return to capital. Too frequently the learning process is disregarded: in effect, its costs are assumed to be unacceptably high. The process can take many forms, from learning by doing to formal education and, if need be, learning from examples set by foreign enterprise. If liberalization makes loan funds accessible to enterprise and clears various markets of distortions that suppress enterprise, someone—lender, borrower, or government—finds the learning process to be profitable.

A lamentable example of repression of efficient loan demand appears in the wheat-producing areas of North and Northwest India. The effect of the green revolution has been disappointing. Conditions of land tenure have permitted consolidation and expansion of large holdings but have prevented development of small farms. Loans on cheap terms have encouraged capital-intensive techniques by the larger enterprises while capital rationing has barred the small enterprise from the savings market. The income distribution has been twisted toward increasing inequality, and the owners of large farms have responded with luxury consumption and with higher rates of savings that flow into more tractors, more expensive homes, and luxurious automobiles. Potentialities exist for raising savings rates of small farmers, diverting the savings of the wealthier farmers, and utilizing the savings flow for efficient investment in new stages of the green revolution. They can be realized if deposit rates are raised at financial institutions, if loan rates are raised to induce economies in capital inputs and substitution of labor for capital, and if loan demand for finance of small farming can be stimulated by adjustments in land tenure, by extension services, and by encouragement of the learning process in other ways. Absorptive capacity for heavier savings flows exists even in the midst of dire poverty.[13] Precedent can

[13] B. S. Minhas, *Mass Poverty and Strategy of Rural Development in India,* Economic Development Institute, International Bank for Reconstruction and Development, March, 1971.

be found in Mexico, for example, for measures that India might adopt in order to realize the savings, investment, employment, and distribution effects of liberalized finance in its northern regions.[14]

Loan-Rate Differentials and Subsidies. Capital may be homogeneous putty in the world of Wealth View, but it is an heterogeneous array of buildings, machines, inventories, and people in the lagging economy. There may be one yield rate on capital and one appropriate loan rate in perfect savings markets, but the capital markets of lagging economies are in bits and pieces, so segmented that the highest loan rates are substantial multiples of the lowest. The segmentation and rate differentials are partly expressions of portfolio preferences among savers and financial institutions between the loan opportunities proffered by investors, partly the result of gaps in information and blockages in communication between portions of the capital market; and they are also imposed by monetary authority.

Authority in lagging economies dictates explicit loan rates on the organized markets, making fine distinctions according to maturities, borrowers, and lenders, size of loans, and other criteria. Excess demands for loans are cleared by rationing in conformity with the Plan, with an eye to borrowers' records of debt payment, sometimes on the basis of political affiliation, too often according to side payments that borrowers may offer. The auction is not the paradigm of these capital markets.

Interest rates are a favorite vehicle for subsidy of investment. Investment in general is subsidized, at savers' and labor's expense, by

[14] Describing Mexican experience, Leopoldo Solis has reported: "Thus, some economic sectors that had not been considered attractive credit risks, despite being key sectors for development, can now obtain credit through the mediation of the monetary authorities, who have resorted to diverse mechanisms in order to facilitate their access to credit. The natural resistance of the commercial banking sector, which normally wants to invest in activities that constitute a low risk or of which it has previous knowledge, has thus been overcome" (Leopoldo Solis, "Mexican Economic Policy in the Post-War Period: The Views of Mexican Economists," *The American Economic Review,* Supplement, June, 1971). For an account of resistance to development of loan markets in Malaysia, see Bank Negara Malaysia, *Annual Report and Statement of Accounts,* 1970, p. 15.

the low mean level of real rates. Investments in particular are subsidized by the lowest charges in the rate structure, and their prior claims to rations are based on the central bank's guarantee of repayment, for example, or by assurance of rediscountability on cheap terms. This technique of subsidy must be the first-worst way of extending an economy's production capabilities: it advises savers and investors that savings are plentiful, more plentiful relative to labor than in developed economies, with the result that savings become more scarce and their employment more tightly concentrated in subsidized investment. To use the price of the scarce productive factor as the vehicle for subsidy is to convey a false message about relative factor availabilities. There is the objection, too, that because savings are fungible, the subsidy may not reach the final product for which it was intended.

An obvious alternative for interest rates at subsidy levels is the direct payment of subsidy from the government's tax revenues. The subsidy can be allowed according to demonstrated differences between investors' private rates of return and estimated social rates. A second alternative is often feasible, and that is to remove distortions in relative prices, other than interest rates, that affect investment's profitability. For example, an interest-rate subsidy may appear to be appropriate for construction of power generators, but the need for it disappears when power is appropriately priced to its users. Again, the interest-rate subsidy may be superfluous for import-substitution industry if the foreign-exchange rate is made less adverse for exports. Distortions in relative prices imposed by the Power Board generate distortions that seem to justify intervention by the Monetary Board. The first-best way out is to let prices resume their function of clearing excess demands in interrelated markets.

It is characteristic of ministries of finance to insist on borrowing at subsidy rates of interest, possibly to avoid an increase in tax collections or in the rate of inflation or in prices charged by public corporations. Governments miss the point that subsidy rates of interest do impose a tax, on savers and workers. Moreover, these rates of interest mislead the government as well as the private sector into production of the wrong products at the wrong prices for the wrong markets. In both higher tax revenues and wider profit margins of public corporations, governments have alternatives to cheap interest that do not shrink and waste the savings flow. Financial reform does not exempt the government sector.[15]

The term structure of interest rates in lagging economies extends to a very near horizon, a matter of months, on free or unorganized markets. It starts high with the shortest maturities and ascends higher still. There are rates at long term in the organized sector, all dictated—for mortgages, government bonds, or pension and social-security funds—and all far below the structure on the curb. This temporal pattern is hardly to be explained by any persuasive expectational hypothesis of savers' and investors' behavior. It is possible that sophisticated capital markets would derive a pattern of security yields declining with maturity in lagging economies, because sometime capital-labor ratios must rise and yields to investment must fall. However, the same capital markets would be more likely to call out an ascending pattern reflecting risk aversion to the familiar uncertainties of wealth holding. Time and liquidity preference would dominate the effect on interest-rate structure of potential economic growth.

Monetary and other financial reform can be expected to extend capital-market horizons and divert savings into contracts at longer term. A reduced variance of the inflation rate moderates borrower and lender risks. Confidence that the monetary system will grow in real terms permits borrowers to expect that loans will be extended and increased at a price. The expanding financial system can assume some responsibility as a secondary buyer of long-term securities so that savers sacrifice less liquidity as they extend terms of their portfolios. This does not mean, of course, that it should attempt to peg security prices.

There is a role for insurance by the financial system of borrower and lender risks in markets for savings. For example, borrowers may not be able to foresee renewal terms, and savers can rarely find

[15] For further discussion of loan-rate subsidy, see Chapter 6, pp. 158–159.

in lagging economies the information necessary for careful choice among securities. The financial system presumably has clearer expectations and access to richer stores of information and can supply loan insurance. Needless to say, it should charge for its services a price generally adequate to cover its costs and losses. Free guarantees and free insurance on the capital markets are indirect subsidies that twist and distort the allocation of savings. Moreover, prices charged for them are incentives to capital-market development.

The Organization of the Monetary System

Monetary systems have numerous feasible designs. Some criteria for choice among them are reasonably clear. A society with a socialist bent wants its banks nationalized, but a capitalist society can consider its banks to be the fulcrum of private enterprise. An open society with strong commitments to the international division of labor accepts an external target rate of inflation and, given its money-demand function, leaves the nominal-money stock for determination by the balance of international payments. The society wishing to detach itself in some high degree from the world outside draws its own price-level trend line and uses domestic control instruments to supply appropriate growth in nominal money.

Within any of these broad contexts criteria for organization can be based on considerations of optimality in the markets for money and savings. The first criterion is the unambiguous designation of the monetary authority, the one agency with money illusion. The second is sensitivity of the system to the authority's control instruments. The third is competitiveness of the system, or simulated competitive behavior, to narrow spreads between loan and deposit rates. The fourth is operating efficiency to economize on factor inputs, and a fifth is responsiveness to technological changes that can increase real money demanded. A sixth is allocative efficiency in both a static sense of capacity to rank alternative uses of money holders' savings and a dynamic sense of capacity to find and induce an increasing flow of loan opportunities. A seventh is solvency: money holders must be protected against default in the monetary system. Finally, the design of the monetary system should not have undesired effects on the distribution of income and wealth. In the remainder of this section we consider applications of these criteria on the markets for money and capital.

Organization on the Market for Money. A monolithic governmental monetary system would score high on some of the criteria. Only the government bank would issue nominal money, with its branches supplying payments services. All money would be high-powered, and issue of nominal money would bring inflation-tax receipts into the government budget. This style of monetary system could manage nominal money precisely, avoiding the loose linkages of pluralistic systems between high-powered money and bank money. If one may judge from countries' revealed preferences among monetary systems, it is inferior on other criteria.

All money might be low-powered but based on reserves of one hundred per cent against the private banks' issues of both currency and deposits. The monetary authority would monopolize the system's purchases of securities in the capital market, paying in high-powered reserve money that only commercial banks would hold. It would pay reserve-deposit rate to commercial banks from its own earnings. Given competitive chartering of the commercial banks, these earnings adjusted for the banks' operating costs would be passed on in deposit interest to money holders. The banks would be the system's deposit window, and the monetary authority would be the loan window. There is a new market, for bank reserves, with supply wholly at the dictate of the monetary authority and demand by commercial banks arising from the opportunity for profit from the spread between two deposit rates. There is also a market for bank charters, and the optimal price on this market is zero. There is a market for bank equities where price is the discounted value of competitive earnings from provision to the public of payments services.

At the extreme of decentralization all money might be low-powered, and the commercial banks might be both deposit window and loan window. The monetary authority would impose its will on the stock of nominal money by supplying reserves to the commercial banks through rediscount, setting the supply arbitrarily, and calling out a rediscount rate that would induce the commercial banks to maintain the appropriate reserve ratio. The banks' demand for reserves would be generated by prospects of net settlements among themselves in clearing house. The authority's abdication from any role in the capital market would reflect confidence in the competitive banking system's allocative efficiency.

The typical monetary system is more intricate than any of these three models. The central bank issues demand debt that serves both as money and as bank reserves, and bank reserves may include treasury bills or other instruments. Money is supplied, too, by commercial banks. The central bank, commercial banks, and other institutions share the loan function. The first effect of such arrangements is to multiply the determinants of change in the stock of nominal money. The public's choice between money that is a claim on the monetary authority and money that is a claim on commercial banks affects the share of the former that drifts into the bank's reserves. The commercial banks' preferences between reserve balances and primary securities or between reserves in one form and another affects the relationship between the nominal amount of the monetary authority's control variable—for example, commercial bank deposits with the central bank—and the money stock. The preference of the ministry of finance between issues of bonds and issues of bills affects the supply of assets that commercial banks demand, under compulsion of reserve requirements or not, as a condition for incurring debt in money form. The stock of nominal money is buffeted by portfolio choices in various sectors, and its relationship with the control variable is attenuated. The second criterion of organization, sensitivity of the monetary system to controls over nominal money, is abused in this tinker-toy design of monetary systems.

As loopholes in control are discovered in the complex monetary system, techniques of control are multiplied. For example, markets for government securities are organized so that there may be open-market operations by the central bank. Reserve requirements become more complex; rediscount rules and rates became more numerous. And, of course, price fixing over loan and deposit rates and other financial prices becomes more pervasive. The social costs are apparent—in expensive administrative structures, expensive measures in private institutions for evading constraints, corruption of regulatory officials, suppression of competition in financial markets, discouragement of operating efficiency and wariness of technological change. Controls over nominal money become overdetermining with the result that some instruments of control are used simply to counteract mischief done by others.[16]

After the monetary authority has plotted growth in demand for real money, elected its inflation rate, and identified the path of growth in nominal money, it should wish to minimize noise and friction in holding nominal money on track. The authority at the apex of a decentralized monetary system needs sole responsibility for one nominal variable, for example, bank reserves, and one relative price, for example, reserve-deposit rate and its negative, rediscount rate.[17] It needs, too, an instrument to enforce competitive behavior among private banks, and competitive charter policy suffices except in the smallest economies. Finally, insurance of private money issue against default belongs in the basic kit of monetary controls. The social advantages of money deepening justify the use of insurance as a means of making money a secure asset and, in effect, of raising real deposit rate. Insurance is a superior substitute for intricate governmental supervision over banking operations, if only because it is likely to interfere less with the allocative efficiency of the monetary system. In view of the externalities of money deepening, a case can be made

[16] How controls give birth to controls has become a matter of concern in the monetary system of the United States. See, for example, "The President's Commission on Financial Structure and Regulation: A Symposium," *Journal of Money, Credit and Banking,* February, 1971, pp. 1–34; William E. Gibson, "Eurodollars and U.S. Monetary Policy," *Journal of Money, Credit and Banking,* August, 1971, pp. 649–665.

[17] Don Patinkin, "Financial Intermediaries and the Logical Structure of Monetary Theory," *The American Economic Review,* March, 1961, pp. 115–116.

for meeting some costs of insurance from taxation. Whether the costs are absorbed in this way or by charges upon banks, the insurance charges should be graded according to the size of net worth and variance of yield within bank portfolios.

Organization on the Market for Capital. Savings ushered into the monetary system through growth in the money stock, in non-monetary debt, and in the net worth of banking are ushered out again mainly to the capital market, in smaller amounts to purchases of the system's own operating assets. The flow to the capital market in the lagging economies has common characteristics. First, it is closely monitored by central authority with regard to both quantity and price. Second, a large share of it is taken into the fiscal budget of government. Third, a portion of it reaches the ultimate destination of investment through secondary intermediaries, each with its sector of investment to supply with rationed funds. Lending done by the commercial banks at their own discretion accounts for a minor fraction of their total assets and serves traditional borrowers in conventional enterprise. The private monetary system has little allocative responsibility.

Reasons averred for this design are numerous, and we mention only a few. For example, unless there were central direction, savings would not flow to destinations preferred in the Plan: the banking system cannot detect on imperfect capital markets the relative social rates of return that the Planning Board sees; the commercial banks are foreign-owned, perhaps, or tied to a small number of privileged borrowers or bound by unreasonable standards of risk-avoidance. Again, there are economies of scale from specialization in loan functions. Third, given the policy choice for subsidy rates of interest and for the rationing that they imply, losses in the lending function should fall on a government agency, and the authority of government is needed to enforce the rules of rationing. The monetary system may be important allocatively in the developed capital markets, but elsewhere its portfolio should be filled with required reserves; with specified holdings of government securities and forced loan to development banks, as secondary intermediaries, and even to investors; and with loans that abide by credit guidelines in one form or another, including preferential rediscount rates.

The reason we suggest for the wallflower role of the monetary sys tem is that the real size of the system has been depressed by deposit-rate policy, that there is excess demand for monetary savings at subsidy rates of interest, that a market mechanism for allocation cannot survive in this context, and that dictated allocation is a political function. Shallow finance implies decreed allocation of finance.

One purpose of monetary deepening is to overwhelm the rationing mechanism of repressed finance, substituting a pricing mechanism and decentralized judgment in ranking competitive bids for savings. The savings effect of deepening implies sufficient growth in the flow of funds to tax the capacity of a few specialized loan windows and to reduce their importance as guardians of an especially scarce resource. The investment effect implies dispersion of savings on less capital-intensive projects than planners relish, with savings being shifted about the capital market to take advantage of yield differentials.

The case for centralized banking is strong in the liberalized market for money because it gives more secure control over growth in nominal money. The case for decentralized banking is stronger in the liberalized market for capital because it provides competitive judgments about loan rates and loan options. Competitive chartering is in order along with other devices to widen participation in the capital market. No obstacles are properly put in the way of development of bill markets where dealers and brokers can complement or compete with the loan windows of commercial banks. A case exists for loan insurance, as we have suggested before. Subsidies can be justified for flows of information to both lenders and borrowers about developments in market for, say, goods and labor that bear on the outcomes of investment opportunities. Significant investment effects of financial deepening depend on the discipline of price in the capital market, on improvement in the assessment and distribution of risk, and on flows of information that reduce uncertainty.

Costs and Profits in the Monetary System. The monetary system is a service industry consisting typically of incorporated firms, some with private and some with public equity ownership. It applies real factor inputs to the process of intermediation, supplying services in the payments process to money holders and services in savings allocation to borrowers, charging the latter loan rate and from revenues paying deposit rate as well as factor returns. Explicit loan rate is decreed in repressed finance at some level below the scarcity price of savings, nominal deposit rate is fixed at zero, and the gap between rates plus some heterogeneous charges for services cover factor costs and profits. Various furtive and unreported revenues and charges are effects of differences between imposed rate ceilings and free rates in street markets.

Despite ambiguities in banking data, it appears that factor costs are high, per unit of real money, for stagnant monetary systems. One assumes that part of the differential can be explained by services for depositors in imperfect substitution for positive deposit rates and by superfluous services that borrowers pay for in partial substitution for higher loan rates. Part of the differential can be explained by costs of land and plant that are attractive dispositions, in an inflationary environment, of stockholder equity. The remainder of the differential is a matter of technological lag in management and of the bankers' freedom from competitive pressure.

It appears, too, that profit return to equity is high. Bankers are seldom insistent upon monetary reform. Because the risk element, except perhaps for foreign banks, cannot be large, the monopoly element of profit must be important. The monetary system discriminates against money holders, but it provides attractive benefits for borrowers, including government, that receive loan rations and for stockholders, again including government. The loan commitment or line of credit and the bank charter are valuable private wealth.

Optimal monetary policy seeks equilibrium on the markets for money and savings that minimizes the gap between loan and deposit rates while it allows supply price for equity in banking. One counts upon competitive pressures to bring about agreements between banks and depositors regarding efficient substitution between pay-

ments services and deposit rate as well as between banks and borrowers concerning substitution between allocative services and loan
rates. The rate gap would be minimized for the quality of product
upon which buyers and sellers agree under competitive circumstances
and subject to specifications in insurance programs for deposits and
loans.

Numerous ways can be found to enliven banking's competitive
spirit. The central bank and the government's commercial banks can
assume the role of market leaders. Private charters can be offered in
larger numbers, but always at a price that appropriates for government at least some of their monopoly value. The "banks" that are
not banks but merely loan windows—institutions for agricultural or,
for example, export credit—can be thrust into the market for money
as suppliers of means of payment. It is hardly necessary that foreign
enterprise should be called in as a competitive catalyst because the
cost of learning by doing in this industry cannot be high.

THE CURB MARKETS

A private money market is thriving in Korea today so that the financial
activities of the country are under what is called a dual system. The financial activities are largely divided into two—one is centered around
banks and other financial institutions which are under the control of the
government, and the other centered around the private money market
functioning to meet money demands outside government control.[18]

The rampancy of various private moneylending agencies not only puts
credit order in confusion but inflicts harm on the public, especially small
business men. Also, there exists the possibility of competition with banks
in some financial activities. Since the private money market indulges in
covert financial activities, it is apt to impose restrictions on the operation
of monetary policy by the government. Moreover, a covert distribution
of money impedes efficiency of capital as a whole. In this connection, it is
necessary to make operation of the private money market overt and
come to the fore of social activities.[19]

[18] Finance Section, Ministry of Finance (Korea), *Outline of Banking System
and Policy of Korea,* pp. 98–99.
[19] *Ibid.,* p. 104.

Curb markets[20] of many styles, each with its characteristic financial assets and institutions and with its own skein of interest rates, can be found everywhere.[21] Their relative importance in the saving-investment process depends on the degree of repression applied to their competitor, the "organized" or "official" financial system. A common view about them is suggested by the second paragraph of the quotation above: if they cannot be suppressed, they too should be "organized." They engage in covert activities, it is said; they frustrate official policy; they finance weddings, funerals, and capital flight abroad; they exact usurious rates of interest; they compete with organized finance and retard its growth.

Data regarding curb markets are scarce and not wholly reliable. They are sufficient, however, to impress one with the vigor of the propensity to save even under trying circumstances. The savings they attract along with other savings that escape from the low returns of organized finance into inventories of real assets and foreign assets must be a multiple of savings that flow on a voluntary basis to repressed monetary systems. The data indicate, too, that productivity of investment is higher than officially approved loan rates suggest.[22] Evidently savings are fungible enough to find some of these

[20] Against the preference for "kerb" rather than "curb," one's defense rests on *Webster's New International Dictionary,* second edition, unabridged.

[21] Hugh T. Patrick, "Interest Rates and the Grey Financial Market in Japan," *Pacific Affairs,* Winter, 1965–66; U Tun Wai, "Interest Rates Outside the Organized Money Markets of Underdeveloped Countries," *Staff Papers,* International Monetary Fund, November, 1957, pp. 80–142.

[22] Sydney M. Robbins, *The Money-Capital Market in Korea,* Agency for International development, June, 1970. Basch and Kybal bring a report from Colombia that might well be reproduced for a number of countries (*op. cit.,* p. 127):

> The interest rates charged by financial institutions have been governed by detailed directives issued by the central bank and, more recently, by the Monetary Board. In fact, the whole credit system is regulated by the Monetary Board; this applies not only to the terms of loans but also to their destinations. Nevertheless . . . their effectiveness on the money and capital markets is open to doubt.
> One disturbing feature of the securities market was the expansion of bills of exchange. . . . These bills, endorsed by commercial banks, yielded the

opportunities despite inhibitions put in their way by official measures: like lovers, savers and investors can arrange their trysts. Descriptions of the curb make it clear, too, that organized finance is spendthrift with its factor inputs. The loan brokers at café tables in Bogotá, the Indian business firms that open their own deposit windows, the peasant cooperative societies, have simple production functions with low input specifications.

A program of financial liberalization has two principal implications for this proletariat of financial institutions. First, the curb should have to face competition from deepening in the organized sector. It can be strong enough to survive the degree of liberalization that governments are willing to accept. Second, the curb should be offered opportunities to become part of an integrated capital market, incurring less risk and lower costs of other kinds as an open rather than covert activity. There may be little that the curb can do for markets at long term, but its participation in markets at short term can assist in reducing spreads between loan and deposit rates, between rates to different classes of savers and investors and spreads between regions.

Each economy is likely to find its own best methods of integrating the curb markets with organized finance. They might include legalizing the curb's contracts and making them enforceable, and laws against usury could be put on the shelf. Cooperative societies could be granted preferential deposit rates and even a variant of rediscount facilities in organized finance. One type or another of financial instrument, from acceptance to commercial paper or negotiable certificates and treasury bills, might be introduced for the curb and trade

---

buyer up to 3 per cent per month. As a result they competed with other investment alternatives, at a time when the central bank was following a policy of credit restriction. Trading in bills of exchange reached its peak in 1966 . . . but as a result of restrictions introduced by the Monetary Board on commercial banks, it practically ceased by 1968. Nevertheless, even larger trading in this nonbank type of credit has developed outside the stock exchanges, in the street market (mercado de la calle).

in it permitted without official intervention.[23] Dealers and brokers on the curb may be assisted in moving into organized finance, including banking. The curb is an underutilized national resource.

NON-MONETARY INTERMEDIATION IN THE ORGANIZED MARKET

The good financial regime, as Henry C. Simons visualized it, would be simple. Coin and currency would be issues of the central bank, and all deposit means of payment together with close substitutes in terms of liquidity would be issued by banks against reserves of one hundred per cent. Banks issuing deposits would take their revenues in the form of service charges against deposit activity. Intermediaries apart from banks, doing the lending that banks do now, would finance lending by issue of their own equity securities.[24] The good financial regime, as lagging economies seem to visualize it, bears little resemblance to Simons'. This section discusses some factors that explain the complex pattern of non-monetary intermediation in financially shallow economies and then suggests modifications that lead toward, but not to, the Simons' ideal. One may note that, however inventive lagging economies have been in designing inefficient financial differentiation, some "advanced" economies surpass them.

Typically but not invariably, the commercial banks of lagging economies pay an explicit deposit rate of zero on demand accounts and offer other deposit-contracts with yields ranked according to maturity and other considerations. They differentiate between money, as the means of payment, and near-monies. One knows that monetary authorities insist upon a deposit rate of zero for money for a composite reason: to sustain public demand for the authority's

---

[23] How quickly an open short-term market can be developed by the curb around an appropriate credit instrument is described by Richard D. Porter in his *Birth of a Bill Market,* Center for Research on Economic Development, University of Michigan, Ann Arbor, Michigan. For a similar Brazilian experience, see David M. Trubek, "Law, Planning and the Development of the Brazilian Capital Market," *The Bulletin,* Institute of Finance, Graduate School of Business Administration, New York University, April, 1971, p. 22.
[24] Henry C. Simons, *Economic Policy for a Free Society,* pp. 64–65; Milton Friedman, *Essays in Positive Economics,* Phoenix Books, pp. 133–156.

own issue of coin and currency, to maintain a margin satisfactory for banks between deposit rate and controlled loan rate, sometimes illusorily to reduce bankers' temptations to excessively risky lending. One does not hear vociferous protests from bankers and finds his way to the suspicion that imperfectly competitive banking firms appreciate zero demand-deposit rate as a device for decomposing their deposit market and, through product and price differentiation, maximizing profit. From the zero nominal rate as base, they can find an ascending scale of rates for successively less perfect imitations of money that, given depositors' elasticities of substitution, satisfy their profit aspirations. To be sure, the banks must have the monetary authority's approval for the rate pattern, but there are ways of modifying effective as distinct from explicit rate, at least marginally, so that the banks and the authority seem to reach an accord. Multiple-product banking in the lagging economy, supplied by a small number of firms with the central bank as market leader, is not grossly unlike the textbook patterns that also fit, for example, the industry of gasoline distribution at retail.[25]

In addition to differentiation of issues within the monetary system, there is differentiation that sets financial institutions apart from the monetary system, denying them the role of money issue. Some of their distinctive issues to savers are near-monies, among them postal savings deposits and savings and loan shares, and some are remote from money, such as pension claims. Doubtless, even under optimal conditions some of this differentiation would survive and other forms would develop. That is to say, some of it does reflect economies of specialization in search and invest, providing savers with combinations of deposit rate and services that they prefer and finding outlets for savings in primary securities with appropriate patterns of yield and risk.

However, some share of this differentiation is of the hothouse variety, contrived in response to inappropriate government policies. It is reminiscent of the tax-evasion industry of lawyers, accountants, and others that flourishes on distortions and complexities of tax law.

[25] C. E. Ferguson, *Microeconomic Theory,* Chapter 12.

A savings-and-loan industry is a case in point. Typically, it is a subsidized and otherwise sheltered medium for giving social favors to residential construction, and it would not be viable without protection. Pension funds are often devices for compulsory savings or for restraint on the mobility of labor, adopted as alternatives to tax and wage reforms.

One can trace some non-monetary intermediation, then, to economic opportunity for specialization in the saving-investment process and some to stimuli from non-monetary public policies. Another part may be emulative, a luxury import from advanced financial systems: some trust arrangements are an example. We suspect that repression of the monetary system is the strongest impulse. Where real deposit rates in the monetary system, on money and near-monies, are negative or only slightly positive and where loans at low rates are reserved for government and other privileged borrowers, there can be attractive opportunities to design for savers financial assets that escape the tightest government controls and to find loan opportunities where rates of return can leave a margin of profit to intermediation. Sometimes these opportunities are found in organized finance, say through cooperative techniques, but they appear too on the curb for investment in real estate, consumer durables, and automobiles, even in capital flight.[26] Governmental constraints create opportunities for financial smuggling.

If there were money deepening and if banks issuing deposit money and other short-term claims were permitted, on a competitive basis, to exert their full comparative advantage, intermediation would fall into an homogeneous pattern. The mosaic of intermediaries issuing indirect financial claims at short term, with this intermediary depending upon a sheltered loan market and that intermediary existing by virtue of subsidy, would be replaced by commercial banks, preferably in competition with an open bill market. The advantages of homogeneity are clear. On the one hand, it can economize resource inputs into finance, some of which are especially scarce in lagging

[26] Fu-chi Liu, *op. cit.*, pp. 32–38.

economies. Again, it can clear pockets of imperfect competition. Homogeneous intermediation in conjunction with a bill market has the capacity to allocate savings more selectively between investment opportunities in different sectors and areas. The point, of course, is not to impose homogeneity or prohibit specialization, but rather to create the environment in which the superior technology wins, given prices of factor inputs and savers' tastes for portfolio diversification.

The comparative advantage of competitive banking would be apparent in a relatively small spread between loan rates and deposit rates on short-term obligations. The advantage diminishes and disappears in markets for longer-term indirect financial assets, remote from money in their various characteristics. There insurance plans, mutual and pension funds, and financieras of various kinds can hold their own. Markets for equities, bonds, and mortgages are complementary with them and with the monetary system as well. Because savers' preferences shift toward the long-term end of the maturity spectrum for financial assets, as planning horizons recede and as wealth increases, generalized banking would diminish in relative importance, not in lagging economies but higher on the growth path.

Partial reform is better than none—fortunately so, because the real thing is hard to get anywhere.[27] Intermediaries designed to benefit one investment sector, one class of saver or another, seem likely to persist even though there are other ways of getting to the same or superior results. As the history of European capital markets suggests, competition in finance is not easily arranged. Governments do insist on decreeing interest rates. International agencies are proposing to transplant financial institutions. A simple structure of intermediation, with generalized banking in markets for short-term indirect financial assets including money and with a few other comparatively sturdy technologies for long-term assets is not yet within reach, but it is a device for estimating how much financial repression remains. Until first-best comes along, even somewhat freer and

[27] That the oldest capital markets cling to their imperfections is clear in Organization for Economic Cooperation and Development, *General Report, Capital Markets Study,* pp. 11–16.

higher interest rates, a little more competition, fewer institutions for preferential finance can deepen financial wealth.

ORGANIZED MARKETS IN LONG-TERM FINANCE

Experiment, possibly reform, is active on the markets for long-term securities in lagging and developing economies, in economies high on the income scale, and in economies that are still poor. Trade and accumulation in markets for equities, bonds, and mortgages are contributing less to rates of saving and allocation of savings than the United States or Colombia, Brazil or Ghana, Pakistan or Korea considers to be feasible. Elaboration of long-term finance is in fashion.

Ingenious new stimuli have been devised for long-term finance. Korea has its annual Day of Securities. Japan grants tax concessions on dividend income, and Brazil has permitted purchase of securities in lieu of tax payments. The Investment Corporation of Pakistan conducts open-market operations in equities to stabilize their prices, and Colombia forces investment in agricultural bonds upon financial institutions. A Malay stock exchange was opened in 1970, and international agencies supply underwriting funds and technical assistance for nascent equity markets.

The path of experiment or reform has not been smooth. The deflated index of share prices declined during 1959–67 from 100 to 5 in Argentina, 39 in Peru, 42 in Colombia, and 47 in Brazil.[28] Option trading still predominates in a number of equity markets, and many markets are accessible only to issues of governments, their agencies, and a small number of dominant private firms. The path of experiment does not cover in lagging and developing economies much of the distance toward the degree of penetration by long-term assets into financial portfolios that is observed in advanced financial systems.[29]

[28] Basch and Kybal, *op. cit.,* p. 79.
[29] Raymond W. Goldsmith, *Financial Structure and Development,* Chapter 8; George C. Maniatis, "Reliability of the Equities Market to Finance Industrial Development in Greece," *Economic Development and Cultural Change,* July, 1971, pp. 598–620; David Williams, "The Development of Capital Markets in Europe," *Staff Papers,* International Monetary Fund, March, 1965, pp. 37–60; Jiro Yao, *op. cit.,* pp. 37–40.

Objectives of Innovation in Long-Term Finance

There is emulation and fashion in crash programs for deepening long-term finance, but other objectives predominate. One of them is "agrarian reform" in the corporation in order to democratize ownership and management of the capital stock in private sectors.[30] This program would break up the autocracy of enterprise in large firms. It implies dispersion of stock ownership and the development of markets that make equities broadly attractive and submit them to comparative evaluations. It implies organization of bond markets for risk-averse investors in corporate wealth and of mortgage markets to finance diffusion of control over real property. These markets and others, it is hoped, would divert savings to newer and smaller ventures not only for democratization but also for innovation of processes and products and for employment of resources previously idle.

This program to disperse control of existing capital is partly an effort to undo the consequences of financial repression and such related policies as foreign-exchange overvaluation. The policies of repression, one knows, result in capital-intensive production on a relatively large scale. Credit rations, import licenses, and tax favors lead to concentrations of economic power. Shifts imposed on terms of trade against agriculture, exports, and labor transfer wealth into narrow ownership. The new measures are partly intended to sweep up the debris from negative real rates of interest and allied devices.

The new measures are being tried, too, because there is dissatisfaction with the structure of claims against enterprise. Debt has piled too high, it is said, relative to equity, and debt at short term dwarfs the accumulation of claims at long maturities. As a result, enterprises are vulnerable to illiquidity, and equity holders are subject to risks of highly leveraged investment. Even a brief run of adversity can put firms at the mercy of creditors, and a mass of debt defaults during some widespread constraint on loans at short term might precipitate a general crisis in cash flows or, possibly, a shift

[30] David M. Trubek, *op. cit.,* pp. 43–44.

of enterprise ownership and control to primarily government leading institutions.

The argument is that the new measures are needed because old techniques of finance have not done enough for growth. Foreign aid is increasingly hard to acquire, and it is unpredictable. Tax-reform commissions have generated no apparent optimism that tax-income ratios can be raised or that the income and inflation elasticities of tax revenues can be increased markedly. Monetary systems in the lagging economies are stagnant, and the yield to inflation taxes has fallen as expected inflation has caught up with realized inflation. Exporters, farmers, and workers put up sturdier resistance against various forms of implicit taxation. Perhaps the lagging economies can use the new instruments of long-term finance to reduce chronic excess demand for savings. If real demand for assets is static at the short end of the maturity scale, try the long end.[31]

A few countries, not the laggards, are coming to innovation in long-term finance because income growth in a context of relative liberalization has generated potential demand for securities on terms that are an acceptable supply price of capital to investors, with and without intermediation. The legal system, the supply of skills, and, for example, communications facilities have reached the capacity of using new financial techniques cheaply. The stock of capital is large enough to bring within reach the scale economies of sophisticated long-term markets. Savers' horizons are so far into the future that current dividend rates are not the principal basis of choice between primary securities. In these economies growth has generated market opportunities for long-term finance, and the innovations one sees are the response.[32]

Liberalization and Long-Term Finance

The repressed, lagging economies have nothing to gain by adding the paraphernalia of long-term finance to their financial systems.

[31] Jean van der Mensbrugghe, "Domestic Savings in Developing Countries," *Finance and Development,* International Monetary Fund and the World Bank Group, March, 1972, pp. 36–39.

[32] Committee for Invisible Transactions, Organization for Economic Cooperation and Development, *Capital Markets Study: General Report,* pp. 219–238.

The demand in real terms for long-term assets does not exist and cannot develop in adequate volume, given the context of financial repression and associated policies in trade, public finance, and other areas. Equities are not a defense against relatively high and unstable inflation nor is indexing of bonds and mortgages.[33] Such inflation, alternately accelerating and slowing down to a stabilization crisis, compromises the real earnings of capital and of claims on it. Monetary reform, with deepening of money, is an indispensable first thing to do. Until it occurs, along with allied reforms, the path of returns to any item of capital stock is a perilous random walk: recurrent overvaluation of the foreign-exchange rate depresses export enterprise; any enterprise is vulnerable to unpredictable changes in credit rations, tax concessions, allowances of foreign exchange, import licenses; specific price controls have arbitrary effects on earnings. Savers' horizons are necessarily short in the repressed economy.

The costs of adding instrumentalities of long-term finance to the shallow financial system are not low. Almost inevitable is a handsome and expensive stock exchange. The thin flow of transactions is congenial to speculative fiascos, even in the equities of the stock-exchange corporation. The concentration of economic power must increase because only the securities of firms with reliable access to wealth and favor can command savers' attentions. Intervention by the central bank to stabilize the equity or debenture market would be one more source of endogeneity in the supply of nominal money. One can imagine also that deposit rates in short-term markets would be held low or reduced to generate demand for long-term issues. This pattern suggests that premature measures to stimulate finance at long term can result in one more turn of the screw against financial growth.

When a less-developed economy has become disillusioned with repressive policies, there is a temptation to install quickly the apparatus of long-term finance. The argument seems to be that if finance finally is deepening at short term or if reform is progressing in

---

[33] Bank of London & South America *Review,* June, 1969, pp. 347–360; Robert P. Collier, *Purchasing Power Bonds & Other Escalated Contracts,* Buffalo Book Co., Taipei, 1969.

the fiscal and international sectors, enough foreign technical assistance or subsidy to underwriting and sufficient tax concessions to "open" companies and to security buyers would lead quickly to deepening at long term. Possibly the tax-credit scheme for the Brazilian Northeast might give the desired momentum or shares of more successful government corporations might be offered at bargain prices.[34]

The brief for expensive, dramatic action to promote long-term finance is not persuasive. One reason is that opportunity yields for tax revenues or foreign aid to subsidize long-term markets are high. The developing economy does not have much largesse, collected in more or less neutral fashion, to distribute among numerous claimants including infrastructure and housing or land reform and agriculture as well as finance. Moreover, subsidies have a way of reaching the strongest as distinct from the intended recipients. Finally, why lavish resources on long-term finance when deepening at short-term is cheaper?

The brief for gradualism in extending the financial horizon is persuasive. Especially if intermediaries' deposit rates are not repressed, there is little for the household sector to gain from participation in a wide range of direct long-term finance. After all, intermediaries do have scale advantages in selecting and managing primary portfolios. A market must exist in the equities of the intermediaries if charters are to be issued competitively. Because scale advantages are least for portfolios of government securities and some few others of gilt-edge quality, perhaps there is a case to be made for open markets in these issues to intensify the competition that intermediaries face.[35] Such markets at long term together with a bill market may be useful devices of financial discipline. Again, there are early steps to be taken in arranging "transactional linkages" between intermediaries with re-

[34] Albert Hirschman, "Industrial Development in the Brazilian Northeast and the Tax Credit Scheme of Article 34/18," *The Journal of Development Studies,* 1968, p. 5.

[35] James Tobin, "Notes on Optimal Monetary Growth," *Journal of Political Economy,* July/August, 1968, p. 858

spect both to new security issues and to secondary transactions.[36] These are linkages that permit intermediaries to optimize their own mixture of assets. The principle suggested here is that the early stages of development in long-term finance should facilitate and exploit economies of intermediation while they take precautions against concentration of power among financial institutions. The first step in financial reform is money deepening, and the second step diversifies intermediation. Creating new Wall Streets comes later, if at all.

SPECIAL BANKS

There has been a proliferation of "banks" that are not banks. Some of them are deposit windows for drawing savings from the public to such other institutions as the central bank or the finance ministry. Most of them are loan windows—agriculture banks, power banks, housing banks, development banks, road banks, and river banks—for disposing of savings that flow from the monetary system or the fiscal budget or foreign sources. Some of them have regulatory assignments in markets for securities, foreign exchange, and goods internationally traded, and a few are managers and guardians of troubled government enterprises.

These banks rarely mount savings campaigns in the lagging economies: they are not established to do better than other savings instrumentalities. Their function is typically allocative. The projects that have concerned them most are financed at subsidy loan rates and are capital intensive in the extreme. Characteristic projects have low explicit yields, but their justification is that returns are higher when they are recomputed at relevant shadow prices. The special lending banks have been too frequently one more device for segmentation of the capital market.

It is not too harsh to conclude that special banks are an instrumentality of repressed finance. However, liberalization of finance opens up most new possibilities for them. They can be used as gen-

---

[36] Kent O. Sims, *The Development of Private Financial Markets in Pakistan,* December, 1970, p. 16.

eralized banks for intensifying competition in markets for short-term financial assets, including money. They can be used as mutual funds, selling participations especially in the equity of government corporations. They can be assigned responsibility for insurance, at a price, of debts or portfolios of private financial institutions. They have work to do in identifying investment opportunities that have been neglected in labor-intensive indigenous enterprise, and some of them have capacities for finding or creating export opportunities abroad. Their own equities may be suitable for attracting savers cautiously to the longer-term end of the maturity spectrum in developing security exchanges. Briefly, they may be useful instruments in liberalized markets for money and capital.[37]

[37] J. T. Dock Houlk, *Financing and Problems of Development Banking* (New York: Frederick A. Praeger, Inc., 1967); Edward Nevin, *Capital Funds in Underdeveloped Countries* (St. Martin's Press, 1961), Chapters 4–5; Paul E. Roberts, Jr., "Development Banking: The Issue of Public and Private Development Banking," *Economic Development and Cultural Change*, April, 1971, pp. 424–437.

6 | Fiscal Policy and Financial Deepening

Financial deepening is one technique for attaining income, savings, investment, employment, and distribution effects that can assist in escape from underdevelopment. Others exist, from land reform and new designs of education to foreign aid and family planning. This chapter is concerned with fiscal technique and particularly with ways in which it complements, displaces, or frustrates the technique of financial deepening. The important point is that development cannot quicken in lagging economies until compatible reforms occur on the fiscal and financial fronts: the treasury and central bank must discover that they are natural allies.

The first section of this chapter is concerned with government manipulation of deposit and loan rates as instruments of tax and subsidy. These financial prices are used as fiscal instruments to raise or conserve government revenue and to reach various regulatory objectives. The second section explores briefly the interdependence of financial and fiscal techniques in the saving-investment process. They can be regarded as substitutes at the margin of capital accumulation, but steady growth of an economy seems to require their employment as complements: growth needs both of them, and strength of one improves performance of the other.

TAX AND SUBSIDY OF INTEREST RATES

Real deposit and loan rates are relative prices of financial assets. If finance were costless, if financial markets were perfectly competitive and if government did not find occasion to intervene, deposit and loan rates would be equal and would approximate marginal rates of return to capital. Government does intervene in the structure of real interest rates, distorting the structure as a way of imposing taxes and granting subsidies.

Deposit-Rate Tax: Budgetary Considerations

In its third five-year development plan, the government of Korea commits itself to "keep neutral in money supply by maintaining a balanced budget and an appropriate scale of government finance."[1] In its second plan the government of Malaysia gives the same assurance: ". . . the task of mobilizing financial resources will be pursued in such a way as to sustain the stability and strength of the monetary and financial situation of the country."[2] Both governments, it appears, are pledged to do without the inflation tax as a source of revenue. They will resist the temptation to follow the path taken by Chile in 1951–55, for example, when the tax on cash balances yielded revenues equal to nearly one-fourth of government revenues from all sources.[3] They will transgress this Friedman rule:

Governments tend to look little farther than the next election. If that election is close, an increase in the rate of monetary expansion is bound to provide the government with more revenues. The negative effects on revenue, let alone on more fundamental economic and social matters, will come later.[4]

[1] Government of the Republic of Korea, *The Third Five-Year Economic Development Plan, 1972–1976*, p. 140.
[2] *Second Malaysia Plan, 1971–1975*, p. 76.
[3] John V. Deaver, "The Chilean Inflation and the Demand for Money," in David Meiselman (ed.), *Varieties of Monetary Experience*, pp. 47–48.
[4] Milton Friedman, "Government Revenue from Inflation," *Journal of Political Economy*, August, 1971, pp. 853–854.

Private wealth in the form of real money balances is a tax base that numerous finance ministers have not overlooked, with or without elections imminent. There are various ways of extracting revenue from it to finance a fiscal deficit. Metal coins can be debased and the metal recovered from any stock of nominal money—by primitive carving away of coins' edges or by more subtle ways of modern metallurgy—can be sold for what the transaction will bring into the exchequer. Two other techniques are more prevalent. The first, a "surprise" inflation tax, reduces real deposit rate *ex-post* on money balances without affecting the rate anticipated for the future. The second, a "trend" inflation tax, reduces real deposit rate realized and expected.

We may suppose that the surprise tax is imposed after a period in which nominal deposit rate $\underline{d}$ and real deposit rate $d = \underline{d} - \dot{P}$ have been zero, with expected inflation P^* also at zero. The real money supply has grown to $(M/P)_t$, and there is equilibrium on all markets, including the market for money. Then government securities are issued to the monetary system, and the system pays for them with an increase of 10 per cent in nominal money. Government expenditure of these proceeds from borrowing imposes excess supply on the market for money, excess demand on other markets. Nominal money in the public's balances is raised to 1.1 $(M)_t$ and, if the real stock of money demanded remains constant, the price level rises to 1.1 $(P)_t$ so that the real stock of money reverts to its initial level. Holders of money balances have been taxed by a reduction in real deposit rate from zero to *minus* 10 per cent, and government has received revenues of $\dot{P}$ $(M/P)_t$. If fiscal budgets were reported in real terms, with sources of revenue appropriately identified, the budget for this episode would report a surprise inflation tax equal to 10 per cent of real money balances rather than government borrowing and growth of 10 per cent in nominal money.

The surprise tax repeated often enough leads money holders to revise price-level anticipations to $P^* = \dot{P}$. It becomes a trend tax to which money holders adjust by reducing real deposit rate expected to $d = \underline{d} - P^*$, in equality with real deposit rate realized. Depending on the elasticity of real money demanded to the fall in real-deposit rate, there is erosion of the tax base, and each rate of trend tax yields lower real revenues for government than might be expected from a surprise tax at each level of other factors, including non-monetary wealth, affecting real money demanded. A government bent only on maximizing the yield of trend tax, without regard for growth in real money, puts the tax rate at the level where elasticity of money holders' response to it is unity.[5] Obviously, a government reaching for revenues from the inflation tax does not restore the tax to money holders by compensatory adjustment in nominal deposit rate. The inflation tax is a reduction in real deposit rate.

Real deposit rate can be reduced for the government's benefit without inflation. Government may force its debt upon commercial banks at rates of interest below free-market levels. The savings in interest cost, borne by money holders if deposit rate is reduced correspondingly, by bank stockholders if bank profits are affected, or by bank borrowers if banks raise private loan rates, are the equivalent of revenues from the inflation tax. Alternatively, the central bank may supply reserves to commercial banks by purchase of government securities and pay reserve-deposit rate less than free-market rates. A reserve requirement can be imposed to limit the bank's evasion of the tax.[6] Inflation, forced investment, and reserve requirements are devices by which government can depress real deposit rate as a fiscal measure.

Non-monetary financial assets of the public are vulnerable to tax through real deposit rate, with or without such compulsion as reserve requirements to reduce evasion. Mandatory private contributions to social security funds are investments in government securities bearing taxed real yields.[7] At times, governments impound profits of expatriate enterprise and allow to them a rate of return that is below

[5] Milton Friedman, *op. cit.,* p. 49.

[6] Harry G. Johnson, "Problems of Efficiency in Monetary Management," *Journal of Political Economy,* September/October, 1968, p. 977.

[7] Roberto Alemann, "Economic Development of Argentina," in Committee for Economic Development, *Economic Development Issues: Latin America,* p. 23.

an equilibrium level. Postal savings deposits rarely escape the deposit-rate tax assessment. Insurance companies are subjected to liquidity requirements that force upon them low-yield treasury bills or bonds. Government as financial authority manages real deposit rate to bring in revenues for government at debtor.

Not all revenues from the deposit-rate tax flow into the government budget. Private borrowers at banks collect revenues from the inflation tax on deposit balances if their loan rates are not fully adjusted to the rate of inflation.[8] Bank stockholders collect the revenues when loan rates, in contrast with deposit rate, are fully adjusted. In a number of lagging economies profit rates on banking net worth or total assets are high even though the real stock of deposits is small in relation to national income and despite the fact, too, that bank operations are not economical. The reason turns out to be that banks are collecting the inflation tax for themselves. Borrowers and stockholders of other financial institutions can realize similar advantages from any rise in $\dot{P}$ relative to nominal $\underline{d}$, and these advantages can be capitalized for sale as private wealth.

Governments extract revenues from private financial accumulation by explicit taxation as well as by the inflation tax and by compulsion on savers to hold, directly or indirectly, government securities bearing nominal rates of interest below free-market levels. In the schedular style of income taxation, which predominates over the global form in economies at relatively low income levels, rates of assessment against income from financial sources are high relative to rates applied against other incomes, and the rate of progression is steeper.[9] For one reason, financial income is easier for the tax collector to detect than, for example, profit income or even wages and salaries in the private sector. For another reason, financial income seems to connote greater ability to pay tax than comparable labor

---

[8] It has been estimated that 72 per cent of revenues realized from the inflation tax on money balances in Chile during 1929–55 did not accrue to government, flowing instead as subsidies principally to borrowers at banks. Deaver, *loc. cit.*

[9] Richard A. Musgrave, *Fiscal Systems,* pp. 188–191.

income does. After real deposit rate has been whittled away by inflation, by low yields on compulsory investment in government securities, and by income tax, the residue hardly provides a strong incentive to save.

Budgetary stringency in the government sector is chronic among the low-income countries, lagging or not. The case of Ghana is illustrative:

It is estimated that during the 1960's as a whole, when the wealth of the country, as measured by the gross national product, was rising at the annual rate of 2.5 per cent per annum, the current costs of government increased at a rate of 10.5 per cent per annum. At the same time the government's income by way of taxation rose by an average of 10 per cent per annum, thus leading gradually to increasing difficulties in finding the resources to finance the development program.[10]

Finding resources for government's current and development budgets has involved growth in public debt at a rate faster than growth in national wealth, in principal bases of taxation and in fiscal revenues. Service on the public debt has become an impediment to development policy. Deposit-rate tax in one form or another is an obvious and common solution. There can be few parallels for Japan's use of the tax in 1945, when the nominal stock of money was approximately doubled to repay all long-term public debt.[11] However, more restrained use of the tax is no less common, it would seem, when domestic debt imposes transfer burdens on the fiscal budget than renegotiation of terms with foreign creditors when service of external debt strains the developing economy's international budget. When compounding of savers' financial claims on government seems to threaten a desired growth rate in government expenditures for other things than debt service, how easy it is simply to tax the savers!

Some costs of this solution have been discussed in earlier chapters. An inflation or other tax on money balances has its adverse income,

[10] Republic of Ghana, *Budget Statement for 1971–72*, p. 27. For a discussion of comparable experience in Peru, see Antonin Basch and Milic Kybal, *Capital Markets in Latin America* (special complimentary edition), p. 140.
[11] Michael W. Keran, "Monetary Policy and the Business Cycle in Postwar Japan," in Meiselman (ed.), *op. cit.*, p. 170.

savings, investment, employment, and distributive effects. Deposit-rate taxation on other financial assets reduces real amounts of them demanded by savers, penalizing the financial technique of capital accumulation. Evasion of the tax dissipates savings in consumption or diverts them to self-finance of investment, the curb markets, and capital flight abroad. Uncertainty on savers' part about future levels of deposit-rate taxation must be one reason for short financial horizons in lagging economies. The tax is objectionable on grounds of equity if only because savers with relatively low incomes have fewer alternatives of evasion. Equity is not served when proceeds of the tax accrue partly to private borrowers and stockholders of financial institutions. No other feasible tax is neutral, but the biases of deposit-rate taxation in any of its forms should motivate any minister of finance to look for substitutes.

Deposit-Rate Tax: Regulatory Considerations

Since 1965 the Board of Governors of the Federal Reserve System has been especially busy with manipulation of deposit rates at financial institutions in the United States. It has raised and lowered rate ceilings in its Regulation Q, created new categories of deposits and deposit rates and managed banks' reserve requirements with a view to affecting the deposit rates that banks are prepared to pay. Each adjustment can be regarded as a tax or subsidy to induce changes in relative demands among financial institutions and their depositors for various types of financial assets. The ultimate objectives apparently have been to affect savings allocation, profits of some financial institutions and perhaps distributive equity. Deposit rate has been used as a control instrument for multiple purposes and not simply for the one objective of financial deepening. The Federal Reserve is not unique among monetary authorities in managing deposit rate now as tax, now as subsidy to change patterns of financial behavior.[12]

[12] John L. Scadding, "The Fiscal Element in Monetary Policy," *Journal of Money, Credit and Banking,* May, 1971, pp. 391–411; James Tobin, "Deposit Interest Ceilings as a Monetary Control," *Journal of Money, Credit and Banking,* February, 1970, pp. 4–14; Milton Friedman, "Controls on Interest Rates Paid by Banks," *Journal of Money, Credit and Banking,* February, 1970, pp. 15-32.

Deposit-rate ceilings were first imposed by the Federal Reserve, on statutory authority of the Banking Act of 1933, for protection of commercial banking profits. It imposed imperfect competition on the market for bank deposits, demand and time alike, with the effect of subsidizing bank stockholders.[13] As one might expect, given the large number of banks in the United States, there has been non-price competition for deposits, and some of the subsidy has been restored to depositors. Beginning in July, 1966, a new objective emerged, and authority to set rate ceilings was extended over a wider range of financial institutions. The new objective was to protect savings and loan associations and savings banks against rate competition by commercial banks, the beneficiaries to include both stockholders in these institutions and borrowers in the mortgage market.[14] A third objective emerged in 1968 when rising rates of interest in open markets induced a shift by asset-holders away from term deposits in banks to markets for commercial paper and Eurodollars in particular. Then the authorities lifted ceilings on deposits of larger size and longer maturity to protect banks against deposit liquidation and the balance of payments against capital outflow.

This series of experiments with rate ceilings has been one of the more dismal episodes in American central banking. Evasion of the ceilings and adjustments to them have been expensive; for example, in costs of spreading branches of American banks abroad. Subsidy of mortgage rates of interest is an inefficient device to protect less well-to-do consumers against rising costs of housing or the construction industry against slumping demand. Equity suffered when ceilings on large deposits were put more than 50 per cent above ceilings on small deposits in order to limit the flight of funds from banking. Changes in the public's relative demands among financial assets weakened the processes of control over nominal money. Dollar bal-

[13] The subsidy might have taken the form of a deposit rate paid by the Federal Reserve on bank reserves, but then the burden of the subsidy would have fallen upon the government primarily rather than upon bank depositors.
[14] James Tobin, *ibid.,* pp. 9–10; William E. Gibson, "Eurodollars and U.S. Monetary Policy, *Journal of Money, Credit and Banking,* August, 1971, pp. 649–665.

ances in flight from deposit-rate ceilings intensified inflationary pressures abroad. One must look far and wide for a clearer demonstration that deposit rate cannot perform its normal function as a price for savings and a variety of other functions as well, from subsidy of financial institutions and of housing construction to constraint of international capital flows. One instrument, one function is a rule not to be violated with impunity.[15]

Jeremy Bentham could find no answer to the question:

. . . why the legislator should be more anxious to limit the rate of interest one way, than the other? Why should he set his face against the owners of that species of property more than of any other? Why should he make it his business to prevent their getting *more* than a certain price for the use of it, rather than to prevent their getting less?[16]

Perhaps, though one may doubt it, Bentham's ire over the tax on deposit rate would be soothed by differentiation of the tax that occurs widely, not just in the United States. Frequently deposit-rate ceilings are arranged to direct savings among allocations. For example, penalty ceilings have been set on foreign deposits with banks in Germany and elsewhere to repel inward capital flows. More generous ceilings and hence a lower tax on deposit rate are commonplace for institutions that supply agricultural or housing credit or loans to indigenous small industry. The tax is frequently less on deposit rates at cooperative societies perhaps because there is patently so little reason for taxing savers' right-hand pockets for the benefit of pockets on the left.

For regulation of savings' uses, perhaps with benefits for economic equality among savers, the differentiated deposit-rate tax ranks as an inferior instrument. As has been suggested in Chapter 5, it encourages hothouse differentiation of financial institutions with effects of raising factor costs in finance and of reducing competition in financial markets.[17] Once a differentiated tax has brought about

---

[15] Harry G. Johnson, *op. cit.*, pp. 980–981.

[16] W. Stark, *Jeremy Bentham's Economic Writings,* Volume I, p. 133.

[17] See above pp. 140–141; Organization for Economic Cooperation and Development, *Capital Markets Study, General Report,* pp. 13–16, 231.

institutional adjustments, the invention of a new intermediary perhaps, the tax is there to stay and cannot be adapted easily to changing goals of savings allocation. Furthermore, the tax affects only one source of finance so that its impact on allocation can be evaded by adjustments in flows of savings through other channels. The incidence of the tax is unclear so that who benefits or suffers from differentiation must usually remain a mystery.

Subsidized Loan Rate and Credit Rationing

Loan rate is prevented, especially in lagging economies, from doing its job of reporting capital's marginal product in alternative uses and of equating demand for investment with the savings flow. In organized markets, it is an administered price set at differential levels that require complex rationing techniques to resolve excess demand for funds.[18] In traditional or curb markets, it is a flexible price at very high levels. The administered rate confers a subsidy on rationed investment from revenues supplied partly by the deposit-rate tax on savers. The flexible rate imposes a tax on demand for funds, excluded from the organized market by rationing, for the benefit of savers with access to curb-market facilities. Extending subsidies and imposing taxes, loan rate is transformed from a financial to a fiscal instrument in the saving-investment process.

Fiscalized loan rates, fixed to monitor subsidies rather than to clear capital markets, have common characteristics among countries. They are differentiated in intricate ways, and there seems to be an inherent momentum toward more refinement. Differentiation is both by source of funds and by use as well as by lending institution. The rates are inflexible: ration rather than price adjusts to changes in excess demand. The rationing function is parceled out to closely regulated, specialized institutions. Subsidy by loan rate is a matter of very fine tuning or twisting indeed.

While Korea has been active in interest-rate reform, its loan-rate structure is still a striking illustration of subsidy technique. Table I

18 See above, pp. 81–88, 125–128.

Table I   The structure of administered loan rates in Korea
(*per cent*)

Lender	Source of Funds	Type of Loan	Loan Rate	Number of Changes after 1965
Bank of Korea	Bank of Korea	Advances to government	2.0	0
Bank of Korea	Bank of Korea	Loans for exports	3.5	0
Bank of Korea	Bank of Korea	Rice lien loans	4.0	0
Commercial banks	Banks	Loans for exports	6.0	1
Agricultural Cooperatives	Government	Warehouse construction	8.0	0
Korea Development Bank	Foreign		10.0	1
Medium Industry Bank	Government	Cooperatives	10.0	1
Korea Housing Bank	Bank of Korea	Apartment loans	18.8	0
Medium Industry Bank	Bank	Small industries	20.0	0
Commercial banks	Banks	Discount of bills	23.0	3
Trust accounts	Bank of Korea		29.5	3
Life Insurance companies	Insurance companies	Mortgage loans	36.5	1

SOURCE: The Bank of Korea, *Monthly Economic Statistics*, Number 6, 1971, pp. 43–47.

lists only a sample of Korean rates effective in mid-1971. The rates are nominal, bearing an inflation premium of about 10 per cent.

In this sample, eight varieties of financial intermediary, utilizing savings from private domestic, government and foreign sources, divide the capital market into segments, with negative real loan rates reserved for some of the segments and real loan rates that approximate the scarcity price of savings exacted of others. All of the rates are immobile at the decreed levels. According to planning priorities and other criteria, changes in excess demand at each rate have been cleared by rationing. The intensity of excess demand has been affected by peripheral benefits for successful borrowers, benefits including tax concessions, import licenses and tariff preferences, loan guarantees and others. Loan rates in Korea bear little resemblance to auction prices, on the organized markets, and most of them are remote from both the marginal rates of substitution of Korean savers between present and future consumption and the marginal rates of transformation of Korean producers between present and future final outputs. It has been estimated that in 1969 loan-rate subsidies amounted to 8 per cent of all loans outstanding at Korean banking institutions, to 17 per cent of "preferential" loans.[19]

Arguments in defense of such distortions as these in the loan markets have been honed to a sharp edge by reiteration in many places. For example, entrepreneurs may raise their own and aggregate savings to qualify for loan rations and associated benefits: the negative effect on total savings of deposit-rate taxes may be less than the positive effect of loan-rate subsidies. Again, these distortions may counteract and neutralize others: perhaps cheap loan rates for exporters compensate for an overvalued rate of foreign exchange, cheap loan rates to farmers for import duties on fertilizer. Still again, the infant-industry argument may be brought to bear in its various forms. Loan-rate subsidy may compensate producers of new exports for costs of sales promotion abroad or producers of new products in general for learning costs. It may overcome myopia and risk-aversion of entrepreneurs in connection with new ventures and unfamiliar techniques. Possibly it can give black entrepreneurs a running start in competition with whites or Malayans with Chinese. To these arguments can be added a justification in terms of externalities, that is of tangential benefits to the economy at large. The loan-rate subsidy may be the inducement that employers need to train the labor force in marketable skills or it may generate linkages between branches of industry that pay off in economies of scale. Briefly, the loan-rate

---

[19] Research Institute for Economics and Business, *A Study of Money Market and Industrial Investment Financing in Korea,* November, 1970, Sogang University, pp. 99–103.

subsidy is said to be a bonus to investors who commit resources and accept risks in changing the economy's structure. The capital value of the subsidy and associated favors is also, of course, a bonus that the political party in power can use, without cost to itself, for attracting support.

The classic charge against the subsidy is that it impoverishes an economy: it deepens the imperfection of the capital market—"the most fundamental of all kinds of market imperfection."[20] It induces excess demand for the factor, capital, that is scarce and increases excess supply of complementary factors, labor in particular, that are plentiful. It distracts an economy from the processes and products that make best use of relative factor supplies and shrinks the frontier of production possibilities. Given relative factor supplies, appropriate public policy does not distort relative demands for them but instead seeks to improve factor quality and mobility and to encourage adoption of superior pertinent technologies. A common rejoinder to this charge of impoverishment is that the Plan ignores distorted market prices for labor and capital, allocating capital instead according to shadow prices which do allow suitably for the economy's pattern of resource availabilities. Then the loan-rate subsidy imparts no bias to employed factor proportions and is simply a useful spur to entrepreneurship.[21]

Perhaps plans would be less perishable if they did not work at odds with objective market prices, present and anticipated. When planning prices and market prices diverge, there are opportunities for private profit from smuggling in various ways. Of all markets, the savings market is most vulnerable to evasion of planners' mandates. One is not surprised to learn that business firms with loan rations are sometimes lenders concurrently on the curb market or speculators in their own equities on the stock exchanges or investors through subsidiaries in projects that rank low in national planning priorities. Bias in relative factor prices results in inferior factor allocation, Plan or no Plan.

[20] John Hicks, *Capital and Growth*, p. 203.
[21] Jan Tinbergen, *The Design of Development*, pp. 39–41.

The loan-rate subsidy is of dubious efficiency for stimulating entrepreneurship and for forced feeding of infant industry. It can be capitalized in the market value of corporate equities, and original owners can walk away with the capital gain. The subsidy accrues to promoters of new firms, but high returns to promotion should not be confused with high returns to entrepreneurship or with compensation to infant industry for its learning costs.[22]

Loan-rate subsidy is frequently differentiated according to sources of loan funds. The subsidy may be larger when the funds are from government, for example, or from foreign aid programs. Perhaps this is an exercise in cost-plus pricing, with loan rates intended to reflect different degrees of resistance by ultimate savers to tax. It is an irrational exercise, whatever the motive. Savings are homogeneous and, like wheat or rice or crude oil of given grades, cannot vary in potential utility according to suppliers' political or income status, age or location or passivity to tax. There is just one cost that is relevant for pricing a unit of savings to some use, and that is the opportunity cost of foregoing an alternative use.

Governments are particularly demanding of loan-rate subsidy for themselves. It seems to be a cardinal point of fiscal policy in lagging economies that finance ministries should borrow cheaply. Hard-pressed for revenues, the ministries must economize and where better to do it than in the savings market? Low rates for treasury bills can be decreed for the banking system, and longer-term securities can be thrust into social-security funds, pension funds and portfolios of insurance companies. Savers are captive taxpayers. The results are that government does not consider carefully enough the opportunity cost of savings in planning its expenditure budget; that savers in lower-income categories are discriminated against; and that the long-maturity segment of the capital market is closed to private securities.[23] There is rarely public accounting for the subsidy and the

[22] Ian Little, Tibor Scitovsky, Maurice Scott, *Industry and Trade in Some Developing Countries: A Comparative Study,* pp. 217–221.
[23] Harry G. Johnson, *Money, Trade and Economic Growth,* pp. 160–161; Gunnar Myrdal, *Asian Drama,* Volume III, pp. 2087–2096.

deposit-rate taxes that finance it. It is not reported in fiscal budgets and is obscured by accounting convention.

There are substitutes for loan-rate subsidy that impose less bias on relative demands for capital and labor, create fewer benefits for promotion and corruption, do less injustice distributively and cost less to administer. Government can provide data and training for unfamiliar production processes and markets and assume other costs of market development. It can insure new firms against some contingencies. On a temporally diminishing scale, it can provide tax refunding or tax relief when new industry has profits to report, putting its subsidies on an *ex-post* rather than *ex-ante* basis. For funds to support its program, there are tax techniques that do not, in the manner of deposit-rate tax, repress the financial technique of moving savings to investment and retard money deepening.

Fiscal Aid to Finance

Finance is taxed in lagging economies and others too. It is subsidized in the same markets. Tax-*cum*-subsidy, a favored instrument for patching imperfections in markets generally, seems to be in style especially for financial markets. Subsidies to finance, like taxes there, are sometimes explicit and appear in government budgets, sometimes distributed through channels that are difficult to trace. This section considers a sample of subsidy techniques and their objectives, then turns to costs, and the conclusion is that, if fiscal repression of finance were eased, much of the apparatus for subsidy could be dismantled.

For "reinforcement of personal savings," the Japanese government has granted a variety of tax concessions for savers' income from both primary and indirect financial assets. There has been tax exemption for income from savings deposits and bonds in relatively small denominations. Life insurance premia to a maximum have been deductible from taxable income. Concessions are allowed on dividend income and for capital gains on securities. The example set in Japan and other advanced and growing economies has been followed where development is halting. Argentina is a case in point, granting tax exemption for most varieties of non-monetary indirect financial assets. Governments have been optimistic that, at a cost to their own scarce savings, some larger increase in private savings could result from tax favors that raise effective deposit rates. In their "reinforcement" campaign, Japanese authorities incurred the cost of tax concessions amounting during 1958–63, for example, to fifteen per cent of total personal-tax revenues.[24]

Subsidy of deposit rates of interest in the organized financial sector is used to divert funds from the curb. Whether or not subsidy is effective in increasing total savings, it may entice savings from the anarchy of the curb into the orbit of control by central authority. Savings can be drawn, too, from currency hoards that "are liable to be dishoarded more easily than financial assets."[25] Since savings are scarce, the argument goes, they should be within reach of financial authority's allocative techniques.

The gift of scarce charters to private financial institutions is defended on the grounds that it increases savings facilities and intensifies competition with the curb, hoarding and capital flight. The gift is a subsidy at the expense of government and taxpayers, that may attract infant financial enterprise into agricultural areas or, perhaps, fishing villages, to experiments with new savings techniques and to loan ventures with new industries. Private financial enterprise receives, free of charge, a degree of monopoly which presumably bears an appropriately high return of social as well as private benefits.

Subsidy from domestic and foreign fiscal sources has been used in dramatic, even flamboyant fashion to extend the maturity spectrum of capital markets. Governments which force private savings into social security funds and tax them there, by low or negative real yields, simultaneously reach into the public budget for funds to support nascent stock and bond exchanges—a tax on one long-term asset of the

[24] Ryutaro Komiya, "Japan" in The Brookings Institution, *Foreign Tax Policies and Economic Growth,* p. 57.
[25] Anand G. Chandavarkar, "Some Aspects of Interest Rate Policies in Less Developed Economies: The Experience of Selected Asian Countries," International Monetary Fund, *Staff Papers,* March, 1971, p. 57.

public-*cum*-subsidy for another. Under its Capital Markets Law of 1965 and Decree Law 157 of 1967, Brazil has diverted savings into the stock exchange by fiscal methods of which the most dramatic is the tax credit for purchases of mutual-fund shares.[26] France has granted tax advantages for savers to buy "L'Emprunt Pinay," a bond indexed to gold.[27] Central banks here and there have absorbed losses to support market prices of bonds, equities and mortgages, attempting to overcome risk-aversion against long-term commitments.

Deposit-rate tax has been used to discourage some allocations of savings. Subsidies are added to deposit rate for the benefit of other allocations. They change the structure of effective deposit rates so that loan rations can be more generous for various classes of investor. To increase the chance that savings do reach desired destinations, specialized intermediaries are designed to administer the subsidies for housing, small industrial firms, small as distinct from plantation agriculture. A new investment priority generates a new segment of the capital market with new financial institutions to disburse a subsidy. As priorities change, financial systems are dotted with increasing numbers of institutions that depend on preferred fiscal status: the art of closing down obsolete institutions is underdeveloped.

Some subsidies for finance increase inequality of income and wealth distributions. Tax concessions for life insurance premia do not reach the poor nor do underwritings of equity issues and market support for industrial debentures. There have been attempts to make the technique of tax-*cum*-subsidy in finance less regressive. For example, preferential yields have been paid on government debt in small-denomination savings certificates; cooperative societies receive

[26] David M. Trubek, "Law, Planning and the Development of the Brazilian Capital Market: A Study of Law in Economic Change," New York University, *The Bulletin*, April, 1971, pp. 58–60; Banco Central do Brasil, *Relatorio de 1970*, May, 1971, pp. 60–80; David T. Kleinman, "Foreign Aid: the Case of Brazil," Industrial Management Review, Winter, 1969, pp. 47–66.
[27] Claudio Segré, "Capital Markets in Developing Countries: Institutional Problems and Growth Prospects," Inter-American Development Bank, *The Mobilization of Domestic Resources in Latin America*, p. 14.

favors; deposits with building societies are granted special tax treatment or special status as loan collateral. Subsidies to reduce inequality are generated by subsidies that increase inequality.

The list of objectives for financial subsidy stretches farther than this. Deposit insurance is financed in different degree by government budget. Government deposits are placed with financial institutions to improve their earnings. While some foreign savings are blocked against repatriation and taxed, others receive concessions, in terms of deposit rate and exemption from tax, as a way of strengthening the international accounts. There appears to have been no careful review anywhere of aggregate fiscal benefits for finance, but so many reasons for so many devices of subsidy could be found in few other industries.

The burden of proof that subsidy to finance bears an adequate yield for the community and not merely for the direct beneficiaries must be on the subsidy's proponents. Since both the financial system and the fiscal system are frail in lagging economies, penalizing either for the advantage of the other is not an obviously efficient way of developing the total saving-investment process. Finance is a market phenomenon and remains shallow unless its relative prices, deposit and loan rates, are permitted to express the costs of eliciting savings and the productivity of investment. The common practice of distorting these prices by tax and undoing some of the damage by subsidy puts a heavier burden on the saving-investment processes of private self-finance and foreign investment or aid.

The theory of monopolistic price discrimination appears to fit many of the features of fiscal-financial tax-*cum*-subsidy.[28] It visualizes the monopolist, best represented by government authority in the present case, as seeking to divide his market into fragments. By differentiating his product, he may be able to limit a price reduction, when he wishes to expand output, to some of his customers, maintaining his charges to others: each price reduction has a smaller negative effect on total revenues. One may use parallel reasoning for

[28] For application of comparable reasoning in a narrower context, see pp. 139–140.

monopsony. By differentiating inputs and segmenting their market, the monopsonist may be able to limit a price increase, when he wishes to expand output, to some of his suppliers: each price increase has a smaller positive effect on total costs. Government authority in finance faces borrowers on the organized market as a monopolist, threatened only by the curb market's competitive vigor, and splits the market so that reductions in loan rate can be discriminating. The authority faces depositors as a monopsonist in the purchase of savings and splits the market so that increases in deposit rate can be discriminating. The authority can appropriate for financial industry the surpluses that would accrue under competitive conditions to infra-marginal borrowers and depositors when loan rates are reduced or deposit rates increased. Alternatively, it can distribute the surpluses among preferred customers and suppliers—borrowers and depositors—on criteria to its taste. With its fiscal instruments, the authority can refine in still closer correspondence with its taste the degree of discrimination between customers and suppliers. Whatever the market, for finance or bicycles or shoes, monopoly-monopsony is socially impoverishing. Finance cannot deepen optimally under a regime of price discrimination in differentiated markets.

The resource costs of price discrimination in conjunction with subsidy are not cheap. There are costs of imposing regulation, complying with it and evading it. The segments of financial industry are too small in the usual case to realize potential economies of scale. Some non-price attractions to depositors are expensive in buildings and labor force.

The distributive balance of tax-*cum*-subsidy is patently regressive despite gestures of compensation toward depositors and borrowers in lower-income classes. Taken in conjunction with monopoly benefits for the relative few from import licensing and tariff preferences, with benefits from invulnerability to taxation of properties that the poor cannot afford, the benefits from free financial charters, loan rations, subsidies to stock markets and the like make up a package of regressive measures that cannot be consistent, in the long run, with social equity and stability. The transfer of government savings through financial subsidy is a set-back to government investment in the social facilities that should accompany population growth, industrialization and urbanization.

Fiscal subsidies and penalties on finance preserve the fractionalism, whether dualism or worse, that costs lagging economies the benefits of the common-market principle. They tend to widen the gaps between rich and poor, modernized and indigenous industry, city and countryside: the rich receive their credit rations; modernized industry is encouraged in its capital-intensiveness; the city grows around the nucleus of urbanized infrastructure and government offices of economic administration. They are only a part of the policy package that leads to these and associated results, and replacing them with policy that unifies capital markets and deepens finance is only one element of comprehensive reform. However, their bias toward fractionalism is clear.[29]

COORDINATION OF FISCAL AND FINANCIAL STRATEGIES

Too often in lagging economies fiscal and financial policies and techniques are pitted against each other: deposit-rate tax and loan-rate subsidy are cases in point. The quotations below indicate the point we wish to make now, that financial deepening and fiscal strength are mutually dependent.

. . . the problem of inefficiency in the financial system can not be solved by the improvement of financial institutions and policy alone. The improvement of financial system should be considered together with the measures to improve the related non-financial policies. It would be meaningless to push the improvement of the financial system without taking corrective measures on foreign exchange rate, foreign loan policy, domestic tax government incentive policy, fiscal policy, etc.[30]

In the particular case of Chile during 1960 and 1961, President Alessandri had a golden opportunity to capitalize on a situation in which the

[29] H. Myint, *Economic Theory and the Underdeveloped Countries,* Chapter 14.
[30] Research Institute for Economics and Business, Sogang University, *op. cit.,* p. 120.

rate of inflation was kept below 10 per cent for two consecutive years. This opportunity was eroded through a failure to reform the fiscal machinery. As a result, the chance to bring about a permanent stabilization of the Chilean price level was lost. Again a very promising effort at stabilization by the Frei administration in Chile, successful at slowing inflation substantially by 1965 and 1966, had to be effectively abandoned in 1967, solely on fiscal grounds.[31]

In countries with per capita incomes at various levels, there is continuous experimentation with financial and fiscal instruments of capital accumulation. Accumulation is financial-intensive in some countries at some stages, fiscal-intensive at other places and times. For example, among twelve relatively advanced economies during 1960–64, funds collected by the consolidated financial sector varied as a percentage of gross savings from 35 per cent in Norway and 44 per cent in the United Kingdom to 60 per cent in Belgium, 66 per cent in Japan and 71 per cent in Spain.[32] There is substitutability at the margin between instruments, as there is between labor and capital in the production function for output of goods and services. Just as capital and labor are complementary in the growth process, growing together in a more or less balanced way, financial and fiscal deepening go together.

The Fiscal Base

The aggregate demand function for real values of financial assets is the base or "handle" for the financial way of eliciting savings. Real deposit rate and improvements in the menu of financial assets are the instruments that "tax" the base. A primary objective of financial policy is to make the base larger, to deepen it, and to make it elastic in degree higher than unity to the community's growth in terms of income and wealth. The base is less elastic and may even erode as the result of uncompensated inflation or political uncertainty. It varies

[31] Arnold C. Harberger, "Economic Policy Problems in Latin America: A Review," *Journal of Political Economy,* July/August, 1970, Supplement, p. 1012.
[32] Organization for Economic Co-operation and Development, *Capital Markets Study, Statistical Annex,* pp. 84–85.

with income distribution between poor and rich, agriculture and industry, domestic and foreign recipients. If one probes deeply enough, he can discover social and cultural determinants of the base that help to account for differences in demand for financial assets between Japan, for example and West Africa. In the centralist society that limits private incomes to the wage bill, demand for financial assets provides relatively little leverage for deposit rate. Where the state takes responsibility for various personal exigencies of citizens, the role of insurance and other precautionary savings is minimized. The size and elasticity of the financial base are subject to a barrage of influences that affect the sequences of choice between financial and fiscal techniques of capital accumulation.[33]

The fiscal base for extraction of savings in the public sector includes a much thicker catalogue of items than the financial. Few classes of transaction, income and wealth have missed inclusion in it somewhere or sometime. It is potentially more elastic than the financial base to growth in income and wealth. The tax base in Japan has risen so rapidly that a "tax-cut policy" has been adopted, in successive years from 1950, raising exemption minima for income taxation and reducing progressivity of tax rates without reducing the government's share in national net savings.[34] However, in lagging economies, the base is sufficiently shallow and inelastic that finance ministries find it necessary to tax and shrink the financial base. They impose a multiplicity of taxes, many of them with yields that cannot be much in excess of collection costs.

Tax bases are shallow for a multitude of reasons. The major one, of course, is poverty. Costs and imperfections of fiscal administration are another, and we consider them in more detail below. The point to be stressed here is that public policy lets tax base slip away. Governments substitute import quotas and licenses for tariffs, and

[33] Basch and Kybal, *op. cit., passim;* Raymond W. Goldsmith, *Financial Structure and Development,* Chapter 9; Jiro Yao, *Monetary Factors in Japanese Economic Growth,* pp. 45–48; W. Arthur Lewis, *The Theory of Economic Growth,* Chapter V.
[34] Ryutaro Komiya, *op. cit.,* pp. 53–54; Jiro Yao, *op. cit.,* p. 30.

what might have been revenue for treasuries is diverted to importers or to monopsonistic firms that buy from them. They extend tax concessions to persistently infantile industry and sometimes tax too gently the exploitation of natural resources for export. They allow themselves to be committed, in the heat of political campaigns, to exempting various properties from the base. Pieces of the tax base are used as bargaining counters between government and numerous private interests some of whom can and many of whom cannot extract from the base a higher rate of saving than the government's own.[35]

Tax bases have ways of eroding relative to income and wealth: without increases in rates of tax, revenues can fall absolutely or relatively. Such experience as Mexico's during 1939–50, when tax receipts rose one-third less rapidly than national income, is not unusual.[36] The persistent decline during 1964–71 in Ghana's real fiscal revenues per capita can be traced both to shrinkage of the base and to reductions in tax rates. In these countries and others, two factors are mainly responsible for the erosion. First, the values of products subject to indirect taxation decline relative to total output because sources of supply are depleted, because demand is income-inelastic or because substitutes appear. In one sense or another, components of the base are inferior goods.[37] Second, monetary values assessed for the tax base are not adjusted to inflation so that the real value of the base diminishes when the price level rises. As an illustration, Malaysia's revenues from income taxation are vulnerable to a rising price level because a lag approaching eighteen months separates assessment and collection. Inflation yields real revenues from a part of the financial base—the money supply, for example—but it reduces real revenues from parts of the fiscal base. When the fiscal base is both income-inelastic and inflation-inelastic, the peak-employment

[35] Stephen R. Lewis, Jr., *Pakistan: Industrialization and Trade Policies,* pp. 138–159.

[36] Timothy King, *Mexico: Industrialization and Trade Policies since 1940,* p. 94.

[37] S. R. Lewis, "Revenue Implications of Changing Industrial Structure: An Empirical Study," *National Tax Journal,* December, 1967, pp. 231–244.

fiscal surplus becomes smaller as rates of growth in real income and the price level are higher, especially if revenues from the inflation tax are counted in the surplus. Such a fiscal base automatically constrains capital accumulation and is automatically destabilizing in the short run.

Consumption expenditure is a fiscal base that meets neatly the criteria of depth and elasticity to say nothing of equity.[38] The expenditure tax exempts savings; it induces saving; with subsistence consumption also exempted, it bears on income-elastic and inflation-elastic components of consumer outlay. One can appreciate why Ceylon and India adopted it in 1960 and 1962. Why they abandoned it is also clear: ". . . it is doubtful whether any revenue net of costs of collection was realized."[39] Its administrative cost is prohibitive in the developing economy.

Reform of fiscal technique in the lagging economy can focus on two immediate objectives, a discrete enlargement of the tax base and an increase in the marginal revenue rate or ratio to national product. The common view seems to be that these first steps in sharpening fiscal technique must precede financial deepening:

As development progresses and a reasonable degree of price level stability is maintained, the private savings rate may be expected to rise substantially. This will ease the pressure on public (and foreign) savings. But the rise in the private savings rate cannot be legislated. It takes time. Not only must the public gain confidence in price level stability, but savings habits and institutions must be developed. This suggests that public saving must carry the major weight during the earlier phases of the plan, with private savings assuming a greater share later on. To accomplish this, an unusually high marginal revenue rate will be needed over the next few years.[40]

Which comes now, which comes next in Chile, Korea, Kenya, or elsewhere is less important than that both fiscal and financial bases are in need of depth and elasticity.

[38] Nicholas Kaldor, *An Expenditure Law;* Nicholas Kaldor, *Indian Tax Reform.*
[39] Ursula K. Hicks, *Development Finance: Planning and Control,* p. 106; Antonin Basch, *Financing Economic Development,* p. 96.
[40] R. A. Musgrave, *Revenue Policy for Korea's Development,* p. 5.

Fiscal Slippage

There is still no confident answer for Nicholas Kaldor's plaintive query, "Will the underdeveloped countries never learn to tax?" In choices at the margin between financial and fiscal technique, high unit costs of finance and generous margins of profit, shared sometimes with borrowers and government, seem to give an advantage to fiscal technique—until there are taken into account the slippages of revenues from the fiscal process. These slippages, too numerous to consider exhaustively here, begin with the phrasing of tax law and regulation which creates a thriving industry of tax avoidance and evasion.[41] They include the losses of revenue from shortcomings in valuation of income or property or turnover as well as from the administrative costs of inefficient bureaucracy. Paid-in taxes net of collection costs can be a small fraction of yields intended and expected by parliaments.[42]

"Tax effort" may be least affected by slippage in the developing economy with a large share of internationally tradable goods in its total output and total usage of goods and services. Exports of raw materials, coming to ports by trail, railroad, and pipeline can be taxed at port of exit. Imports are accessible to the tax collector. Alternatively, government import and export corporations can monopolize international trading and produce tax revenues in the form of differences between buying and selling prices. But there is slippage. Smugglers collect the taxes when the rate of return to their industry is made sufficiently high by a combination of official tariff rate and overvalued rate of foreign exchange. Government export corporations, paying formula prices to producers of coffee or cocoa or other

[41] Nicholas Kaldor, *Essays on Economic Policy,* Volume I, p. 216. An Indian economist has complained regarding estate duty and taxes on gifts, wealth, and expenditure in his country: "We must stop caricature of these taxes. They exist only in name. They must be made effective sources of revenue." L. Sinha, *Capital and Employment: Problems of a Developing Economy,* p. 94.
[42] Albert Hart is "inclined to argue that the most promising progressive tax for Latin America would be a tax which consisted of *collecting the difference between what is now paid and a decent approximation of the tax which the law calls for.*" (His italics.) Albert G. Hart, "Fiscal Policy in Latin America," *Journal of Political Economy,* July/August, 1970, p. 878.

items, are not invariably successful in winning gross profits from spot and forward prices on international markets. Some of them do not have economical storage facilities, and exportable crops deteriorate in the jungle or at dockside. More than one marketing board has withheld its revenues from the ministry of finance or incurred debts to the monetary system for the benefit of its own establishment.

A "rise in the private saving rate cannot be legislated." Fiscal slippage in its numerous forms indicates that a rise in the government's saving rate requires something more than a new statute. There is no apparent reason why a tax rate should be more efficient than a deposit rate in diverting income from private consumption to savings. In some circumstances of underdevelopment, the force of compulsion by tax impresses savers less than the force of persuasion by relative price.

Government Enterprise

Among both lagging and succeeding economies, there are state firms in numerous industries, of diverse size and degree of monopoly. There is state participation, sometimes dominant and sometimes passive, in mixed enterprise: "business and government get pretty mixed up with each other," as W. Arthur Lewis has put it. Some of this enterprise is a colonial heritage; some of it represents first steps toward socialism; other parts are demonstrations of government grandeur; others are take-overs from unsuccessful or foreign ownership. However, the bulk of it is an expression of faith that governmental can surpass private enterprise in extending the economy's frontiers of production possibilities and social welfare.

Saving has been a low-priority objective of public enterprise. During 1963–69, public corporations in Korea supplied only a small and diminishing share of total gross savings—7 per cent in 1963 and 4 per cent in 1969.[43] In South Asia, West Africa, Latin America, the prevalent experience seems to be that, even when it is favored by

[43] Research Institute for Economics and Business, Sogang University, *op. cit.,* p. 8.

loan-rate subsidy, tax concessions and other exemptions, public enterprise earns negligible or negative profits.[44] There are cases where the explanation of low profits and low savings is to be found in technological and managerial factors: costs of the state mining corporation rise as ore deposits are exhausted, and costs of the state railway rise because its depreciation and maintenance allowances have not been adjusted for inflation. There are more cases where the explanation is that costs are inflated or sales prices are held low to provide subsidies for suppliers or customers or both. State policy in the monetary system, of disequilibrium pricing, is policy also in government's non-financial enterprise.

Public enterprise has not characteristically economized savings. It has favored capital-intensive technology. With rationed access to capital at subsidized loan rate, it has characteristically preferred processes that economize on manpower. Yet, where unemployment in the urban labor force has created social tensions, state enterprise has provided employment by adding personnel that is excessive for its technology. Wages paid for the superfluous manpower are at relatively high levels, above any defensible shadow price, determined under the urban enclave's minimum wage laws or agreements. Disequilibrium pricing by state enterprise occurs on markets for both savings and labor—cheap for the former, dear for the latter.

State firms have privileged access to foreign savings. They are favored with rations of undervalued foreign exchange as well as with tariff exemptions and import licenses. In other instances, they pay low regulated prices for inputs of domestically produced raw materials. When they provide services to each other, prices are low and the services come on ration. They escape tax on the argument that it is pointless for the state to tax itself. Briefly, the prototype firm is accorded cheap buying prices for services other than labor. With cheap buying prices and low targets for retained earnings, it is in position

[44] "Throughout most of the region (South Asia) goods and services from the public sector have been priced so low that rates of return on capital invested have been lower than the rates of interest prevailing on the capital market." V. V. Ramanadham, *The Finances of Public Enterprise*, p. 53.

to supply output for the private sector at low average disequilibrium prices.

The selling prices are commonly differentiated by class of buyer, and rations are adjusted accordingly. Sometimes foreign enterprise is the beneficiary, sometimes enterprise of indigenous ownership that lacks experience and needs learning-by-doing, sometimes export industry. The price schedules tend to have the pattern of differentiation that applies also for bank loans, foreign exchange, and other items with administered allocations. Whether in India or the Philippines, Uruguay, or Colombia, government firms are in the business of receiving and extending subsidy. There is growing disenchantment with this design of public policy. Stock markets are being developed partly in the hope that they may transfer ownership of government firms into private hands. Here and there, public firms have raised their relative selling prices. It is becoming evident that administered disequilibrium pricing has contributed to capital shortage, underemployment of labor on balance and distributive inequity. Until reform is more drastic, however, some of the capital accumulation and capital conservation that public enterprise might do must be done instead through refinement of financial technique and financial deepening.

Fiscal Perversity and Loan Rate

Financial technique in the saving-investment process allows relative price, in the form of loan rates, a principal role in discriminating between investment alternatives for scarce savings. It puts savings into a capital market and depends on the market's breadth and competitiveness to find uses for them where marginal social productivities are highest. Mistrust of this technique is based on two main considerations. First, so it is said, participants in a capital market cannot see an appropriate ranking of social productivities or they disregard it and attend to a ranking in terms of private advantage. Second, demands for savings in a capital market are interest-inelastic so that loan rate has no power to discriminate. The conclusion follows that little is to be gained by development of the capital market; that private perceptions of investment productivity should be corrected by various interventions; that some inevitable residue of private myopia should be neutralized by either or both rationing of savings at rigid loan rates and transfer of the investment function to government. Practice of this principle has not worked out well in the non-socialist economies that concern us.

Participants in the small, segmented markets for savings are not blind to investment opportunities that reflect resource availabilities and final demands for output. They are distracted and confused by fiscal and other perversities that affect relative marginal yields for different kinds of wealth. These signals tell them that superior yields are to be earned by building excess plant capacity because depreciation allowances in the tax laws are so generous; that labor is expensive because there is an employment tax; that investment in urban areas is best because subsidized electric power is there. The distorted yields that they see do produce bias in the capital market, but the distortion is based on fiscal perversity and not the market's ineptitude.

Participants in the capital markets may abuse them by monopoly power. A competitive ranking of yields can diverge from a monopolistic ranking. One financial solution is to deepen finance so that more buyers and sellers of loan funds have access to the markets, and another is to reduce the differentiation of financial institutions that breaks the market into detached pieces. Another solution calls for direct action against monopoly power that derives from fiscal perversity. Turnover taxation provides a bonus for vertical integration. Tax exemptions discriminate for established investors at the top of the scale in terms of profits. Failure to tax real property, capital gains, and higher incomes allows market strength to accumulate. Capital markets are vulnerable to monopoly that could be weakened if there were fewer fiscal devices to generate monopoly.

Capital markets may be myopic to externalities or undervalue public goods or misrepresent the best interest of one generation relative to the next. The cure is not subsidized loan rate, with rationing, in shallow capital markets. If some kinds of capital formation pollute the environment, they may be discouraged best by competitively high loan rates and a specific tax on pollution. Government may be more discriminating in its choice among public goods if it regards tax revenues not as free but as scarce savings that should be valued at competitive loan rate. If private savers and investors shy away from long commitments, at least part of the reason can be found in erratic use of the inflation tax and in unpredictable *ad hoc* adjustments of the tax structure.

Interest-inelasticity of demand for savings was a myth, rejected by Lord Keynes, that neo-Keynesian dogma seized upon in explana tion both of alleged secular stagnation in advanced economies and of underdevelopment.[45] The implication of interest-elasticity is that loan rate has power to discriminate between competing bids for savings, increasingly without assistance from devices of rationing as finance is deepened and the capital market unified. It cannot discriminate between social productivities of investment, however, if competing bids are affected by fiscal interference with productivity. Mexico's Law for the Development of New and Necessary Industries and legislation like it in many countries puts a fiscal veil over relative productivities that even the largest of capital markets could not lift.[46]

Reform on Two Fronts

Where capital accumulation lags and is misdirected, financial and fiscal structure and policy are jointly at fault. Fiscal punishment is meted out to the financial system by deposit-rate tax and loan-rate subsidy. The fiscal system is not deep or elastic enough to help as it might in eliciting savings. It distorts savers' demands for financial assets and choices by financial institutions between loan options. Punishment is meted out the other way, by the financial system to the fiscal. Inflation shrinks the fiscal base and reduces its elasticity, and financial administered pricing, aversion to risk and inflexibility create opportunities for fiscal perversity. Principal reforms that are due

---

[45] "The interest-inelasticity of investment . . . did not enter into Keynes' analysis at all." Axel Leijonhufvud, *On Keynesian Economics and the Economics of Keynes,* p. 405.

[46] Timothy King, *op. cit.,* pp. 96–106.

in finance have been discussed in earlier pages. Though fiscal phenomena are not the main concern for us, a few notes may be appropriate to indicate the kind of fiscal reform that can help to liberate finance.

There are things that can be done quickly with an inefficient fiscal system.[47] Numerous taxes that yield small returns net of exemptions and administrative costs can be eliminated. Delays from tax assessment to collection can be reduced, very substantially if withholding can be applied to some forms of income. Tax administration can be tightened. Schedular taxation of income can be rationalized, with fewer distinctions between sources and less discrimination against income from financial assets. Property taxation can be more productive if title records are brought up to date and valuations are reviewed. The network of subsidies can be simplified, if only by elimination of subsidies that evidently have not given the desired stimulus to output or that are merely enriching profits of established enterprise. Pricing policies of government enterprise can be rationalized, with benefits that are especially significant in an inflationary context. Tariffs can be an efficient substitute for import licensing, and more sophisticated sales programs must increase revenues of government export corporations. In every nook and cranny of the fiscal system, there are small improvements that potentially add to an impressive sum.

Meanwhile first steps can be taken with major changes. Despite strong opinion to the contrary, the case is persuasive for a value-added tax as centerpiece of the fiscal scheme.[48] With exclusions of

[47] S. Malcolm Gillis (ed.), *Fiscal Reform for Colombia: The Final Report and Staff Papers of the Colombian Commission for Tax Reform,* International Tax Program, Harvard University; Albert G. Hart, *op. cit.;* Richard A. Musgrave, *op. cit.*

[48] R. W. Lindholm, "The Value Added Tax: A Short Review of the Literature," *Journal of Economic Literature,* December, 1970, pp. 1178–89 and December, 1971, pp. 1173–79; Mel Krauss and Richard M. Bird, "The Value Added Tax: Critique of a Review," *Journal of Economic Literature,* December, 1971, pp. 1167–73; Ronald I. McKinnon, "Export Expansion through Tax Policy: The Case for a Value-Added Tax in Singapore," *The Malaysian Economic Review,* October, 1966, pp. 1–27, and April, 1967, pp. 36–38.

agricultural and retail enterprise, the value-added tax can be imposed at a uniform rate on total sales of a widening circle of enterprises. Each taxpayer would assume a role in tax administration and enforcement, since his own tax can be reduced by the amount of value-added tax collected against his inputs. The potential base is wide and elastic to both real growth and inflation in the economy. Applied at a uniform percentage, its distortions of relative price are minimal. Value-added taxation does not provide opportunities for avoidance, evasion, and slippage that are so offensive to equity.

The global income tax has an illusory advantage of progressivity in lagging economies with relatively low mean levels of income. Given difficulties with its administration, even when there is automatic correction of tax debts for inflation, other ways of matching taxation with ability to pay are superior. For example, specific taxes can be collected on luxury items at retail, and more capital gains can be reached. If subsidies are economized and if public enterprise abandons the principle of cheap pricing with rations for the privileged few, the outcome for equity is more substantial than one can expect from high marginal rates of income taxation that are rarely effective. There is so much to be done for equity by deepening of finance and other nonfiscal reform that fiscal change can stress other aspects of fiscal effort.

There are clearly evolutionary improvements to be made in the style of public debt and especially in the mode of its pricing. Loan-rate subsidy for public securities, at the expense of financial institutions and savers, would be the first casualty, and the second would be the captive markets where public securities are forced into private portfolios. Rates of interest more closely related than at present to scarcity prices of capital, with at least some of them escalated to change in the price level of domestic goods, must persuade savers to divert a larger share of their funds voluntarily to the public sector and must induce there more rational savings allocation. An open market for treasury bills may provide healthy competition for the curb.

The Trade-Off Illusion

We have emphasized that fiscal reform and financial reform are complementary: each reenforces the other. A different view can be found, that there are trade-offs, with financial repression and especially inflation enhancing fiscal adequacy. Inflation reduces unemployment rates, the argument goes. The effect is to increase real income, even in the long run, deepen the base for ordinary taxation and so to raise revenues from explicit taxes as well as from the inflation tax.[49] Again, according to the Wealth View of money, inflation increases the stock of physical wealth per capita, with evident advantage for the tax collector.[50] Still again, since all feasible taxation has its inefficiencies, second-best policy may stipulate some use of the inflation tax.[51]

One is aware that public authority in various economies has a revealed preference for inflation and against compensatory measures that would protect financial growth. Apparently price-level stability or full compensation for instability is utopian. Given the weight of doctrine in favor of trade-offs between financial and fiscal reform and the preponderance of financially repressive policy, the view that financial and fiscal systems should be corrected in tandem—"all at once"—will have its critics. However, if one believes that Phillips curves tend to be perpendicular in the long run, that the Debt-Intermediation View describes finance more accurately than Wealth View; and that experiments in maintaining a low and steady rate of inflation have been productive, he will continue to insist that the governor of the Central Bank and the minister of finance are not natural enemies.

[49] James Tobin, "Inflation and Unemployment," *The American Economic Review*, March, 1972, pp. 1–18.
[50] Edwin Burmeister and Edmund Phelps, "Money, Public Debt, Inflation and Real Interest," *Journal of Money, Credit and Banking*, May, 1971, pp. 153–182.
[51] Jagdish Bhagwati, *The Economics of Underdeveloped Countries*, pp. 113–123.

7 | Financial Deepening in the Open Economy

Previous chapters have discussed financial deepening with slight reference to external trade. Now trade is admitted on both current and capital account, and we consider its interdependence with domestic finance. The theme is to be that shallow finance and distorted trade go together as do deepened finance and liberalized trade. It may be redundant to add that financial and trade reform implies improvement too in fiscal effort. The finance minister who dashes around the London-Paris-New York circuit to fund a mass of expensive suppliers' credits dashes home again to decide how high the inflation tax must be.

The first section below is concerned with the foreign-exchange market and with its relative price, the foreign-exchange rate, for domestic in terms of foreign money. The lagging economy imposes disequilibrium on this market as it does on domestic markets for money and other finance and attempts to clear excess demand with a variety of interventions. The second section is concerned with reciprocal effects of distortion in domestic finance and international trade on current account. Flows and flights of savings through the balance of payments are discussed in the third section, and the final section considers reform in the lagging economy's international sector. Analysis is directed to the long run, to issues of growth and stagnation rather than stability or instability. Moreover, it has to do with the "small" economy that is more or less open to a larger world where its amounts demanded and supplied exercise, in the main, little effect on price behavior.

THE FOREIGN-EXCHANGE MARKET

As we know, money in the closed economy has three prices. One of them is simply unity in terms of the money-of-account—one won, for example, or one guilder. The second is the reciprocal of a comprehensive price index $1/P$ and represents money's exchange value against a basket of goods and services. The third is deposit rate including the marginal advantages in costs avoided by holding money, the expected rate of change in P and any explicit interest allowance by the monetary system on money balances. When an economy is opened, its money becomes a tradable, and a market appears to determine a fourth price, the foreign-exchange rate against external money. In fact, there may be multiple markets on which domestic and external money trade against each other, each with a rate of exchange; for example, official and black or spot and forward markets. In this section, we consider alternative styles of foreign-exchange market.

Colonial Money

One can trace a virtually continuous spectrum, from full monetary integration toward autarchy, for the capacity of an economy to regulate its own money stock.[1] At the extreme of integration, there is a California, for example, with its monetary system linked at a rigid rate of exchange to the monetary system of the remainder of the United States and with the rate held at par by clearing and collection arrangements that amount to a foreign-exchange market. Not far away along the spectrum, one may find a Malaya of the colonial period, its dollar rigidly linked to sterling under the administration

[1] Egon Sohmen, *Flexible Exchange Rates* (rev. ed.), Chapter VII.

of a currency board.[2] It can be useful to explore briefly this colonial extreme of monetary integration and dependence.

Within the "currency area," comprising the colony and the center to which it is attached, one can define two regional demand functions for money, each written conventionally:

$$(1) \qquad M_d = Pl\,(Y, i, \underline{d})$$

That is to say, the stock of nominal money demanded depends upon the price level positively, on real income and the nominal deposit rate of interest $\underline{d}$ positively, and on loan or "bond" rate of interest i negatively. There are two regional supply functions as well, each in this form:

$$(2) \qquad M_s = Pm\,(\underline{R}, i, \underline{d}, q)$$

Nominal money supply depends positively on nominal high-powered money $P\underline{R}$, defined as liabilities of the central bank in the form of coin and currency and the commercial banks' reserve balances. It depends positively on loan rate of interest i, negatively on deposit rate of interest and on reserve requirements q. Aggregate $P\underline{R}$ is determined by the center's monetary authority. Full monetary equilibrium implies that banks in center and colony wish to hold the quantity $P\underline{R}$ that has been supplied and that $M_d = M_s$ aggregatively and for each region.

The colony shares all markets with the center, we assume, and its resources are mobile so that no regional differences exist for per capita income and wealth. The colony is small in the sense that its excess demands on any market have a negligible effect on levels of trading and price. The center's interest rates and price level are the colony's too, and they are imposed upon it by the center's economic size. The colony is not sheltered against the center's influence on each market by economic distance, that is by costs of inter-regional transactions.

One may disturb the initial equilibrium by an increase in the re-

[2] Frank H. H. King, *Money in British East Asia*, Colonial Research Publication No. 19, p. 37.

serve base $P\underline{R}$. Banks respond to surplus reserves by portfolio expansion with the result that there is excess money supply and excess demands on the common markets for securities, goods, and productive factors. In a new equilibrium, the increment in nominal money is distributed between colony and center according to their relative amounts of real money demanded, and the increment in nominal reserves is distributed according to the relative tastes and reserve requirements of banks in the two regions. In clearing house, the foreign-exchange market for this case, no unresolved balances remain at the foreign-exchange rate of unity.

One may disturb the initial equilibrium by a shift of liquidity preference against $P\underline{R}$ on the part of the colony's banks—an expression of domestic monetary policy. The result is excess supply of reserves that is absorbed by expansion of nominal money for the monetary system as a whole. Securities are transferred into the portfolios of the colony's banks without significant effect on common-market levels of interest rates, commodity prices and output. These banks have reduced their lending to the center's monetary authority, displacing its deposit balances on their balance sheets with loans to other sectors, possibly to investors in the colony.

One may disturb the initial equilibrium by a shift of liquidity preference on the part of the colony's money holders. An autonomous increase in the real stock of money demanded implies excess supply by the colony on common markets for goods, securities, and productive factors. It is resolved by an inflow of reserves and domestic expansion of nominal money. The center is protected against disturbance either because it is large enough to absorb the growth in total real money demanded as just one of many random disturbances or because the monetary authority can expand total $P\underline{R}$. The colony has exported capital to the center, increasing its lending through the media of reserves, coin, and currency.

In this model, the stocks of reserves and nominal money for the currency area are determined by the center's monetary authority, according to its target for the price level and according to real stocks of reserves and money demanded. The colony decides for itself the real stocks of reserves and money among its assets, but its price level and scale of nominal money balances are imposed on it. Its choice of R and M/P can be accommodated by any combination of PR, M, and P that the center elects. In view of its smallness, its nearness and the rigidity of its foreign-exchange rate, it can have no nominal-money policy of its own. It is autonomous insofar as the real values of reserves and money are concerned.

For all practical purposes, the moneys of center and colony are one money, with the exchange rate between them frozen by legal sanctions of the center's monetary authority against balances at clearing house that are not absorbed by transfers of reserves between banks. It does not matter that one money may be called, say, dollar and the other pound, that the dollar issues of the colony's banks may not have legal-tender powers in the center or that each exchange between dollar and pound is subject to a service charge.[3] At an exchange rate of 1 : 1 or any other ratio, they are perfect substitutes. Moreover, the ratio of their real as distinct from their money-of-account price, the purchasing power parity, must be identical with the exchange rate and no less stable, given the full mobility that prevails in markets for output and resources. There can be no forward premia or discounts in the foreign-exchange market since open and competitive markets for financial assets keep interest rates at a common level.

Satellite Money

There are lagging economies within currency areas of the colonial type. Appalachia, Northern Ireland, and Sicily are cases in point. However, their backwardness is imposed upon them by immobilities and by a decision at the center to apply resources for development

---

[3] Before the Federal Reserve, there seems to have been a wider variation in the San Francisco price of New York exchange than was characteristic for the Malayan price of sterling. Regarding the latter, King reports, "The effect of exchange costs on the loan and investment policy of the banks cannot but be marginal, and it is wise to look upon the banking system of the Malayan area as one which is almost, but not quite, identical with that of the United Kingdom." Frank H. H. King, *op. cit.,* p. 79.

in other regions. The lagging economies that concern us have monetary sovereignty and misuse it. We can move one step closer to a prototype for them by assuming a currency area of two economies each with its monetary authority. Again, one economy is large, one small, and initially there is full integration of markets for output, resources, and financial assets: everything is a tradable. The small economy resembles independent Malaysia more closely than colonial Malaya. There are resemblances with Costa Rica and Panama.

The lesser or satellite monetary authority of the currency area can specify and defend the rate of exchange between domestic money and money of the center. Since there is just one rate of exchange between the two monies, the satellite's choice prevails.[4] The implication is that the satellite has its choice among levels of prices, in terms of domestic money, for non-monetary tradables. Commodities priced at one unit of the center currency may be priced at any figure of the satellite's choice in its own currency: it can move decimal points to right or left, as it likes, in specifying exchange rate and price level. Money holders' demands for real balances in the satellite currency can be satisfied by as many or as few units of nominal money as the authority desires. Furthermore, the authority can select among rates of price-level inflation. It can specify a rate of change in the spot foreign-exchange rate and price level and, given real rates of interest in the common capital market, can put nominal rates of interest where it wants them to be. If it decides upon relative inflation, its foreign-exchange market can quote forward premia for the center currency so that nominal rates of interest appear to be the same at home and abroad. If it decides upon relative deflation, forward discounts for the center currency dispel money illusion among borrowers and lenders. We suppose that the satellite considers these options and elects a rigid parity of exchange, in effect delegating control over nominal money, the domestic price level and nominal rates of interest to the center. One advantage of this choice is that it diverts criti-

---

[4] Solution of this "redundancy" problem is not always so simple. The United States has succeeded, in a crisis context, with measures to impose its preference among values of the dollar on the foreign-exchange market.

cism of money management to the center: the satellite authority can plead *non mea culpa* when the price level misbehaves. When this choice is made, under our assumptions, the satellite authority has nothing more to do.

With a touch more of realism in the assumptions, the authority can be given tasks of real money and real financial policy. For example, it may be supposed that private international trading generates some random pattern or some seasonals of excess demand or supply for the center currency on the foreign-exchange market. If there were a perfect common capital market, such disturbances could be resolved at the rigid spot exchange rate by short-term borrowing from the center or short-term lending to it by traders or banks. Some of them could be settled from liquid reserves in the private sector. When the capital market is imperfect and when private opportunity costs of holding external reserves are high, there are advantages for the satellite economy if the monetary authority takes residual responsibility for clearing the foreign-exchange market by changes in its own net external assets. One advantage can be that foreign lenders anticipate less risk on commitments to the satellite and stand ready to lend more and charge lower rates of interest. In effect, the authority can use its reserves to improve the functioning of the capital market. Again, import prices for goods and services may be lower when prompt settlements of debts are assured, and there may be fewer interruptions of trade while credits are arranged. The authority's reserves can improve the markets for goods and services. There are real social yields to official reserves just as there are to private money balances.

Electing a fixed exchange rate, the satellite authority cannot do as it likes with its aggregate portfolio, but it can decide the division of its portfolio between reserves of net external assets and domestic assets: it can exercise reserves policy. At the margin of substitution, there are social yields from additions to reserves, as we have seen. There can also be costs. An addition of reserves is a capital outflow to the center, a diversion of savings from domestic capital formation that might be but apparently seldom is compensated by interest earned in the center on reserve balances. Reserves policy involves a difficult choice, in the present model, between advantages of perfecting commerce with the center and of retaining domestic savings for domestic investment. One can understand why ministers of finance, frustrated in use of the inflation tax by a fixed rate of exchange against the center, may have little patience with reserve accumulation. It forces government securities out of the monetary system's portfolio, and proof may not be easy that the same securities can be more easily marketed in the open capital market if the foreign-exchange market's capacity to transfer debt service is supported by a strong reserve position.

With increasing economic distance between markets of center and satellite for output, resources, and securities, both the utility and the opportunity cost of reserve accumulation increase. Reserve accumulation can help with smooth absorption of balance-of-payments surplus, and decumulation can economize on measures to shrink a deficit. We return to this point shortly, but it is worth stressing here that wealth in the form of reserves has its pay-offs and its costs, helping with integration of markets in the long run, with stability of markets in the short run.[5]

The satellite authority, having decided on the rigid exchange rate and settled its reserves policy, has an opportunity to apply real money policy domestically. Through issue of charters, it can affect competitiveness in domestic financial industry and the level of deposit rates, given loan rates in the common capital market. Since local money is a tradable, domestic banks can compete with banks of the center in satisfying aggregate demand for money through the

[5] The following citations are a small sample from the extensive literature on optimality in reserve accumulation. Peter Barton Clark, "Optimal International Reserves and the Speed of Adjustment," *Journal of Political Economy*, March/April, 1970, pp. 356–376; Robert Clower and Richard Lipsey, "International Liquidity: The Present State of International Liquidity Theory," *The American Economic Review*, May, 1968, pp. 586–596; Herbert C. Grubel, "The Demand for International Reserves: A Critical Review of the Literature," *Journal of Economic Literature*, December, 1971, pp. 1148–1166; International Monetary Fund, *International Reserves: Needs and Availability*, Washington, D.C., 1970.

currency area. Intermediation services are a component of national income, and Switzerland like Hong Kong, for example, and Singapore have proved that it can be substantial. For the open economy, financial depth implies gains from export growth in intermediation and efficient import substitution. Liberalization of finance is one technique of export promotion. One must add, of course, that export promotion and import substitution can be inefficient, yielding a smaller return in value added for employed resources than an alternative use, possibly in education or civil service. When this is the case, liberalization of finance implies import of financial services, the cost covered by nonfinancial exports of comparative advantage. For many or most small economies, an efficient financial system may include both domestic enterprise and foreign, the optimal division of the market depending on factors of scale, for example, and technical sophistication. Indigenous banks and a foreign stock exchange are one of many imaginable combinations.

Autonomous Money

The two monetary regimes already considered are designed to take full advantage of integration, with the widest matrix of transactions. Gains from integration are undeniable for the small economy, but domination by the large economy has its costs. We consider now a change in the foreign-exchange market that sacrifices some benefits of full integration to reduce or to avoid some costs. It is a band of fluctuation in the foreign-exchange rate around a rigid parity in the style of Bretton Woods.

The band is a range of fluctuation in money's price between two "points" at which the monetary authority enters the foreign-exchange market to clear excess demand with purchases or sales of external assets. Excess offers of domestic money depreciate its relative price in money of the center to "borrowing" point at which the domestic authority imports savings either by sale of assets or by floating debt. Excess bids appreciate domestic money to the "lending" point at which the domestic authority exports savings either by purchase of external assets or by repayment of external debt. Between the points, change in money's price is given the opportunity to initiate adjustment mechanisms that shrink excess demand. Mistrust of these mechanisms and interference with them accounts for much of the difficulty that lagging economies experience with their international trading.

Adjustment may be expected in private asset portfolios. When the center currency appreciates, exporters in the small economy may accelerate shipments from inventory, and importers may defer new purchases abroad. Investors in the small economy see, through the filter of the foreign-exchange market, a decline of interest rates in the center and can be expected to accelerate borrowing and repatriation of the proceeds. Savers may take advantage of the opportunity to shift from foreign to domestic financial assets. In the relatively developed foreign-exchange market, of course, speculators may take short positions in the center currency, long positions in the money of the small economy and generate a forward discount for the center currency that eliminates differentials in interest rates between the two areas. In each case, however, the speculative-adjustment mechanism depends on expectations that the spot exchange rate will recover toward parity, and it depends on costs incurred in portfolio changes.

The "gap" of excess demand at parity and the depreciation it imposes on the small economy's money may induce corrective adjustment by substitution in trade. Exportable output in the small economy may be diverted to the center's markets. Imports may be displaced by competing domestic outputs in the small economy. Relative change in prices of tradables and non-tradables tends to move the current international account into surplus. This price-adjustment mechanism is effective according to pertinent price elasticities.

Exchange depreciation imposes on the small economy an inflation in prices of tradables and, depending on their importance in total trade, in the general price level. The effect is to reduce the real stock of money and of other financial assets valued in the domestic money-of-account. This impoverishment can assist in balance-of-payments adjustment if holders of financial assets reduce demands for exportables and for imports. As a wealth-adjustment mechanism, it can eliminate some excess demand for the center's money in the foreign-exchange market.

Finally, there is an income-adjustment mechanism to account for. Increases in domestic prices of tradable goods relative to factor price are a stimulus to employment of underemployed resources. This widening of profit margins for producers of exports and of substitutes for imports generates adjustments on the supply side of the goods markets that work with substitutions on the demand side to clear the small economy's external deficit. To be sure, multiplier effects of increased output on demands for tradables tend to widen the deficit unless they are absorbed by rising tax revenues or counteracted by the impact of rising domestic income upon interest rates.

Changes in the foreign-exchanges price of the small economy's money within the band tend to mobilize the speculative, price, wealth, and income adjustment mechanisms in stabilizing fashion.[6] If the mechanisms are too frail in either direction, the principle of the band requires the monetary authority of the small economy to resume the role of satellite. It has come to the end of its tether of autonomy and is required to reduce excess supply of domestic money on the foreign-exchanges by releasing reserves and to reduce excess demand for domestic money by absorbing reserves.

For some developing economies, the costs of reverting to a common currency at a fixed upper or lending point on the foreign-exchange market can support a strong case for exchange-rate float. These economies have set inflation targets for themselves, and they have been sheltered against external inflation both by their economic distance from the center and by shifts in their import menu to cheaper goods. Persistent inflation in the world outside, at a pace exceeding their own, eventually forces growth in external reserves upon them and corresponding pressure for accelerated monetary expansion. It raises prices of traded goods, and monetary expansion

[6] Ronald I. McKinnon, "Portfolio Balance and International Payments Adjustment," in Robert A. Mundell and Alexander K. Swoboda, *Monetary Problems in the International Economy,* pp. 199–234.

supports sympathetic rises in prices of non-tradables including wages. One cost of the fixed lending point in the foreign-exchange market is that domestic savings are drawn, through reserve accumulation, to the center economy. Since the tax base is inelastic to inflation, a second cost is that inflation shrinks the real size of the government budget. There is a third cost, that the inflation tax imposes distributive inequities on savers, commonly in the lower-income classes, whose financial assets are not escalated. A fourth cost appears when producers in import-substitution, injured by rising prices of imported inputs, ask for and receive concessions of subsidy through, say, loan rates, tax rates, tariff rates, and other trade limitations. Without exhausting the list, one more cost may be mentioned, that lag in adjustment of nominal domestic rates of interest to inflation diverts private savings from the small economy to the center at least until doubts have arisen that the exchange parity will hold. For so long as domestic deposit rates stay beneath old ceilings, the attractions to savers of foreign assets at rates adjusted to inflationary expectations are irresistible. Each of these costs is a burden on the domestic capital market.

There is a comparable case for mobility of the borrowing point on the foreign-exchange market when the center economy has shifted to a lower price-level target. A reduced rate of monetary expansion in the center deflates prices of tradables and, drawing reserves from the small economy, induces monetary contraction there that generates excess demand for money and excess supply of non-tradables. Rigidities in their prices and especially in wage rates, given the usual minimum-wage laws, increase levels of unemployment that tend already to be high. The private savings flow is diminished by decreasing output, and government savings are pared by diminishing revenues and rising costs of welfare. Pressures develop for autarky of trade with further protection of imports and bias against exports. Monetary instability from the center requires sacrifices from satellite small economies whether the disturbance involves acceleration or deceleration of the center's monetary expansion.

At either borrowing or lending point, small economies have been vulnerable to destabilizing speculation. It has been observed above that the speculative adjustment mechanism can assist in reducing a discount from parity of the small economy's currency, but the necessary condition is that speculators attach small probability to depreciation below the band. On this condition, they are ready to take long positions in the currency and wait for its appreciation back toward parity. Doubts of the currency's strength are easy to arouse. Small economies commonly do not maintain impressive external reserves, and a persistent drain can give speculators pause. When special measures are taken to stop exchange depreciations, perhaps tightened import controls or bids for new international loans, speculative preference shifts against the currency on all markets. On the foreign-exchange market, long positions can be liquidated quickly, and there can emerge a shift of both foreign and domestic funds to the center. On domestic markets, a reduction in real money demanded can intensify inflationary pressures, with obvious effects on excess demand for foreign exchange. Effects on domestic finance are adverse: demand shifts away from it so that even stock market indices turn down.

"Fundamental disequilibrium" fuses opinion in favor of adjusting a band. It has been the case on too many occasions, however, that a step upward or downward of the band is deferred until a speculative debacle proves that disequilibrium really is "fundamental." Since disequilibrium of the foreign-exchange market within a narrow band of rates is inherent in immobility of real resources and differences in inflation targets between centers and satellites, a floating exchange rate that averts speculative mass attacks seems to be essential. Resource immobility in the context of various relative changes in the real growth paths of economies linked by trade makes monetary one-ness a costly fiction. It may be helpful to consider a few illustrations.

Change in production technology sometimes diffuses slowly from one economy to another. With, say, Japan in mind, we may imagine relatively rapid technological progress combined with high savings rates in a satellite. New technologies implemented by growth in the stock of physical capital and in the labor force can so reduce factor costs in production of tradables, both for export and for import-substitution, that the current account of the international balance of payments develops a growing surplus, given world prices of tradables and a fixed exchange-rate band. Reserves are drawn from abroad. If public policy resists a compensating decline of domestic assets in the monetary system's portfolio because it would reduce the savings flow into domestic capital formation and the growth rate of output, the inevitable result is inflation in the satellite's price level for non-tradables on markets both for output and for factors. The inflow of reserves might be frustrated by external investment if it were not inhibited by immobilities in resources and policy. The purchasing power parity of the satellite's currency, measured in terms of supply prices of tradables, has appreciated, and a fixed band works to reverse this appreciation by raising domestic prices of factor inputs. A free foreign-exchange rate would accommodate appreciation, reduction in domestic prices of tradables, and relative stability in prices of non-tradables. It would attract technological innovation, savings and labor to the domestic sector.

Small economies have been known to raise real supply prices of exports. Ghana, for example, restricted use of fertilizers, pesticides, and other inputs for cocoa production during the early 1960's and suffered a decline in output that encouraged production in competing areas abroad. There was, it appears, a permanent fall in Ghana's share of total cocoa supply at each level of prices in the London market. The cedi's purchasing power parity, again measured in the supply price of a tradable, depreciated. The fixed band for the cedi's price in terms of sterling cost Ghana significant loss of reserves and, given resistance of public policy against internal deflation, a significant increase in external indebtedness as well. A free foreign-exchange rate would have accommodated depreciation, increase in the domestic price of tradables, and relative stability in prices of non-tradables. It would have supplied incentive to measures for reversing misguided cocoa policy.

Relative changes in the real-income paths of center and small economies can be the result of shifts in terms of trade. Decline in "world" prices for the small economy's exports relative to its imports, a deterioration in terms of trade, reduces relevant purchasing power parity and generates excess supply of satellite money on the foreign exchanges. When immobilities stand in the way of development of new exports or import substitutes or of change in the mix of imports, it is not difficult to argue the case for fundamental disequilibrium and exchange depreciation. If there is enrichment in terms of trade, exchange appreciation is the appropriate defense against general inflation of prices in the small economy.

Destabilizing speculation in capital and foreign-exchange markets, divergence in rates of inflation and real growth between center and small economies and shifts in terms of trade are strong talking points against satellite money and for the alternative of full autonomy behind a floating exchange rate. There are others. For example, international corporations make large transfers of savings that small economies may absorb with less shock if the foreign-exchange rate is permitted to help with the process. Again, waves of migration generate flows of remittances which may be transferable with less disturbance across a flexible relative price for money. Fixing exchange rates at the upper and lower limits of narrow bands sacrifices one instrument of relative price in making adjustments between economies that are imperfectly integrated in real terms and in policy, and gains from full monetary integration may not be worth the price.

Disequilibrium Money

Foreign exchange difficulties are not a temporary exigency but a normal and permanent condition in very poor countries. . . .[7]

The lagging economies have designed their own characteristic foreign-exchange market. It is a disequilibrium market where "difficulties" generate chronic excess demand for center money. Now and again—each ten to twelve months in Brazil during 1964–68—excess demand precipitates a crisis that is resolved temporarily by substantial devaluation below borrowing point and by other measures of

[7] Gunnar Myrdal, *Asian Drama,* Volume III, p. 2082.

emergency hue. Fundamental disequilibrium is one characteristic of the lagging economies' foreign-exchange markets. A second is perhaps no less inhibiting to growth: unpredictable change in the relative price of domestic money and *ad hoc* patterns of intervention to stabilize it. Disequilibrium, arbitrary intervention and risk are the trademarks of the lagging economies' foreign-exchange markets.

There is a scenario for disequilibrium money that opens on this identity:[8]

$$
(1) \qquad
\begin{matrix}
B \\ \text{Trade} \\ \text{Balance}
\end{matrix}
\quad = \quad
\begin{matrix}
Y \\ \text{National} \\ \text{Income}
\end{matrix}
\quad - \quad
\begin{matrix}
E \\ \text{Usage or} \\ \text{National} \\ \text{Expenditure}
\end{matrix}
$$

Attention is focused on the current account of the lagging economy's balance of payments where disequilibrium appears as a negative B, representing unsustainable excess of aggregate demand for goods and services relative to national output or excess of desired investment relative to savings. In view of the monetary authority's slim stocks of international reserves and limited borrowing capacity in outside capital markets, a regime of quantitative restrictions on imports appears, in effect a regime of multiple exchange rates for imports. Then export subsidies are applied to help with the exchange gap, in effect a regime of multiple exchange rates in the export sector. The third stage brings substitution of tariffs for other restraints on imports, with government appropriating importers' monopoly revenues. Finally, there is a devaluation, a write-down of money's relative price in center currency, and then the process is touched off again because not enough is done to limit "usage" relative to output. This scenario is life-like, but it is incomplete because it neglects the role of markets for money and capital.

[8] Jagdish Bhagwati, "The Theory and Practice of Commercial Policy: Departures from Unified Exchange Rates," International Finance Section, Princeton University, *Special Papers in International Economics,* No. 8, January, 1968, pp. 48–49; S. C. Tsiang, "The Role of Money in Trade-Balance Stability: Synthesis of the Elasticity and Absorption Approaches," *The American Economic Review,* December, 1951, pp. 912–936.

A richer scenario for disequilibrium money can be developed from the following expression for current and capital accounts combined in the international balance of payments, with only transactions between monetary authorities omitted:[9]

$$(2) \qquad B = R_f + R_r - P_f - P_r = R - P$$

Here R_f are receipts by residents of payments from foreigners, and P_f are payments by residents to foreigners. R_r and P_r, identically equal, are payments and receipts between residents. Policy in lagging economies adopts an ostensibly fixed parity against center money on the foreign-exchange market, with a narrow band between lending and borrowing points. Then it generates excess demand for foreign exchange by driving B to negative levels. It induces excess offers of payments P from domestic money balances relative to bids in all markets for receipts R that restore balances: it imposes excess supply on the market for domestic money. There are three solutions for which makers of policy in lagging economies have deep distaste. Excess demand for foreign exchange might be cleared by drawing down the monetary authority's balances of reserves, but reserves are an expensive use of resources, and the lagging economies choose low reserve targets. Excess supply of domestic money might be cleared by reducing the rate of growth in nominal money and by other measures to increase real money demanded, but there are strong objections to monetary restraint as a cure for external deficits and, as we know, real-money policy is not deepening. Finally, the foreign-exchange rate might be permitted to float downward, but this is regarded as both disruptive of growth and ineffective. With exchange parity fixed, reserves meager, and domestic monetary policy ruled out as an instrument of control over the foreign-exchange market, lagging economies resort to a characteristic pattern of interventions in the foreign exchange and other markets.[10] According to this scenario, the interventions collapse in due time under the pressure of excess demand for foreign exchange and other rationed

[9] Harry G. Johnson, *International Trade and Economic Growth,* pp. 135–168.
[10] Frank C. Child, "Liberalization of the Foreign Exchange Market," *The Pakistan Development Review,* Summer, 1968, pp. 167–168.

goods. Devaluation ensues; there may be an interval of monetary restraint; and then the sequence is repeated. Policy in the lagging economies makes a gesture of integration with the center economy, but its bias is autarchic. The fixed parity with a narrow band is illusory.

The Apparatus of Exchange Control. Excess money supply presses on all markets in lagging economies, and there is a common pattern of devices to suppress its effects. On markets for goods, it drives the price level higher. For some goods, however, authority steps in with price ceilings to support money's relative price $1/P$. Ceilings are most common for prices of "necessities," including wage goods and services of public enterprise. There is rationing of supply at the ceiling prices, and there is subsidized supply. Unsatisfied demand for goods seeks black markets and finds them, and government has a familiar battery of penalties for black marketeers.

Excess money supply drives nominal rates of interest higher once inflation has come to be expected. Again, authority steps in with price ceilings, this time to hold down money's opportunity cost and keep real interest rates low. The ceilings are lowest for loans that qualify as "necessities"—loans to new enterprises, possibly exporters and farmers and always government. There is rationing of loans, and the lending is subsidized. Unsatisfied demand seeks black markets and finds them, and authority brings penalties to bear. This same pattern of disequilibrium pricing in an inflationary context is repeated in markets for relatively scarce labor skills, for physical capital such as housing and for scarce natural resources such as urban space.

Obviously the pattern is repeated in the foreign-exchange market in order to support the price of domestic in terms of center money. Excess domestic money supply that generates excess demand on domestic markets spills over to the foreign-exchange market. There it is met with the familiar response of price ceiling, rationing, subsidized supply, and black markets. Distortion of money's relative prices—price level of output, real deposit rate, and foreign-exchange rate—pervades the entire market structure.

The art of managing excess-demand disequilibrium in any market is not the invention of lagging economies. It had been refined and polished before its vogue in India and Pakistan or, say, Chile and Colombia. There is space here to mention only a few of its features that one observes among countries and among markets. One common feature is differentiated pricing, with exchange rates or loan rates, for example, designated by sources of supply and categories of demand. The differentiation may be explicit or effective price differences may be created on foreign-exchange markets by exchange-retention schemes, differential tariffs on imports and subsidies on exports, as on loan markets by compensating-balance requirements and maturity differentials. At one extreme of the price scale, of course, there is the infinitely high ceiling imposed by prohibition on purchase.

There is always differentiated rationing at each of the various stipulated prices. Rationing by the random technique of the queue does not comply with a pattern that control authority deduces somehow, possibly from standards of optimality set down in a plan or from political pressure. In effect, a dual payments mechanism instituted, with payments not only in money but also in ration certificates or licenses, and authority finds it difficult to repress a "foreign exchange" market between the multiple means of payment. The rations or licenses are private wealth, and the temptation is strong for holders to maximize their value by trading. It is recognized occasionally, as in the case of export bonus-voucher schemes, that trade in an open market for the "second money" can ameliorate some of the effects, in terms of equity or allocative efficiency, of rationing.

Rations in one market are linked with rations in other markets. The manufacturer who receives a foreign-exchange ration receives too, if control apparatus has been synchronized, a loan ration, electricity ration, import and investment license. He receives other concessions, say in taxes and tariffs, that lower his effective cost for producing a priority output. His excess demand for any input including foreign exchange is increased by disequilibrium pricing for other inputs.

Disequilibrium Money and Market Structure. There seems to be a dual effect of controls associated with disequilibrium money on market structure. One is a centralizing effect. On major markets, one or another government agency confronts a number of applicants, for privileged access to rationed supply, that must be small, given the administrative costs of regulation. Government as the monopolist of ration tickets, investment licenses, export bonus vouchers, and other "second monies" deals, if only for reasons of administrative economy, with an oligopsony of bidders for privilege. Part of the explanation for capital-intensive production in economies with ample labor supply is that relative prices are wrong, as in the case of the price of savings relative to the price of labor services, but part of it must be that government and enterprise economize in management of the disequilibrium system by concentrating savings among a few outlets. Capital-intensive production implies economies of scale in administering disequilibrium.

A second effect is to fragmentize market structure by multi-monetizing the economy. Money in the usual form ceases to be the only means of payment and in some markets cannot be used as the medium of exchange unless it is combined with ration tickets in some guise. Its exchange value *vis à vis* some other goods varies among money holders. The amount of money demanded in one form, say, currency, relative to amounts demanded in checking balances depends on relative advantages in illegal domestic transactions and in capital flight. Money's utility in search-and-bargain is reduced: multi-monetization is a variant of demonetization. Moreover, factor costs of the payments mechanism are raised by expenditures on managing and using complex money. The result must be that some of money's income effect is lost. The disequilibrium system is not money deepening.

"Normal and Permanent" Disequilibrium Money

It is a matter of observation that excess demand for foreign exchange and disequilibrium methods for repressing it happen in coincidence with relatively high rates of monetary expansion in lagging economies and relatively high rates of inflation. Agreement is easy on this empirical point. There is not consensus, however, about the role of monetary phenomena in causing excess demand for foreign exchange or removing it. We turn briefly to views that excess demand for foreign exchange is based on real, non-monetary phenomena and that monetary cures for it, including exchange depreciation, are either irrelevant or harmful. Sometimes the point is added that excess supply of domestic money and excess demand for center money trace to common causes.

One model, without monetary variables, constructs a poor economy that is striving to lift its growth rate of output from zero to some target level.[11] Initially there are no savings flowing to investment, but the marginal propensity to save is positive. An average propensity equal to the marginal would supply savings required for target growth of income. Until income has risen to the level at which this equality is reached, income growth at the target rate generates excess demands for savings. Since excess demand can be supplied only from abroad, by foreign investment or grants in aid perhaps, it can be interpreted as excess demand for foreign exchange. The savings gap is also a foreign-exchange gap. Disequilibrium in the market for savings and foreign exchange is temporary, to be overcome by priming the income pump from which domestic savings flow. The model visualizes the marginal rate of savings and the output-capital ratio as constants, subject to no manipulation of financial variables.

A second real model conjures up two chasms or gaps that a poor economy must jump on its way to steady growth at a target rate—both a savings gap and a foreign-exchange gap. Despite an adequate average propensity to save, the economy may slip off its growth path into stagnation and unemployment if it is deprived of foreign exchange from an inflow of loans or grants. The source of trouble is growth requirements for imports, in more or less fixed proportions to output, that export capacity cannot satisfy at relative prices prevailing for tradables abroad. It is limited trade opportunity that inhibits growth, not a shortage of domestic savings and not excess

<hr>

[11] Ronald I. McKinnon, "Foreign Exchange Constraints in Economic Development and Efficient Aid Allocation," *The Economic Journal,* June, 1964, pp. 396–400.

money supply. The inhibition is not to be overcome, for countries below some critical level of per capita income, by substitution among export alternatives, by import substitution, or by improvements of efficiency in export production and import use.[12] As Myrdal puts it:

In the final analysis, then, it is the low level of their exports and the difficulties in the way of raising it at any rate of exchange—together with their great poverty and their desire to plan for development—that compels India and other South Asian countries to take steps to preserve foreign exchange for imports of essential consumer and development goods.[13]

The real explanation for disequilibrium comes in other packages.[14] Capacity to earn foreign exchange, it has been said, is constricted by the advanced countries' trade barriers or by technological displacement of poor economies' exportables. An elasticity pessimism darkens prospects that developing economies can stimulate exports or economize imports by any among various adjustments in relative prices. It is alleged that market failure frustrates rational adjustment in the balance of payments of the poor economy, that peasants do not sense economic opportunity in new export markets, that aristocracy thinks only of ostentation and that speculators are merciless in their attacks on weak currencies.

There are then two views of disequilibrium money. According to one, chronic excess demand for center money is a product of policies that discourage and repel savings, misallocate resources among tradables and non-tradables, generate excess supplies of domestic money and try to resolve disequilibrium in many markets by admin-

---

[12] There is an indefinitely large number of two-gap models. See, for example, Hollis Chenery and Alan Strout, "Foreign Assistance and Economic Development," *The American Economic Review,* September, 1966, pp. 679–732; Lauchlin Currie, *Accelerating Development: The Necessity and the Means;* McKinnon, *op. cit.,* pp. 400–403; Richard R. Nelson, "The Effective Exchange Rate: Employment and Growth in a Foreign Exchange-Restrained Economy," *Journal of Political Economy,* May/June, 1970, pp. 546–564.

[13] Gunnar Myrdal, *op. cit.,* p. 2080.

[14] Economic Commission for Latin America, *Economic Survey of Latin America,* 1964.

istrative intervention. According to the other, disequilibrium money is an attribute of poverty, which inhibits saving; a result of technologically imposed lags in development of exports and substitutes for imports; one manifestation of inflation that is structural in origin. In the latter case, equilibrium is a luxury that can be afforded when income has passed some critical level, when industrial growth has opened some bottlenecks and when, insofar as inflation is concerned, effective incomes policies can be applied. Transition through the dis equilibrium phase of growth depends on a push from outside, say, through tariff concessions on current account and aid or soft loans on capital account. Exchange rate depreciation cannot be significant for long in clearing excess demand for foreign exchange though "reluctant adjustment" of parity and the band may be unavoidable now and again if only as a condition for obtaining outside aid, deterring capital flight and mobilizing domestic savings through temporary redistribution of domestic incomes.[15] We return to discussion of "normal and permanent" disequilibrium shortly.

TRADE POLICY AND FINANCIAL GROWTH

Financial repression, exchange-rate disequilibrium, and policy bias against comparative advantage in international trade are interlocking restraints on development. Distorted prices of savings and foreign exchange misdirect demand and supply among tradables and domestic goods. Interventions in flows of trade on current account provide new incentives for financial repression and impose implicit multiple pricing on the foreign-exchange markets. There is a combination of financial, foreign-exchange, and trade policies in restraint of growth.

Effects of Financial Repression upon Trade

By reducing domestic savings, shallow finance has led to distortion in trade. Savers have responded to low and unstable real rates of return on financial assets as one would expect, by shifting demand to imports of consumables, to consumables with high import con-

[15] Jagdish Bhagwati, *op. cit.,* p. 62.

tent, and to domestic goods with export potentialities. By its effects on income distribution between the poor and the well-to-do, agriculture and industry, wages and rents, shallow finance has increased the imported share of consumption.[16] Countries that plead shortage of foreign exchange have made the shortage worse by damping domestic savings.

Since financial and fiscal systems have fallen short of feasible results in raising national savings rates, techniques of self-finance have been used. These techniques include various kinds of discrimination against export production and against industry that is judged competent to do without protection. Production with comparative advantage in trade has endured negative protection and taxation so that import-substitution might be financed from its own profits. In a distressingly large number of instances, the result has been a net sacrifice of foreign exchange. Foreign exchange has been lost in order to increase savings that might have been raised by financial and fiscal devices.[17]

Subsidized loan rates impose bias on trade. They divert savings into capital-intensive products and processes.[18] One result, of course, is to sacrifice the lagging economies' relative advantage in labor supply, space and other natural resources. Another result is that savings are guided into relatively non-malleable capital, and the capacity of lagging economies to cope with changing patterns of demand in both domestic and foreign markets is reduced. Again, subsidized growth in plant and equipment imposes a growing burden on the balance of payments of imports in the form of spare and replacement parts. Preferences of various kinds accorded to these so-called essential items are negative protection for industry with export potentialities. In addition to its effect on capital-labor substitution, subsidized loan-

[16] Ian Little, Tibor Scitovsky, Maurice Scott, *Industry and Trade in Some Developing Countries,* p. 63.
[17] Stephen R. Lewis, Jr., *Pakistan: Industrialization and Trade Policies,* pp. 148–150.
[18] Jeffrey G. Williamson, "Capital Accumulation, Labor Saving, and Labor Absorption Once More," *The Quarterly Journal of Economics,* February, 1971, pp. 40–65.

rate shifts demand to fixed from working capital. Frequently the resulting economies in working capital are pushed so far that work stoppages occur in industries producing tradable goods. Then unit costs of output rise, and potential buyers look to other sources of supply. With no pretense that this list of distortions from subsidized loan rate is complete, we add just one more. Evidence is accumulating that exports have been promoted, in India and Korea and elsewhere, to limits at which social yields on export investment are negligible or worse. One reason must be access to savings on giveaway terms. Finance cannot be blamed entirely when exports valued f.o.b. in international prices are worth less than imported inputs valued c.i.f., but it is not blameless.

The story of distortions in trade that result from disequilibrium pricing in the market for foreign exchange has been told too often for repetition here. Multiple explicit and implicit exchange rates, increasing in number and confusion with each degree of relative domestic inflation and accompanied by skeins of tariff and license schemes, guarantee irrational choices among trading opportunities.[19] Their unpredictability, from one tariff circular of the Commission on Trade to the next or from one schedule of foreign-exchange allocations to the next guarantees that investment in trading industry will be vulnerable to risk.

Effects of Trade Distortion upon Finance

Financial policy distorts international trading by the lagging economy, and trading policy reciprocates with distortion of finance. The feedback from trade to finance obstructs financial deepening in a number of ways. For example, any trade policy that selects inefficiently among alternative opportunities for investment of savings reduces loan rates that financial institutions can realize and deposit rates that they can pay. It forces financial institutions, in effect, to

[19] I. M. D. Little, "The Influence of Economic Policy in Less Developed Countries on the Capital Intensity of Investment, and Growth of Employment," Food Research Institute, Stanford University, December, 1971, pp. 4–5, 16–17.

report to savers that opportunities for use of their savings are unattractive. To illustrate, some trade policy provides incentive for excess capacity in industry, hence to high capital-output ratios that imply meager rewards for savings invested. Road-rolling equipment rusting in open fields and modern rice mills operating on fractional shifts are judged unable to generate appropriate reward on savers' financial claims.[20] Overdue loans with liens on such capital equipment hardly put banks in position to bid full-liquidity rates of interest for deposits.

Investors' pay-out horizons are short in lagging economies. Physical investment at long term is either classified as infrastructure and done in the public sector or it is on private initiative with public subsidy. Private preference for commitments at short term can be explained in part by impatience to augment present low levels of consumption, in part by opportunities for shallow investment.[21] This preference also reflects aversion to risks of instability in public policy including trade policy. Ghana, for example, has applied effective protection of 4,000 per cent on domestic value added in some industry, negative protection in other cases, and the degree of protection has changed from one year's tariff schedule to the next.[22] Instability and notionality in trade policy shorten investment horizons for both physical and financial wealth.

Tariffs in lagging economies have not been a dependable fiscal resource. Revenues have tended to shrink as imports are displaced by protected domestic production. Import licenses have diverted revenues to importers. Protected industries have demanded and received tariff concessions on imported inputs. From still other reasons for slippage we select one, that revenues from some forms of duty are inelastic to inflation of the domestic price level. Whatever the reason, tariff revenues have lagged in real terms. Their shrinkage

[20] Jagdish N. Bhagwati and Padma Desai, *India: Planning for Industrialization*, Chapter 18.
[21] Irving Fisher, *The Theory of Interest*, pp. 176–177, 382.
[22] Ghana's tariff manual, first published in 1966, was amended extensively at least seven times by mid-1971.

has increased government's reliance on the inflation tax and government's demands upon the financial system for real private savings at subsidized loan rates.

Tariffs, quotas, and licensing systems are used as instruments of capital accumulation. Sometimes their objective is to increase private savings for self-finance of investment. Sometimes the objective is to make one form of capital more attractive and another form less so in order to change the ranking of investment opportunities. They are used in combination with financial instruments including subsidized loan-rate and credit rationing. The combination is not congenial for financial development, and the restraint imposed by these linked instruments can be traced in shallow finance, idle capital, underemployed labor, and foreign-exchange scarcity. If tariffs were demoted to the fiscal function, deepened finance could perform better in the saving-investment process.

INTERNATIONAL CAPITAL FLOWS

Financial repression and fiscal inadequacy help to create a savings gap at rates of growth in national product that approach the aspirations of developing economies. Planning ministries compute the savings deficits, and international agencies propose decades of dedication by advanced economies to finance the deficits. We consider briefly impacts of financial distortion, including multiple disequilibrium rates of foreign exchange, on capital flows in the lagging economies' balances of payments. Then we turn the cause-effect relationship around and consider biases imposed on financial development by international capital movements. The point to be made is that these movements cannot keep closed the savings gap that domestic policy creates in lagging economies.

Effects of Financial Repression upon Capital Flows

Low real ceilings on rates of interest in lagging economies stand in sharp contrast with rates of return to savers in organized capital markets of the advanced economies: relative prices on the capital markets invite savings to run up-hill, from areas of scarcity to areas of comparative plenty. In June, 1970, maximum deposit rates of interest at commercial banks were 3.5 per cent for Ghana, 7.5 per cent in the United States where inflation was occurring at roughly one-third of Ghana's rate, and similar pairings could be quoted for Colombia and Germany or India and France. This differential understates the disadvantage to savers of lagging economies. If one allows as well for the probability of explicit devaluation of the new cedi or peso or rupee and of constraints still to come on convertibility between currencics, the differential widens. One needs no further explanation for overinvoicing of imports, underinvoicing of exports and persistent balance-of-payments debits for "errors and omissions." Brazil was acutely aware of the differential's magnetism for capital flight when, in 1964 and 1968, it linked nominal yields on "readjustable" treasury bonds to the dollar-cruzeiro exchange rate and exempted from taxation the adjustment for exchange depreciation.[23]

Financial repression imposes a consistent bias, then, for export of domestic savings. Its effect, too, is to induce cycles of savings flows, tides in and out that cannot be absorbed by efficient adjustments on current accounts for trade. As excess demand accumulates on the foreign exchanges before a reluctant adjustment of the exchange rate, savers foresee and respond to prospective devaluation. When the devaluation has been done, providing usually a safety margin of undervaluation, savings return. Each return inflates bank reserves, and nominal money increases at a rate that cannot be matched by growth in real money demanded. Then momentum builds toward a new climax of overvaluation and depreciation. There is reiterative shock in the capital accounts of the balance of payments that must increase risk aversion to domestic investment.

When exports to open international markets are discouraged by distortion of exchange rates, bilateral trading becomes more attractive. Agreements are signed on terms that deteriorate as an exchange crisis deepens. Then exports are shifted to the bilateral account, but

[23] Bank of London and South America, *Review,* June, 1969, pp. 347–350.

goods and services expected in return are not always available on schedule and according to specification. The result is that the lagging economy builds credit balances abroad, exporting savings to bilateral trading partners while it appeals with growing urgency for imports of savings in multilateral trade. Normally, one understands, the credit balances yield no interest. Their domestic counterpart is bank credit for exporters, monetary expansion, and a further aggravation of foreign-exchange scarcity.

Policy in the lagging economy represses organized domestic markets for savings and generates black markets. There is a parallel on the international front. While a Mexico or a Taiwan can buy savings on competitive terms in foreign-capital markets, the lagging economy cannot. It drives itself out of the open market and into a number of peripheral markets—"brown" if not "black." There suppliers' credits are taken, short in term and bearing interest rates that are a multiple of open-market rates. The credits are not always available for finance of imports that comply best with domestic requirements. Service on this debt can quickly become a burden so severe that the lagging economy seeks funding for it on another peripheral market, for soft loans on government account.

Korea has concocted a policy brew that attracts foreign savings in overwhelming amounts. In 1966-68 alone, commercial loan agreements at maturities of three to seven years, in the main, increased from a small base of $78 million to $939 million, with import arrivals on current account absorbing approximately $535 million.[24] Domestic loan rates at banks had been raised in 1965, to 28 per cent and more for nonpriority loans, and rates on the curb market were 2 to 5 per cent monthly. When loans from abroad were offered at rates in the range of 8 to 10 per cent, subject to guarantee in the foreign currency by the Korean government or banks at moderate charges, the flood of capital was on. Foreign lenders were drawn by

[24] Data for Korean capital imports have come mainly from Gilbert T. Brown, *Pricing Policies and Economic Development: Korea in the 1960's.* The Johns Hopkins Press, in press; The Bank of Korea, *Review of the Korean Economy,* 1969.

the differential between their domestic rates of yield and Korean rates. Korean borrowers were drawn by the differential between costs of guaranteed loans and charges by domestic lenders on both organized and curb markets. The lenders were safe against default and exchange risk, and the borrowers seem not to have taken seriously the prospect that depreciation of the won might increase their effective interest costs.

Korea imposed disarray on money's relative prices, and from it arose an illusory view on the part of both borrowers and lenders regarding relative returns to savings in Korea and abroad. The borrowers were offered terms that represented the real yield r_f at the margin of investment in other countries *plus* an allowance P^*_f for anticipated inflation abroad. Their alternative domestic terms represented the real yield r_d at the margin of investment in Korea *plus* an allowance P^*_d for anticipated inflation in Korea. These options for borrowers may be written:

(3) $$r_d + P^*_d > r_f + P^*_f$$

The differential was high indeed, and the capital market set about to reduce it by savings flow. Charges by Korean government and banks for loan and exchange guarantees did not close the gap. Requirements for advance deposits by borrowers against loan-financed imports were insufficient. A freely floating foreign-exchange rate for the won would have reduced the gap quickly. In perfect markets, the excess of P^*_d over P^*_f would have been compensated by an expected rate a^* of appreciation in the won price of foreign exchange, with approximation to this equality:

(4) $$r_d + P^*_d = r_f + P^*_f + a^*$$

Given the forward premium on center money, the flow of savings would have responded to the differential in real productivities of investment, r_d and r_f. To be sure, the won was floating but under such restraint by Korean reserve accumulation that its spot rate of depreciation was no more than one-third of the margin between P_d and P_f—realized rates of inflation, perhaps much the same in relation to expected rates.

The flow of funds through this contrived, peripheral market did contribute to Korean capital accumulation, but with disturbing effects. As a relatively minor matter, Korea was borrowing funds at loan rates of interest and relending them abroad, at lower deposit rates of return, by a build-up of reserves in the Bank of Korea. Korea engaged, that is to say, in expensive intermediation. It is more important that overvaluation of the won accelerated growth in nominal money and in the pace of domestic inflation, from 11 per cent for the consumer-price index in 1967 to 16 per cent in 1970. The effect was to widen the interest-rate differential in (3) above and to increase Korea's magnetism for foreign funds. The effect was explosive, and it set the stage for both an increase in government interventions and a more substantial but still insufficient rate of exchange depreciation. Other adverse consequences are clear. Under guidance of selective tariff protection, the bulk of imported savings flowed to import-substitution industry, especially to fertilizer and cement production and to oil-refining. As the Bank of Korea puts it: ". . . such borrowings are low in production effect and so it can be anticipated that the improving effect of foreign capital on the balance of payments will be reduced."[25] Service on debt incurred during this episode of disequilibrium money is a burden on exports high enough "to give pause to both Korean officials and to foreign creditors."[26]

Effects of Capital Flow upon Finance

Inequalities of endowment the world over require, for welfare maximization, the flow of capital across national boundaries. With no intent of challenging this precept, one can argue that rescue capital for low-income economies which insist on disequilibrium money and related distortions tends to retard financial deepening and allied development. It is a reprieve from pressure to raise domestic tax rates, improve performance of government corporations or apply remedial measures of real finance policy. Projects deemed

[25] Bank of Korea, *op. cit.,* p. 120.
[26] Gilbert T. Brown, *op. cit.,* p. 3.

eligible for aid from abroad can be rounded up quickly, and foreign funds to finance them can defer for a while unification and reluctant adjustment of the foreign-exchange rate. At the bargaining tables for soft international assistance, which may be regarded as one of the brown or black capital markets that accompany financial repression and disequilibrium money, excess demands for savings and foreign exchange can be financed in an economically comfortable and politically gratifying way.[27]

Reluctant adjustment of the foreign-exchange rate, in a regime of discquilibrium money, is accompanied by surges of capital inflow. Part of the flow is repatriation of domestic funds, picking up profits of exchange speculation. Part of it typically is rescue capital from foreign governments and international agencies. Some of the proceeds are used to repay supplier credits and to consolidate debt abroad. Some of the proceeds are used to restore reserves. Normally there is also a substantial transfer of imports to renew supplies of "essential" goods and of imports in other classifications that qualify for low tariff duties. The effect is abrupt downward pressure on prices of goods that command the least tariff protection—the economy's most efficient firms and industries. For the long pull, the succession of balance-of-payments crises, ostensibly resolved by reluctant adjustment and capital inflow, drives savings away from outlets of comparative advantage and decreases rewards that can be paid to savers.

Bargaining in the brown market between the lagging economies and potential lenders does not always make available generalized

---

[27] K. G. Griffin and J. L. Enos, "Foreign Assistance: Objectives and Consequences," *Economic Development and Cultural Change,* April, 1970, pp. 313–327; Charles Issawi, Mitchell Kellman, Simon Rottenberg, "Foreign Assistance: Objectives and Consequences: Comments," and J. L. Enos and K. B. Griffin, "Foreign Assistance: Objectives and Consequences: A Reply to Our Critics," *Economic Development and Cultural Change,* October, 1971, pp. 142–158. Gunnar Myrdal has remarked, "Not least in India one often hears the suggestion that financial crises may not be entirely bad, as they induce the Western countries to come forth with assistance." *Asian Drama,* Volume I, p. 635, n. 1.

purchasing power abroad that can be put to uses best for growth.[28]
Foreign governments may agree to lend if the "aid" is tied to exports of their own at prices above free-market levels, in effect ex-
acting a rate of interest above the explicit contract rate. A greater
cost can be that aid goods displace potentially competitive domestic
output. In this case, the lagging economy should prefer fungible
savings for uses of its own choice, but it accepts instead savings
embodied in forms that suppress domestic industry. It sacrifices
comparative advantage for short-term assistance in its balance of
payments. In other cases, savings come embodied in capital equipment that is, or might once have been, optimal in the donor's economy but not in the lagging economy. To illustrate, the import may
be construction equipment that is right for office buildings in San
Francisco but hardly for warehouses in the Philippines or schools in
Thailand. If the equipment is to be used at all, complementary domestic resources must be drawn from potentially better uses. Briefly,
full costs of capital inflows do not appear even in the fine print of
brown-market contracts between the lagging economy and either
donor governments or foreign private direct investors. Nationalization of private capital is partly expression of resentment over terms
accepted, possibly in contracts for exploitation of bauxite deposits
or hardwood forests or oil pools, when the lagging economy was in
especially severe foreign-exchange shortage. Old brown-market contracts are torn up, but a new set is signed when crisis recurs. There
cannot be significant financial growth in the lagging economy for so
long as domestic opportunities to invest are displaced by foreign aid,
biased by it, or sold cheaply to foreign developers.

Inflows of aid have inflationary potentialities. A government receiving foreign funds may transfer them to the central bank and
spend the domestic proceeds on local development effort with low
import content. There is domestic monetary expansion, and excess
demand for local goods bids their prices higher. Some growth in demand is permitted to spill into markets for tradables, and the increment in reserves is drained away. The episode does not end in mone-

[28] H. Myint, *Economic Theory and the Underdeveloped Countries,* pp. 44–46.

tary stability for any of various reasons including inflation-inelasticity of tax revenues. The grant from abroad is a tax on foreign savers to finance some miscellany of imports to the lagging economy, and it is the occasion for a new levy of the inflation tax on domestic savers. Incidents of this kind demonstrate the "seamless web" that binds all elements of finance—international, fiscal, monetary—in restraint of growth.

THE CHOICE OF POLICY

Lagging economies have had their choice among styles of linkage, through the foreign-exchange market, between their domestic markets for money and the center's market. Some of them, at one stage or another, have experienced the range of styles from colonial money to the other extreme of disequilibrium money. Their choice has fallen on disequilibrium money, with occasional reluctant devaluation. In this section, we review the case for disequilibrium money and, in consideration of its costs, cast a vote for the floating exchange rate and allied reforms.

The Untouchable Price

The case for disequilibrium money denies the existence of equilibrium on markets for domestic money, savings, and foreign exchange in poor economies: equilibrium is a phantom goal for the economy lodged at some low level of income per capita and aspiring to some politically minimal growth rate of income. Excess supply of money, excess demand for savings and foreign exchange are structural defects, attributes of poverty, that only higher income can repair. In circumstances of disequilibrium, relative price is ineffective as an instrument of development, and intervention to clear excess demands is inevitable. In particular, change in the foreign-exchange rate is ineffective at best, disruptive economically and socially in the usual case. This is the untouchable price, and sometimes "devaluation" is the forbidden word.

As we know, defenders of disequilibrium money count on two

rigidities. One affects the domestic saving rate. Allegedly, the marginal propensity to save is a constant not susceptible, in the private sector, to inducements of relative price including real deposit rate or, in the public sector, to broadening of the tax base, for example, or corrections for revenue slippage. One puts this contention aside after examination of experience in Taiwan, Korea, Indonesia, and, among others, Brazil of late years. The second rigidity pertains to factor substitution in the production process. Linear programs of growth disclose foreign-exchange gaps—excess demand for imported inputs—that cannot be closed by changes in ratios of labor cost to capital cost or of prices for imports to prices of domestic substitutes or of export prices to costs of domestic inputs. This contention has been discredited by the extraordinary growth of new exports, on occasion even excessive growth, where incentives of relative price have been provided and by adjustments of factor combinations in production that can be observed where distortions in relative price have been relaxed.[29] The "constants" that support the case for "normal and permanent" disequilibrium money are not constants after all.

Other arguments mustered in favor of disequilibrium money can be put in a packet labeled "Devaluation does not work." Whether for Argentina in 1958-59, 1962 and 1965, for example, or for Ghana in 1967 and Chile or Colombia repeatedly, devaluation on the foreign-exchange market and allied measures including deceleration in growth of nominal money have not resolved satisfactorily, we are told, excess demand for foreign exchange. For one thing, it redistributes wealth and income regressively. Raising prices for tradables relative to non-tradables, it is a tax especially on labor. Price increases along with monetary restraint reduce the real stock of money and the flow of bank credit so that unemployment rises. Resentment of the working class against both a cut in real wage rates and loss of jobs naturally provokes social unrest. Moreover, workers lose money illusion in successive devaluations and respond with

[29] Jeffrey G. Williamson, *op. cit.*; Michael Roemer, "The Neoclassical Employment Model Applied to Ghanaian Manufacturing," Development Advisory Service, Harvard University, 1972.

demands for money-wage increases that destroy any stimulus to growth in total output.[30]

The reply must be that measures to defend an overvalued currency are inequitable. Monopoly rents accrue to holders of import licenses, credit rations, and other second monies. Business concentration and monopoly power is a corollary of detailed government intervention. Opportunities for speculative gain are opened on the foreign-exchange and other markets. Export industry and workers in it are discriminated against. It is normally luxury goods that benefit most from import-substitution. Moreover, it is not devaluation that taxes: devaluation merely makes explicit the tax that has been concealed in scarcities imposed by public policy. The present generation is taxed by measures that force it to a lower welfare surface, and future generations are forced to share in the tax by accumulation of debt on international brown markets. The special burden of exchange-rate adjustment on labor's employment rate can be temporary, while the rate of growth in money settles down to a lower level and foreign markets are opened for exports, but the burden of unemployment in capital-intensive production is permanent.

A second charge against devaluation is that it accelerates inflation. Sophisticated labor responds with wage-push, and the Phillips curve drifts rightward. The unemployment sequel of devaluation raises government's welfare costs, its deficit, and its demands upon the monetary system for use of the inflation tax. Flight capital returns from abroad so rapidly that it swells reserves of the monetary system and forces monetary expansion. Disequilibrium on the foreign exchanges is endogenous to the economy's underdevelopment, and it is bound to be rejuvenated by inflation.

The response must be that devaluation acknowledges inflation and that, if inflation resumes, the cause is growth in nominal money

---

[30] Oscar Braun and Leonard Joy, "A Model of Economic Stagnation—A Case Study of the Argentine Economy," *The Economic Journal,* December, 1968, pp. 868–887; Richard N. Cooper, *Currency Devaluation in Developing Countries,* International Finance Section, Princeton University, Essays in International Finance, No. 86, June, 1971.

supplied relative to growth in real money demanded. The monetary incontinence typically can be traced to a "strange tolerance of public deficits," and the lag in growth of real money demanded can be traced to government's failure in implementing policies complementary with devaluation.[31] Reluctant adjustment of the foreign-exchange rate is commonly a shock treatment, to retard growth in external debt, and is not combined with measures to increase public and private saving, activate the export trades, induce efficient factor substitutions, and dismantle the intricate array of distorting price signals.[32] It is a traumatic experience, violent enough to provoke bankruptcies in critical economic sectors and too violent for smooth reallocations of resources from one pattern of production to the more efficient pattern that fits resource endowments.

Devaluation cannot be a clean break with the past. It is followed by echo disturbances, including inflation or decline in exports, from stimuli preceding devaluation.[33] Sometimes these effects of old policies causing excess demand for foreign exchange are misinterpreted as effects of exchange depreciation. Beef and hide exports have tended to continue their decline after devaluation in Argentina not because of devaluation but because ranchers were rebuilding the herds of cattle that earlier public policies had taxed and decimated. Inflation has not stopped abruptly with devaluation in Chile because effects of inflationary price expectations linger. Exports of hardwood logs did not respond to devaluation in 1967 of the Ghanaian cedi

---

[31] Mario Henrique Simonsen, "Brazilian Inflation: Postwar Experience and Outcome of the 1964 Reforms," in Committee for Economic Development, *Economic Development Issues: Latin America*, p. 325.

[32] Ian Little, Tibor Scitovsky, Maurice Scott, *op. cit.*, pp. 327–329, 362–391, 468.

[33] John V. Deaver, "The Chilean Inflation and the Demand for Money," in David Meiselman (ed.), *Varieties of Monetary Experience* (Chicago: University of Chicago Press, 1970), pp. 7–68; Carlos F. Diaz-Alejandro, *Exchange Rate Devaluation in a Semi-industrialized Country: The Experience of Argentina, 1955–1961* (Committee for Economic Development, Supplementary Paper No. 21, August, 1967); Robert A. Mundell, "Growth, Stability, and Inflationary Finance," *Journal of Political Economy,* April, 1965, pp. 97–109.

because fiscal inefficiency had permitted deterioration in transport facilities from forest to port.

A third indictment of devaluation is that it increases the burden of external debt expressed in center money. After all, it is pointed out, the domestic value of debt service does rise. Government as debtor must collect more in tax revenues, and private debtors must raise prices on their products or economize on local costs to meet foreign claims against them. One replies that the increase in debt burden is nominal and not real, just one aspect of the general write-up in nominal values that results from excess money supply in the debtor country. With prices of tradables given in the center economy, the real volume of increase in exports to the center or of decrease in imports, to finance debt service, is no larger for the debtor economy after devaluation. Moreover, the effect of liberalizing measures including devaluation stimulates exports and encourages efficient domestic competition against imports so that the proportion of debt service to national product is reduced.[34]

The case against devaluation includes a fourth count, that devaluation done once increases the chance, as speculators and international investors see it, of devaluation a second and more times. A currency with such prospects is said to be easy prey for destabilizing speculation. The decisive rejoinder is provided by experience with flexible exchanges in Canada and Lebanon, for example; Brazil and Chile during recent years; or Austria and Russia during the nineteenth century.[35] Speculators attack a currency because it is vulnerable, as indicated by a discrepancy between decreed parity and purchasing-power parities in commodity and capital markets, and not because a decreed parity has changed. They seek out a currency that is futilely resisting a substantial reluctant adjustment.

The international investor would prefer, other things being equal,

[34] Richard N. Cooper, *op. cit.,* pp. 17–18.
[35] Leland B. Yeager, "Fluctuating Exchange Rates in the Nineteenth Century: The Experiences of Austria and Russia," in Robert A. Mundell and Alexander K. Swoboda (eds.), *op. cit.,* pp. 61–89; Milton Friedman, *Essays in Positive Economics,* pp. 157–203; International Monetary Fund, *Annual Report 1967,* Chapter 4.

a stable exchange rate for transfers of capital and earnings. A stable rate is not inviting, however, when it is likely to be protected by bans on profit repatriation, by repudiation of loan contracts, or by especially severe taxation of foreign enterprise. Measures in defense of an overvalued currency become more painful to the investor than devaluation. Their effect is to raise his supply price of savings severely enough to force the lagging economy into the peripheral markets for international borrowing.[36]

A currency that is allowed now and then to slip in value relative to the center currency is said to lose some degree of its money-ness: a step outside of the fixed band is a step toward barter.[37] If money of the developing economy is detached from a fixed link with the center, it loses some utility as a means of payment, and one effect must be to shift demand toward the center money. The answer, we know, is that methods of supporting disequilibrium money work against money deepening. The disequilibrium system generates multiple monies internally, increasing costs of the payments mechanism and fragmentizing the payments' matrix. It reduces money's real deposit rate, and it increases the variance of the rate. Money holders in Montevideo or Accra, watching black-market quotations in Buenos Aires and Lome for domestic money in terms of center money can hardly regard real deposit rate as a stable price. Comparative aversion to money holding is one of the distinctive characteristics of the disequilibrium money regime.

Another charge against devaluation as one component of the liberalizing program is that it debilitates centrist planning of development. The thrust of chronic excess demand for foreign exchange brings participants in international trade to the planning authority and gives the authority opportunities to scan and control the flow of goods and capital. This point has lost its appeal in the light of

[36] Regarding the country that plays the game of reluctant adjustment, Egon Sohmen writes, "The acquisition of claims denominated in the currency of such a country does not merely involve an exchange *risk,* as it would with flexible exchanges, but an exchange *loss* known with certainty in advance." Egon Sohmen, *op. cit.,* p. 201.
[37] Robert A. Mundell, "A Theory of Optimum Currency Areas," *The American Economic Review,* September, 1961, pp. 657–665.

experience with frailties of public administration in lagging economies. Governments incapable of effective tax collection or efficient
administration of public enterprises are hardly qualified to optimize
international trade by intervention in detail.[38]

Notwithstanding hostility to it, devaluation does recur in the disequilibrium system: the exchange rate, in principle untouchable, is
pushed down in substantial, discrete steps. Managed as it is, costs to
the lagging economy are high. Abrupt devaluations, such as the one
by 90 per cent for Ghana's new cedi in December, 1971, cannot
be turned quickly to the benefit of exports: their short-run elasticity
of supply is not high, and it takes time to generate foreign demand.
It can be immediately disastrous for importers in various categories
and for some import-substitution industry, with bankruptcy of firms
and unemployment of workers the result. Short-run elasticities are
small enough that windfall gains from depreciation cannot take immediate effect in clearing excess demand for foreign exchange, and
windfall losses cannot be ameliorated by diversions of resources to
new products and markets. To make matters worse, abrupt devaluation is rarely associated with other measures to reduce the national
savings deficit. The crisis context is not congenial for financial deepening and acceleration of private saving, more effective fiscal effort,
and reallocation of resources to market opportunities at the new
exchange rate.

The Flexible Exchange Rate

Lagging economies have chosen the worst of foreign-exchange
regimes, disequilibrium money with excess demand repressed inef-
fectively by interventions. Among the alternatives, colonial money
is unacceptable for its sacrifice of sovereignty. Satellite money depends upon a degree of economic integration with the center economy that few developing economies desire or can achieve. Autonomous money gives the exchange rate little scope as an instrument
for closing gaps of excess demand and shifts burdens of adjustment
onto reserves, variations in capital flows, changes in growth rates
of nominal money, reallocations of resources domestically, and

[38] Harry G. Johnson, *op. cit.*, p. 25.

employment rates of capital goods and labor. The ballot here is cast for the alternative of rate flexibility, even in preference to Brazil's "trotting peg."[39] This is not the counsel of despair that it once seemed to be.[40]

Real money policy for deepening the financial system includes specification of a target growth rate, preferably low, for inflation of the domestic price level. One instrument in guiding the price level, given growth in real money demanded, is the growth rate of nominal money. An alternative instrument, for the "small" developing economy, is the essentially inflexible foreign-exchange rate that imports a rate of inflation from the center economy and adapts growth in nominal money to it through balance-of-payments adjustment. There is choice between an autonomous inflation rate, with growth in nominal money domestically imposed, and an imported inflation rate, with growth in nominal money externally imposed. The choice is a matter of indifference for the small economy only when the same inflation rate is to the taste of both domestic and external monetary authorities. When tastes diverge, use of both control instruments —domestic nominal money management and the inflexible exchange rate—provokes a confrontation of monetary authorities with the authority of the small economy inevitably the loser.[41] Out of this conflict, disequilibrium systems emerge. Satellite pricing on the foreign-exchange market is not tenable, with freedom of trade in goods and

[39] J. B. Donges, *Brazil's Trotting Peg,* Institut für Weltwirtschaft, Kiel, January, 1971; George N. Halm (ed.), *Approaches to Greater Flexibility of Exchange Rates,* The Bürgenstock Papers, Princeton, 1970; Ian Little, Tibor Scitovsky, Maurice Scott, *op. cit.,* p. 326.

[40] The case for flexibility is opposed by authority that one challenges at his peril. John Stuart Mill regarded it as "barbarism" that "independent countries choose to assert their nationality by having . . . a peculiar currency of their own." Robert A. Mundell speaks of flexibility as "Balkanization," presumably barbaric, that imposes "exceptionally large" losses in money's potential income effect. John Stuart Mill, *Principles of Political Economy,* edited by Sir W. J. Ashley, new impression, pp. 614–615; Robert A. Mundell, *International Economics,* pp. 182–186, and *Monetary Theory: Inflation, Interest and Growth in the World Economy,* p. 93.

[41] Jagdish Bhagwati, *op. cit.,* pp. 62–63; Peter B. Kennen, "The Theory of Optimum Currency Areas: An Eclectic View," in Robert A. Mundell and

capital, in the presence of chronic differential rates of inflation or of chronic differences in the variability of inflation rates. Flexible pricing is the right answer for the small economy that chooses to do better with the inflation rate than the world outside can do.

Real money policy for deepening also implies free convertibility on the foreign exchanges—no license for this payment or compulsory surrender to the monetary authority of that receipt. Money's maximum income effect and other benefits from financial markets depend on freedom of payment and transfer through the widest efficient matrix of transactions. It is not achieved when payments are forced to run a gauntlet of rationing and are subjected to the costs and risk of black markets. The optimal foreign-exchange market arrives at a single or unified spot rate of foreign exchange rather than at multiple rates in conjunction with interventions to clear excess demands.[42]

Optimal policy requires a clear stipulation by the monetary authority of its inflation target. The appropriate target seems to be an index of non-tradables and specifically of prices for consumer goods. It is the relevant numeraire for bargaining over real rewards to productive factors. In the absence of relative gains or losses in productivity between tradables and non-tradables and with a flexible exchange rate, price levels for the two classes of goods would move along the same path. However, the typical gains in productivity that are achieved, in the course of development, for goods that can flow in international commerce, would result in a lower trajectory for them and possibly in a secular decline.[43]

Alexander K. Swoboda, *Monetary Problems of the International Economy,* p. 54; Ronald I. McKinnon, "Optimum Currency Areas," *The American Economic Review,* September, 1963, pp. 717–724; Michael G. Porter, "A Theoretical and Empirical Framework for Analyzing the Term Structure of Exchange Rate Expectations," in International Monetary Fund, *Staff Papers,* November, 1971, p. 638.

[42] Egon Sohmen, *Flexible Exchange Rates,* rev. ed., p. 187.

[43] Ronald I. McKinnon, *Monetary Theory and Controlled Flexibility in the Foreign Exchanges,* Essays in International Finance, International Finance Section, Department of Economics, Princeton University, No. 84, April, 1971, pp. 23–27.

The flexible exchange rate need not reduce the social rate of return on international reserves, in the portfolio of the monetary authority, to so low a level as to displace reserves completely. At the price of alternative resource uses foregone, each increment in average reserve balances can shrink a little the variance of the foreign-exchange rate around its path of growth and temper the risk of international trading. There are alternative devices including a forward exchange market with private-reserve accumulations, but the likelihood is that they would fall short of optimality from the standpoint of the entire trading community. They are appropriate but insufficient in view of the compounding of costs through the community as a whole when exchange-rate variance increases.

The liberalized foreign-exchange market, with its spot rate free to vary and with full convertibility, generates quotations for forward contracts. Forward premia and discounts on domestic money in terms of the center currency neutralize differences in nominal rates of interest so that savers and investors in either country see only those differences that reflect spreads in real rates of return to capital. Each upward deviation in the small economy's inflation rate from the inflation rate of the center economy produces its forward premium on the center money, each relative decline in the small economy's inflation rate its forward discount on center money. Whatever the forward rate, savings are drawn to the developing economy by the residual margin for real rates of interest. Their direction and volume of flow are not twisted by such illusory spreads in real rates as appear when spot exchange rates are insensitive to relative inflationary experience and especially when savings flow are obstructed by the interventionism of the disequilibrium system. Free convertibility in a regime of flexible spot and forward exchange rates reduces risks in savings flows and must be counted as a particularly vigorous policy instrument for raising savers' real deposit rate into line with savings' scarcity price.[44]

If only the lagging economy could be persuaded into domestic financial deepening and liberalization of the foreign exchanges, it

[44] Egon Sohmen, *op. cit.*, Chapters III–IV.

could be a magnet for foreign savings. Savers and investors abroad could be counted upon to satisfy a larger share of their portfolio demands by direct and indirect investment in the lagging economy's capital stock if they were paid full deposit rate, if the rate of inflation were reduced and stabilized and if the lagging economy were to accept flexible pricing and full convertibility on the foreign exchanges.[45] Acceleration of growth in the lagging economy, from a faster accumulation of capital, would have its cumulative effect in brightening savers' anticipations. At the same time, upward flexibility of the foreign-exchange price for domestic money, in the context of capital inflow, could adjust the flow to the small economy's capacity to absorb funds productively. There need be no capital flows that swamp the domestic monetary system.

The economy that liberalizes can reduce its demand price for foreign savings. Special concessions that are paraded in front of foreign investors can be withheld when it is possible to offer instead competitive rates of interest and assurance of repatriation for profits and debt service across open foreign-exchange markets. Tied aid can be accepted with more reserve, and the begging missions for soft foreign loans can be given better things to do. Sacrifices of sovereignty in bits to foreign savers and investors are a casualty of the financing process that depends solely on attractions of relative yields in the capital-poor small economy.

In that seamless web of finance, foreign-exchange liberalization must imply benefits for fiscal effort in the small economy. Foreign investment can be taxed when the capital market is open and the foreign-exchange market has its flexible pricing and free convertibility. Exporters can get along without their tax remissions when there is not an overvalued foreign-exchange rate to contend with. Importers can be subjected to a uniform revenue tariff at some moderate rate and need not be enriched with the monopoly value of import and other licenses. The infant-industry loophole for losses of tax revenues becomes smaller when domestic production can develop along lines of comparative advantage rather than in ways that seem

[45] Tibor Scitovsky, *Money & the Balance of Payments,* pp. 127–129.

necessary for defense of a disequilibrium foreign-exchange rate. The smuggling that conceals commerce from tax collectors in the lagging economy becomes unprofitable when the effective rate of foreign exchange is permitted to reflect relative profitability of internal and external markets. Both fiscal effort and financial deepening are beneficiaries of foreign-exchange liberalization.

8 | Instability in Lagging Economies

Earlier chapters have been concerned mainly with the low trajectory of aggregative output and income in lagging economies. They have presented the thesis that these economies are tethered to poverty by inept policy affecting particularly the financial, fiscal, and international sectors. Policy sacrifices the leverage for growth that could be realized from financial deepening, improved fiscal performance, and closer integration with external markets. Now we shorten perspective and consider stability in the lagging economies during short periods. The degree of instability has been higher than in developed economies, at least since 1950. Low growth has been unstable growth.

Short-period pulsations above and below the trend line can be blamed partly on the lagging economies' trading partners: there has been transmission of instability from the relatively rich to the relatively poor. Some of the pulsations appear to be echo effects of stimuli that can be traced to the past. Changes in the pace of growth that concern us are "cyclic episodes." Their storm center is the market for capital in the sense of savings. They pass through a standard sequence of phases, from acceleration of economic activity above its norm to deceleration below. They are imposed by public policy: policy reaches in the boom phase of the episode for unsustainable rates of growth in output and generates such excess demand for savings and such drains upon reserves of various kinds that a stabilization crisis ensues, then a retreat to sub-normal rates of growth that last until easing in the capital market clears the way for another impulsive and futile effort toward faster growth than basic constraints permit.

The first section below provides evidence on instability. The second is a brief review of some usual explanations for lagging economies' experience in the short run. Then the outlines of the cyclic episode are traced through the boom, stabilization crisis, recession, and recovery. The fourth and fifth sections analyze destabilizing effects of public policies through each cycle phase. The concluding section suggests measures of policy and control technique to reduce the cycle's frequency and severity.

INDICATORS OF INSTABILITY

It is not difficult to muster evidence of instability in developed economies since World War II. The United States has wobbled through a succession of short business cycles. The United Kingdom is notorious for its habituation to stop-go. France, the Federal Republic of Germany, Japan, and the others have experienced their own brief cyclical swings. Fluctuation has been relatively so slight, however, that the question has been put quite soberly, "Is the business cycle obsolete?"[1] Perhaps, it is sometimes suggested, instability has become a matter merely of change between higher and lower growth rates rather than between boom and depression. Since econometric evidence has mounted that the developed economies are inherently stable, always tending to settle down to the business of steady growth, instability may be merely a transient response to exogenous shock.[2] If this evidence is correct, the community of developed economies may be more stable than its individual members, with random disturbances that stimulate activity somewhere balanced by disturbances that depress activity somewhere else.

[1] Martin Bronfenbrenner (ed.), *Is the Business Cycle Obsolete?*
[2] Bert G. Hickman, "Dynamic Properties of Macroeconomic Models: An International Comparison," in Martin Bronfenbrenner (ed.), *ibid.,* pp. 393–435.

One can feel no comparable assurance that clues to stability have been found by economies at the lower end of the scale in levels of economic well-being and in rates of growth.[3] Pessimism on this count has led to the suggestion that comprehensive planning is fruitless in many or most of the low-income economies.[4] Even staunch defenders of planning grant that its context commonly is crisis in the balance of payments, for example, or the fiscal budget or the inflation rate.[5] At best, the Plan must roll in response to instabilities of behavioral and technical parameters. Its priorities frequently are pushed aside under the stress of emergency, and its long-run horizon is obscured by extemporized responses of public policy to immediate pressures.

Instability has been so chronic and severe in a number of lagging economies, not only in Latin America, that its dynamics are difficult or impossible to deduce with any precision.[6] As a result, there is skepticism that macroeconomic policies for stabilization, in the mode of fine-tuning, have relevance for any immediate future. Paths of excess demands are so affected by lagged responses to earlier disturbance or by instabilities of expectations that any intricate scheme of stabilizers has slight chance of success.[7]

Instability of lagging economies has been especially evident in their relationships with the world outside. For example, export receipts during 1954–66 were less stable, perhaps by one-half, than export receipts of developed and rapidly developing economies.[8]

[3] O. E. C. D., *National Accounts of Less Developed Countries, 1950–1966.*

[4] Albert Waterston, "A Hard Look at Development Planning," *Finance and Development,* June, 1966, pp. 8-13.

[5] Richard D. Mallon, "Planning in Crisis," *Journal of Political Economy,* July/August, 1970, Part II, p. 948.

[6] Arnold C. Harberger, "Economic Policy Problems in Latin America: A Review," *Journal of Political Economy,* July/August, 1970, Part II, p. 1012.

[7] Jere R. Behrman, "Price Determination in an Inflationary Economy: The Dynamics of Chilean Inflation Revisited," Discussion Paper No. 151, The Wharton School of Finance and Commerce, March, 1970, pp. 36–39.

[8] G. F. Erb and Salvatore Schiavo-Campo, "Export Instability, Level of Development, and Economic Size of Less Developed Countries," *Bulletin,* Oxford Institute of Statistics, May, 1970, pp. 263–283; Benton Massell, "Export Instability and Economic Structure," *The American Economic Review,* September, 1970, p. 628.

The experience of lagging economies is replete with episodes of imports carefully conserved to save foreign exchange and of restrictions relaxed extravagantly when foreign exchange is available.[9] Major export crops have been subjected at times to repressive measures, as part of programs to diversify output, and stimulated later for the sake of easing foreign-exchange scarcity, and the effects have been apparent both in international prices of such commodities as cocoa and in crop proceeds. Unpredictability of trading performance has been responsible for accumulation of external debt and of burdensome service on it. The catalogue of restrictions on dealings in the foreign-exchange markets of lagging economies confirms the other evidence that stable growth of trade is still not in sight.[10]

Aggregative data to measure reliably economic instability in a comparative way among economies are not available.[11] Estimates of national product remain so imprecise that error components can dominate short-term changes. However, components of national product that are measured directly and fairly uniformly from year to year, in lagging economies, show the same relative variability, in comparison with their counterparts for advanced or rapidly growing economies, as appears in the international trading accounts. Low trajectories of growth in electric power production, investment in equipment, or, say, housing construction go along with unstable trajectories.

TRADITIONAL EXPLANATIONS OF INSTABILITY

There have been numerous explanations of relative instability in lagging economies. We consider a few here before turning to our hypothesis in the next section. Finding a right explanation is impor-

[9] Ian Little, Tibor Scitovsky, Maurice Scott, *Industry and Trade in Some Developing Countries: A Comparative Study,* pp. 362–391.

[10] International Monetary Fund, *Annual Reports on Exchange Restrictions.*

[11] Simon Kuznets, "Problems in Comparing Recent Growth Rates of Developed and Less Developed Countries," *Economic Development and Cultural Change,* January, 1972, pp. 185–209; Everett E. Hagan and Oli Hawrylyshyn, "Analysis of World Income and Growth, 1955–1965," *Economic Development and Cultural Change,* October, 1969, Part II, pp. 52–61.

tant because it distinguishes policies and instruments that may reduce instability from policies and instruments that make matters worse.

Imported Instability

There is a strong tradition, especially in Latin America, that instability in lagging economies—with Uruguay, Argentina, and Colombia as examples—is imported, imposed from outside rather than generated inside. Allegedly the industrialized countries are inherently unstable, and they transmit instability to their less developed trading partners through both current and capital accounts. Their inherent instability buffets trade with lagging economies in magnified degree because their demands are income-elastic, price-inelastic on current account, and because, on capital account, their exports of savings are vulnerable to wide changes in income and in risk aversion. Moreover, their policies to remedy domestic instability not infrequently have a beggar-thy-neighbor bias both in boom and recession: they may dump goods and savings abroad when that serves their purposes, obstruct trade flows when that is convenient. Experiences of the 1930's are cited, but there are others during World War II and the Korean War and even during 1964–72 when advanced economies responded to difficulties on the foreign-exchange markets by interference with trade.[12]

Some countries have sealed themselves against imported instability and apparently benefited. There were Argentina, Germany, and others in the 1930's. Socialist economies escaped behind a barrier of their own. These drop-outs are precedent for the isolationist tradition that has been strong among lagging economies. Since 1950, import substitution has proceeded rapidly, especially in countries hard hit by adverse trends or pronounced cycles in terms of trade.[13] For a few, it has been compatible with relatively high, though usually decelerating rates of growth in national product. Their experience, together with antipathy to neo-colonial dependence on ad-

[12] Raul Prebisch, *Change and Development: Latin America's Great Task,* Report submitted to the Inter-American Development Bank; W. Arthur Lewis, *The Theory of Economic Growth,* pp. 283–292.
[13] Raul Prebisch, *ibid.,* pp. 53–62.

vanced economies, has accounted for some of the momentum behind restraint of trade and an associated proliferation of direct controls. External factors can account for only a small share of instability in lagging economies since World War II. Cycles have been mild and disynchronous in advanced economies, and "the mechanism for the international transmission of cycles now seems to be highly damped."[14] A world trade model of the International Monetary Fund, fitted to the period 1950–65, estimates an elasticity of less than unity for response of exports from developing countries to industrial production in developed countries.[15] On capital account, annual changes in net imports of lower-income countries were small, averaging $700 million. Stability within the more advanced economies went along with stability in their imports of goods and services from the less advanced and in their exports of savings. The lagging world was bumping up and down in its own succession of waves.

No one denies that some impulses to instability originate in advanced economies and spread along trade channels. Terms of trade have fluctuated, in response to factors of demand as well as to factors of supply, for major producers of coffee, cocoa, rubber, oil, and tin. Inflation has spread from the United States, especially since 1968, to advanced and lagging economies alike. Still these impulses can be blunted and dispersed in the developing economy that permits its foreign-exchange and interest rates to float, generates savings for investment in efficiently diversified agriculture and industry, and settles down to a stable policy for supply of a major export commodity.

There is a second explanation of instability in lagging economies that blames the world outside. An economy that is open necessarily submits, it is said, to external interference with domestic policy. The rules it must accept, for membership in the international trading community, are incompatible with the structure of domestic markets,

<hr />

[14] Richard E. Caves, "Discussion," *The American Economic Review,* May, 1962, p. 124.
[15] Rudolph R. Rhomberg, "Transmission of Business Fluctuations from Developed to Developing Countries," pp. 257–267, in Martin Bronfenbrenner (ed.), *op. cit.*

and the result is recurrent discontinuity in monetary, fiscal, and trading policy. Where inflation is structural, insistence from outside that it be dealt with by restraint on fiscal deficits and on growth in nominal money leads to financial crisis and cessation of growth. Monetary and other policies that may work for advanced economies, the argument continues, are inappropriate for a lagging economy, and some of its instability is allergic reaction.

There is some substance in this argument, too. International agencies and foreign creditors have made unreasonable demands. Among conditions for assistance to a lagging economy in trouble, they have emphasized restraint too much and fiscal, financial, and trade reform too little. Still, the manner that is common for dealing with disequilibrium in international accounts affects advanced and lagging economies alike, and it is optimal for neither. There is no structural peculiarity of a lagging economy that requires special therapy.

Economic Specialization

Insufficient diversification in national product is ranked high among causes of instability.[16] A lagging economy depending substantially on oil or cotton, rice or jute, cattle or sugar is held to be vulnerable not only to vagaries of external demand and competition but to internal disturbance. A crop failure, a technological lapse in one sector, a strike by one union are shocks that can have important aggregative effect. Specialization for the sake of comparative advantage is a risky commitment of national resources, trading away potential stability of income for expected gain in the average level of income. Risk-averse public policy is for diversification. Policy-makers in various lagging economies have been impressed with the prospect that internal diversification wards off shocks from the outside and from the inside too.

Mistrust of "market forces" is strong in some lagging economies. It is doubted that markets relatively free of official intervention can find defenses against external and internal shock. The capacity of open markets and flexible prices to shift demands away from scarce

16 Benton F. Massell, *op. cit.*

outputs or to direct resources, along lines of comparative advantage, to more stable outputs is discounted. Specialization implies vulnerability, it is said, and the lagging economy is not designed to absorb shock or to ameliorate it. Self-sufficiency, diversification through linkages expanding outward from a strategic sector, centralized planning of output at prescribed prices are a shelter against shock and irrationalities of market responses to it.

There has been a remarkable laboratory test of the hypothesis that national specialization, with relatively high ratios of exports and imports to total product, invites instability. During the past quarter-century, some countries in Latin America, including Mexico and then Brazil, have taken the route of relatively heavy dependence on exports and comparatively limited import-substitution while others have taken the other tack.[17] Japan, Taiwan, South Korea, Hong Kong, and Singapore have integrated with the world outside. It seems fair to conclude that, on grounds both of stability and of sustained growth, the import-substitution alternative has come out second best and that, if only through development of regional blocs of trading partners, economic interdependence will be promoted.

Structural Cycles

Aggregate instability has been attributed by most observers to the structure of private-enterprise economies. There are numerous models to explain a common origin of successive, rhythmic departures from growth paths.[18] These models are built around technological inflexibilities and behavioral constants. Delayed responses to stimuli are essential elements of the models, and these may be attributed to technology, behavioral preferences, and imperfect foresight.

There are models of economic development that generate repetitive short cycles. They may specify propensities to save that are fixed or change at a given rate, capital-output ratios that are insensitive to relative price, labor supply that becomes accessible in a pre-

[17] Raul Prebisch, *op. cit.,* pp. 98–100.
[18] For examples, see Bert G. Hickman, *op. cit.,* and R. G. D. Allen, *Macro-Economic Theory,* Chapters 19–20.

scribed flow, rates of external-debt accumulation that take a preordained exponential path. With propensities, ratios, rates, and time lags in suitable pattern, the synthesized economy expands until and excess demand encounters a bottleneck of supply and can be resolved only by general recession of economic activity. Recession continues until there is an excess demand that can be resolved only by general recovery of economic activity. Bottlenecks above trend and bottlenecks below trend keep the economy moving in its distinctive rhythmic pattern.

Whatever their relevance to advanced economies, these models are inappropriate to the lagging economies. Propensities aggregatively to consume or save or import are not constants, even at some "full-employment" proportion of national product to rated capacity of resources. Capital-labor and capital-output ratios are not uniform across the spectrum of industry, and they vary at the margin of growth. Time lags are not constants even in corn-hog cycles and certainly not in responses of manpower supply to changes in real wage rates, of rice planting to changes in fertilizer prices, of money rates of interest to realized inflation.

Especially in lagging economies, market segmentation puts shortperiod instability beyond the reach of explanation by fixed-response models that describe a repetitive wave-like sequence in degrees of resource utilization. Economies with enclaves of modernized industry surrounded by indigenous industry, market-oriented agriculture in the midst of subsistence agriculture, administered capital markets in the midst of curb markets do not resemble a pendulum. The relatively large share of public sectors in lagging economies and the intensity of governmental intervention make it still more fruitless to look for that small number of equations which will define the pendulum's arc.

THE CYCLIC EPISODE

We suggest that instability is episodic in lagging economies. Each episode begins with a shock, internal or external, that drives the economy from its depressed growth path. The shock may strike any market initially, but the effect wears off quickly if capital markets are not involved. When they develop significant disequilibrium, the initial disturbance is followed by a standard sequence of steps back to the growth path. Echo effects may linger, but they are damped and may be counted among the circumstances that restrain growth.

The cyclic episode along with the depressed growth path is a consequence of public policy affecting particularly finance, the fiscal budget and the international accounts. Shocks could be absorbed with fewer and milder interruptions of growth if policy did not distort relative prices, reduce and misallocate savings, shorten horizons for commitments to the future, and, in still other ways, put up barriers to efficiently selective wealth accumulation and deployment. Low growth and unstable growth are joint products of imposed distortion.

Profile of the Cyclic Episode

The aggregative capital market is the storm center of the cyclic episode. This is a generalized account of its role: departure of the economy from trend begins with access for real investment to an accelerated flow of real savings, and the ensuing growth in income above trend generates additional savings flows but at a rate that diminishes relative to desired capital formation: there is increasing dependence on such sources of savings as the inflation tax and foreign borrowing and on disinvestment in one form of wealth to support growth in another: excess demand for savings becomes intolerable, a stabilization crisis is induced, and recession leads the economy back to its growth path. Throughout the process, public policy acts as a drag upon real savings and encourages their allocation to uses with high capital-output ratios.

Flow equilibrium on the capital market may be written:

(1) $c \, \Delta \, F(K, L) = sF(K, L)$

Here c is an index of marginal capital-output ratios that vary over a wide range in the lagging economy, while s is an average propensity to supply savings on the part of domestic and foreign, private, and public savers. The expression on the left of equation (1) is demand for real savings, and the expression on the right is the flow of real savings. Dividing by income, one obtains:

$$(2) \qquad\qquad\qquad cY = s$$

One recognizes, of course, that "equilibrium" on the capital market is imposed by diverse controls on excess demands in all markets.[19]

Especially in lagging economies, c and s cannot be constants. For present purposes, we suggest:

$$(3) \qquad c\,(K, X, r, w, f, v)\,Y = s\,(E, D, r, r_f, d, f, v)$$

Here the capital-output index depends positively on the existing stock of productive equipment K and negatively on its degree of utilization X, positively also on the real wage rate w and on the price f of domestic in terms of foreign exchange, negatively on the real domestic loan rate of interest r. The savings coefficient, relating to all savings sources, depends positively on E and D, representing domestic and foreign equities in K, positively on domestic real rates of interest r and d, negatively on foreign rates of interest r_f and on f. It is net of domestic savings exported. Shocks and discontinuities along with government controls are suggested by v. It is both realistic and important for the analysis below that the arguments in (3) generate increases in cY relative to s, and so in Y relative to the ratio s/c, as Y is raised.

Flows of desired savings and investment represent intentional adjustments in the domestic stock of capital and equity in it, a movement toward stock equilibrium in which domestic K, valued at reproduction cost, is equal to the E and D that wealth holders wish to have as part of their portfolios. In analysis of the long run, one supposes that stock equilibrium is continuously maintained, given restraints imposed by official intervention, by the flows described in (3). In the short run, there can be stock disequilibrium, which de-

---

[19] For a convenient description of simple growth models with c and s as parameters, see R. G. D. Allen, *op. cit.*, Chapter 11.

sired flows of savings and investment are intended to correct, and
flow disequilibrium as well, which frustrates portfolio adjustments.

In Figure VIII.1, the 45-degree ray *ee'* traces both equilibria and
ex-post identities between flows of supply and demand on the capital
market. The curve *tt'* is the result of inserting successive values of Y
into equation (3) as well as into coexistent equations for all other markets. The intersection of *ee'* and *tt'* at point 1 in the chart is the
equilibrium solution for equation (3), indicating the growth rate Ox
in output at which desired savings, for domestic use, and desired domestic investment are realized. We interpret *tt'* as representing the
long-run conditions of accumulation in the lagging economy, and the
trend rate of growth Ox reflects the repressions that we have discussed in earlier chapters. While growth remains at this figure, participants in the saving-investment process are maintaining the balance sheets that they desire in the context of repression.

The curve *uu'* of Figure VIII.2 represents a temporary shift of *tt'*,
the result of a disturbance in the *v*'s of equation (3). There is a wind-

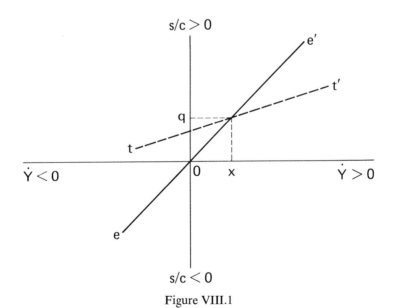

Figure VIII.1

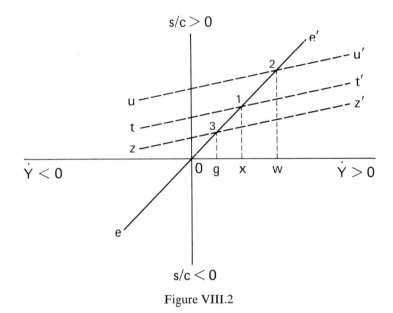

Figure VIII.2

fall of real savings that lifts tt' temporarily, and the desired s/c ratio is raised at each rate of income growth by, say, a bumper crop in agriculture, a short-lived improvement in external terms of trade or a liberalization of terms on outstanding external debt. The growth rate can rise from Ox to Ow without unsustainable distortions of portfolios, but the release is temporary. There is an episodic increase in both sides of equation (3), and in due time uu' must fall back toward tt'. Over the long run, the economy may have a slightly higher income, with growth restored to its old, low rate. Of course, there can be an adverse windfall, with tt' slumping temporarily in the direction of zz'.

The disturbance that raises tt' is a familiar starting point for a cyclic episode in aggregate economic activity in the lagging economy, as we suggest in Figure VIII.3. Starting from flow and stock equilibrium on the capital market at point 1, the economy moves to a position suggested by point 4 where $sc > \dot{Y}$, with excess demand for do-

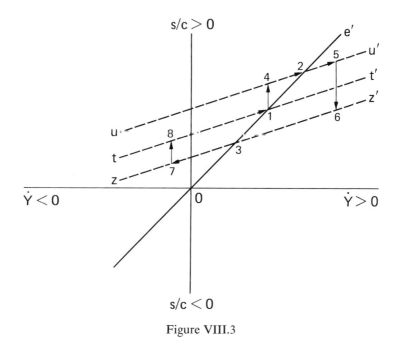

Figure VIII.3

mestic productive wealth or, in Wicksellian terms, with the market rate
of interest r reduced relative to the "natural" rate of return. As desired
growth in physical wealth materializes, Y accelerates to point 2. An
over-shoot occurs, from 2 to 5, because public policy induces or permits acceleration in growth of aggregate effective demand for output
beyond the growth rate Ow. What happens next can occur without the
real windfall that shifts tt', if public policy induces or permits excessive
growth of real effective demand for output that takes the economy
rightward along tt', from the initial equilibrium at point 1. The abnor-
mal growth rate associated with 5 can be sustained for a time but only
at the expense of increasing stock disequilibrium on the capital market.
The margin between uu' and ee' may be closed, at the high rate of
growth in output, by a temporary growth in external debt or, say, by
savings that accrue from unexpected inflation. These solutions for dis-

equilibrium have a short life. The expansion phase of the episode ends, and the economy enters the stabilization crisis.

The crisis is suggested in Figure VIII.3 by the path 5-6. The real windfall has been absorbed, excess demand for savings has accrued and has been resolved temporarily, and now sharp constraint is imposed on aggregate effective demand for output. The curve uu' slumps to zz', overshooting the normal path of tt', and demand constraint must drive the economy to successively lower rates of growth along the path from 6 to 3. The restraint is excessive, with the result that 3 is passed, and the recession ends, perhaps with income falling absolutely, at point 7. In due time, the boom 1-4-2-5, the crisis 5-6, and the recession 6-3-7 are succeeded by recovery 7-8-1 to the steady but still-lagging growth rate. There the economy awaits a new impulse, internal or external, to produce a new episode of instability. It is reasonable to suppose that the low growth rate at position 1 reflects risk aversion by savers and investors to the repetitive boom, crisis, and bust.

PUBLIC POLICY IN THE CYCLIC BOOM

The cyclic episode is the result of random stimuli to real growth and of destabilizing response by public policy. The stimulus opens the way for escape from lethargic growth, but policies that we consider now move the economy to a position of crisis. The analysis begins with financial policy and continues to policy in the fiscal and international sectors.

Financial Policy

The first sign of release to come from the lethargy at point 1 can be an increase in growth rates of demand for real balances of money and other liquid financial assets. The reason for it may be a fall in the expected rate of inflation in response to news of bumper crops, of increases in import quotas, or, say, of success in official negotiations for more generous external aid. Early manifestations of it can be a surge in growth of time and savings deposits, a decline of interest rates on the curb market, a softening of black-market quotations for foreign exchange, or an inflow of reserves into the central bank.

Even at a declining rate of inflation, growth in loan portfolios of financial institutions can be faster: loan rationing can be more generous. Perhaps it will direct savings to investment at reduced levels of c, the incremental capital-output ratio. For example, savings may flow into higher average levels of inventory so that production shutdowns are less frequent and plant capacity can be utilized more intensively. Then both numerator and denominator work for a rising s/c, and finance is assisting the economy along its way to a higher equilibrium growth.

The dynamics of accelerating growth, with a lift from the episodic increase in s/c, must generate a rising flow of savings and of loan bids for them. The flow of savings could be put on a permanently higher level of s at point 2 if deposit rates were raised at financial institutions. More discriminating use of savings and a permanently lower level of c could be assured if real loan rates were raised. There is opportunity for financial deepening that would assist in making the transition from low growth at point 1 to continuing faster growth at 2.

Domestic financial policy in the lagging economy misses its chance for financial deepening. Instead of inducing growth in real amounts demanded of money and other financial claims, as a source of funds for the capital market, it increases growth in nominal money at an excessive pace and so uses the inflation tax to draw savings into investment. New financial institutions may be organized to differentiate financial assets for savers, and an effort may be made to vitalize and develop stock and bond markets, but the effect on the capital market must be slight, given the new impulse to inflation. Investments financed through these institutions are unlikely to be consistent with a declining capital-labor ratio. This pattern of policy drives the economy past point 2, with equilibrium on the capital market, toward point 5 and excess demand for savings.

Without financial deepening, the path of 2-5 implies expectations of higher inflation rates, lower real rates of interest for deposits and loans in organized finance. The widening gap between uu' and ee' can be closed temporarily by a rising inflation tax, by a shift of income to profits and self-finance of investment, by run-down of inventories, and the like. However, accumulating portfolios deviate by a widening margin from desired portfolios. At each higher rate of inflation, real funds become increasingly scarce as the base for the inflation tax shrinks. Completion of capital-intensive investment projects is deferred, and overdue loans multiply. The crisis can be deferred by various expedients but, when it comes, it is the more poisonous. The opportunity for financial deepening having slipped by, the economy must work its way back to retarded growth, represented in the charts by point 1.

Fiscal Policy

Fiscal policy in the lagging economy shares responsibility with financial policy for the repression of s/c that retards trend growth of output. One can charge it, too, with failure to exploit the episodic windfalls, in reaching higher growth rates except during the exhilaration of the boom that ends in the stabilization crisis. Perhaps fiscal policy is so concerned with the Keynesian objective of expanding aggregate effective demand in the short run, as a way of absorbing surplus labor, that it forgets the role of savings and their allocation in supplying labor with productive capital. Problems of supplying output are pushed into the background by preoccupation with demand for output.

The initial windfall of a cyclic episode may accrue to the fiscal budget. Perhaps a rise in foreign prices of exports brings in larger revenues from retention taxes. There may be a minister of finance who succeeds, for a while, in improving tax collection or in forcing a higher degree of efficiency on government enterprise. Whatever the reason, the budget surplus may rise or the deficit decline in real terms, and the economy is on its way along the path 1-4-2. The fiscal savings applied to completion of projects carried over from a previous boom, to replacement of worn and obsolete equipment in gov-

ernment firms or, for example, to cheap storage for perishable agricultural produce can bring down the index of the capital-output ratio.
A lull in the rate of inflation, resulting from growth in the public's
demand for financial assets, can increase real fiscal revenues and, by
raising real rates of interest, induce more careful project analysis in
the government sector.

Unfortunately, fiscal policy in the lagging economy guarantees
overshoot at point 2, and it contributes to widening of excess demand for savings as Y rises. One reason is that the boom inflates
government consumption: the government's own marginal propensity to consume is high. The tax base is allowed to shrink as growth
in the price level picks up speed, and tax rates decay as concessions
are given to private investment. At the same time, work is accelerated on projects that government in any developing country dreams
about—an airport, a new turnpike, a hydro-electric complex, and the
capital-output ratio rises. Prices of government enterprise are not
increased in step with costs. Sensing excess demand in the capital
market, the minister of finance resorts to a number of expedients.

To prolong the episode of faster growth, fiscal authority can be
expected to solicit foreign credits and draw on external reserves.
Normal practice is for it to appropriate a larger share of portfolio
expansion in financial institutions through "forced investment" in
securities of the government itself and its subsidiary enterprises. It
resists rising wage demands in the public sector, and the temptation
is strong to seek an increase in employee's compulsory contributions
to social security funds. When these and comparable expedients become ineffective, the boom has reached its crisis phase and must
stop even though some public construction projects are still just
partly fleshed skeletons.

The fiscal contribution to boom and crisis has an explosive quality. Pressure grows for government expenditure on both current and
capital account—to raise welfare expenditures, for example, and to
reduce the backlog of demands for infrastructure investment. Government is called upon for assistance, through subsidy or loan, in
covering shortages of savings in the private sector. At the same time,
it is vulnerable to fiscal slippage, with erosion of real bases for tax-

ation and borrowing. Sources of savings accessible to government become less productive, and uses of savings become more compelling. Deficit finance depends increasingly on the monetary system, and inflation increases excess demands for savings in both the public and the private sectors. Inevitably, the build-up of experience over a sequence of booms and crises tends to shorten the interval from first windfall to crisis: expectations of the crisis are aroused earlier in the process and are fulfilled sooner.

Policy in the International Sector

Lagging economies characteristically maintain a shallow pool of gross international reserves at the trend rate of growth in national income. Apparently such reserves are a form of wealth that policy-makers credit with a relatively low social rate of return. Under circumstances of disequilibrium money on the foreign exchanges, the scarce reserves are protected by a phalanx of controls over both current and capital items in the balance of payments. There are constellations of relative price, especially with domestic money overvalued at the preferred foreign-exchange rate and with domestic real rates of interest depressed in comparison with rates abroad, that endanger the stock of reserves, but it is sheltered by import quotas and duties, export subsidies, and exchange licensing. One expects to see a burden of external debt that is large in comparison with official reserves and of debt service that is high relative to exports. Some of this debt may be blocked remittances of foreign investors, but the larger share is likely to be debt on official account that has gone through renegotiation at times of crisis. One expects also substantial private reserves of foreign assets, diligently accumulated during years of capital flight.

The windfall that initiates a cyclic episode may appear as an increase in supply of foreign exchange associated with a significant new flow of either domestic or foreign savings. New official credits may be negotiated abroad and, with prospects bright enough, there may even be repatriation of private funds. Since the desired stock of external reserves is small, increase in the saving ratio s tends to be absorbed rapidly by a rise in imports. There is opportunity for re-

stocking of inventories and for other varieties of investment that reduce the capital-output ratio. With s/c rising, the economy is on the
path 1-4-2 of the boom.

The first hazard along the upward swing of activity is that absorption of the external credits by imports may not come rapidly enough.
The flow of reserves has been known to result in accelerated monetary expansion and inflation. While measures to liberalize trade restraints are being considered and cautiously put into effect, growth
of bank reserves can act more quickly in easing constraint on lending by the monetary system to both private and public sectors. As a
result, the rise in s/c that comes from improvements on international
account can be nullified by the fall that comes from domestic monetary mismanagement: $\dot{Y}$ may grow less than $\dot{P}$. Then some part of
growth in external reserves is spilled on diversion of exportables to
domestic markets.

Other hazards appear that carry the boom to its phase of over-
shoot. Savings accruing from growth of exports, foreign credits, or
capital repatriation may be spent on imports of consumables. Because real rates of interest do not rise, savings can flow into investment at high capital-output ratios. Because appropriate explicit or
shadow prices are not attributed to foreign exchange, imports and
savings can flow to projects with small capacity to yield foreign exchange in the future. When traders can foresee overshoot of the
boom, underinvoicing of exports, overinvoicing of imports and
smuggling drain savings away in capital flight. The growth rate of
income rises along path 4-5 with increasing excess supply of domestic money on the foreign exchanges and with increasing excess demand for foreign savings.

Makeshift solutions for disequilibrium can stave off the crisis.
Debt can pile up abroad, with or without underwriting by the domestic monetary authority, and international reserves can be used,
foreign remittances blocked. There may even be ill-advised injections of foreign aid. Imports can be conserved, at the expense of domestic inventories and of capital maintenance. Bilateral trading arrangements may be found for disposal of marginal exports, and some
of them might tolerate, for a while, an accumulation of debit bal-

ances. However, these expedients produce distortions in wealth port-folios, both domestic and foreign, that are not sustainable. At the level finally attained for income growth $\dot{Y}$, the level of s/c desired at prevailing relative prices is so far below the level necessary for con-tinued output expansion that crisis is inevitable. Then a team from the International Monetary Fund arrives.

PUBLIC POLICY IN CRISIS AND RECESSION

Crisis ushers in the solution of last resort for excess demand on the capital market, a falling $\dot{Y}$. in terms of Figure VIII.3, the economy slips from the path uu' past the trend path tt' to the path of depression zz', along a route marked 5-6-3-7. We are concerned here with pub-lic policy in this phase of the cyclic episode. The discussion below deals simultaneously with policies in the financial, fiscal, and inter-national sectors.

There are numerous manifestations of crisis, sometimes including a political metamorphosis.[20] One notes, in particular, changes in relative prices. Market values are marked down for domestic wealth with yields that depend on growth in output, tax favors, cheap ac-cess to complementary inputs including imported items, and cheap financing. The rudimentary markets for long-term securities experi-ence liquidation. Portfolios of financial institutions deteriorate under pressure from borrower bankruptcy and loan defaults. At the same time, there is a shift of excess demand to foreign assets and to in-ventories of goods, especially of goods tradable internationally. Ho-rizons of wealth-holders are shortened for avoidance of risk.

Demand shifts away from domestic money balances as the crisis develops and away, too, from other claims on organized finance. The reason can be that inflation is expected to accelerate, reducing real deposit rates, and it may also be that wealth holders expect blockage

---

[20] Richard N. Cooper, "Currency Devaluation in Developing Countries," *Es-says in International Finance,* International Finance Section, Princeton Uni-versity, No. 86, June, 1971, pp. 28–29. Professor Cooper reports, from his study of twenty-four devaluations during 1953–66, that "chances of ouster for the official immediately responsible seems to increase by a factor of three as a result of devaluation." Governments fell in nearly 30 per cent of Professor Cooper's cases.

of deposit accounts, increases in taxation for wealth holders with assets that are easy to trace or even insolvency of financial institutions. Organized finance shrinks, in real terms, during the transition from boom to recession. Price effects include inflation in the consumer index, in indices for tradable intermediate goods and in black-market rates for foreign exchange.

The crisis is associated with a fall in s/c, the saving ratio declining and the marginal ratio of capital to output increasing. Reasons for the fall in s/c can be found in all sectors. Retained earnings of enterprise must decline with the growth rate of output and as a result of measures that reduce monopoly benefits of import licenses and credit rations. Except for savings on official account, foreign savings avoid the crisis. Government savings tend to be absorbed in losses of public enterprises, as their utilization rates decline, and in meeting wage demands of employees whose real incomes have lagged in the boom. With investment guided more by risk-aversion than by considerations of productive efficiency, c must go up.

Public policy in the crisis is commonly a traumatic assault on the excess demands that policy in the boom has tolerated and stimulated. The growth rate of nominal money is reduced both by measures to cut the government deficit and by new restraints on private lending in the monetary system. Inflation does not stop because there is a carryover from earlier excess money supply, because real money demanded falls, and because the deflationary effects of crisis measures are lagged responses. Sometimes inflation coincident with tightened monetary control is interpreted to mean that inflation is a non-monetary phenomenon, and policy reverts to excessive growth of nominal money.

Fiscal policy is no less punitive at the cycle turn. In contrition for its stimulus to aggregate effective demand on markets for goods in the boom, it finds new revenues by *ad hoc* measures—an increase in its share of revenues from the national lottery and from major export products, higher tax rates on foreign enterprise, special "development" levies. It economizes capital expenditures in particular and defers both foreign and domestic debt service. There seems to be no time for rationalizing the budget by measures that can raise the economy's path of steady growth including measures to broaden the tax base and shelter it against erosion.

The centerpiece of policy in the international sector is, of course, devaluation to absorb the excess demands for foreign exchange that accrue in the regime of disequilibrium money. Possibly devaluation has been preceded by increases in import duties, reductions in import quotas and export subsidies, or export bonus-voucher arrangements, but the real thing affords an opportunity to remove some of the accumulation of specific interventions in trade. Since there are close limits on economizing of imports, if economic activity is not to collapse, and since depreciation cannot revitalize current exports immediately, scarce international reserves are augmented by external credits as well as by deferrals of debt service. Each crisis adds another layer to the burden of external debt and commits still more of future domestic savings to debt service—a reduction in the future value of s.

The trauma of the crisis is the economy's starting point for the long trek back from boom through recession to some semblance of lagging though steady growth. The economy travels along zz' in Figure VIII.3, with levels of s/c continuing for a time to generate excess demands for savings that must be resolved by either one of two strategies. One of them is reform in financial, fiscal, and related policies. The lagging economy chooses the other, of forcing down the rate of growth $\dot{Y}$ by measures directed mainly to restraint of aggregate effective demand. Instruments of restraint do include lower growth rates for nominal money, fiscal conservatism, and the devalued currency, but the temptation seems irresistible to devise a new bundle of specific interventions. Their purpose may be to ease economic burdens on some classes, labor perhaps; revive some pivotal industries, mainly in import-substitution; mend some political fences. They inhibit excess demands selectively.

Selective deflationary controls can be severe for traditional agriculture and industry that has established its comparative advantage. Agriculture can expect restraint on fertilizer imports, shortages of repairs for equipment, and deterioration of storage and transport facilities. Traditional industry, especially if it is foreign-owned, is unlikely to fare better. There is little disposition, on the part of regulatory authority, to experiment with concessions to new industry, especially in unconventional export trades. The bias favors new moves toward self-sufficiency, under the illusion that economic isolation with enough planning can avert repetition of the cyclic episode.

The episode spends its energy in the last stage of recovery to lackluster growth. By this time, lagged responses to abnormally rapid inflation have diminished to minor magnitude, and inflationary expectations have been subdued. Wealth holders of various classes regard their portfolios of assets and debts in the lagging economy as the best attainable base for slow accumulation at the structure of relative prices prevailing, in particular, for savings, capital goods, foreign exchange, and labor. Settled down again at position 1, the economy is ready for the next shock and its cyclic aftermath.

POLICY FOR STABILITY AND GROWTH

The cyclic episode is partly a "political cycle":

Such a cycle may result when exclusive concern with checking inflation (during booms) produces recessions and when exclusive concern with increasing employment (during recessions) produces inflationary booms. More generally, it arises from alternation between undue delay in taking appropriate action and undue severity in whatever action is finally taken.[21]

There are recognition lags and errors, in the central bank and finance ministry or planning board and capital investment bureau, regarding deviations of aggregate nominal effective demand from a path consistent with the lagging economy's characteristic growth rates of output and inflation. There are lags and mistakes in policy implementation that compound instability.[22] This "political" element contributes its share of mischief, but it is hardly all of the story.

[21] Martin Bronfenbrenner (ed.), *op. cit.,* p. vii; Michael Kalecki, "Political Aspects of Full Employment," *Political Quarterly,* October, 1943; Joan Robinson, "Kalecki and Keynes," in *Problems of Economic Dynamics and Planning,* Warsaw, 1964, p. 340.

[22] Thomas J. Courchene, "Recent Canadian Monetary Policy," *Journal of Money, Credit and Banking,* February, 1971, pp. 35–56.

The lagging economy's pattern of response to shock in the short run, it seems to us, is a joint product, along with inhibited growth, of "real" policies affecting especially the financial, fiscal, and international sectors. Their destabilizing effect has two main cutting edges. One is shallow reserves or inventories of working capital, both financial and physical, in the private sector; a small and inelastic revenue base in the fiscal sector; and a thin margin of official external reserves. The other is distortion of critical relative prices—real rates of interest, tax rates, and foreign-exchange rate—in such a way that their cyclical behavior is perverse. Episodic shocks, thin reserves, and price distortions guarantee cyclic instability.[23]

The key to stabilization appears not to be fine-tuning of aggregate demand for output. The prospect for stabilizing effects from schemes to manage markets where developing economies sell their basic exports is inviting but elusive. Timely injections of foreign aid and compensatory waves of private investment from abroad may close disruptive gaps of excess demand or supply on various markets, but costs of absorbing flows of aid and investment are not negligible.

The quantum gain in stability must come from concurrent liberalization of financial, fiscal, and international policy on the part of the lagging economy. Cycles of excess demand, generated in the market for capital and spreading to all other markets, cannot be smoothed without financial deepening, and it is beyond reach in a context of fiscal inadequacy and chronic disequilibrium in the balance of payments. Doing everything almost at once in reform of financial, fiscal, and international economic policy seems to be optimal strategy for both faster and steadier growth.[24]

---

[23] Any precise model tracing the interplay of thin reserves and distorted prices would be complex, to put it mildly. For an interesting partial model, in the spirit of our analysis, see Samuel A. Morley, "The Effect of Government Deficits in an Inflationary Economy," *Ensaios Economicos: Homenagem a Octávio Gouvêa de Bulhões,* Apex, Rio de Janeiro, 1972, pp. 431–452.

[24] This repeats a theme in Ronald I. McKinnon and Edward S. Shaw, "Policies in Restraint of Development," *Program,* International Studies Presidential Advisory Committee, Stanford University, September, 1968.

Author Index

Subject Index

accounts: fiscal, 243; income, 22, 57; international, 12, 13, 166, 197, 198, 246; investment, 23; savings, 23; social, 19, 52
accumulation: financial, 169; wealth, 176
aggregate effective demand, 40, 243
agriculture, 111, 235, 250
Appalachia, 186
Argentina, 142, 216, 218, 231
Austria, 219
autarchy, 69, 193

balance of payments, *see* accounts
Banco do Brasil, 96
bank: central, *see* monetary authority; charter, 19, 43, 55, 64, 123, 129, 134–135, 164, 189; competition, 33–34, 43, 58, 68, 85, 127, 134–135, 139, 141, 156; costs, 58, 64, 66, 133–135; development, 84, 86, 121; equity, 130, 134; monopoly, 68, 92; oligopoly, 139; profit, 133–135, 153; reserves, 129, 184; revenue, 43, 58–59, 64; special, 147–148
Bank of Ghana, 96, 119
Bank of Korea, 97, 212

Banking Act of 1933, 156
barter, 25, 34, 36, 54, 60–61
Belgium, 169
bilateral agreement, 209, 247
bill, 122, 133, 137, 140–141, 146, 161, 180
black market, *see* market
Board of Governors of the Federal Reserve System, 155
bond, 141
bonus voucher, 200–201, 249
boom, *see* cyclic episode
borrowing point, 190
Brazil, 113, 142, 146, 165, 196, 209, 216, 221, 234
Bretton Woods, 190
brown market, *see* market
business cycle, structural, 235; *see also* cyclic episode

Canada, 219
capital: export, 185, 191, 197, 208–215, 210–212; financial, 35; flight, 8, 9, 71, 84, 91, 204, 209, 217, 245; import, 185, 191, 197, 208–215, 222, 232; in production function, 21–22, 55–57; marginal product, 22,

255